D1335334

EUROPE AT WAR 1600–1650

Europe at War
1600–1650

DAVID MALAND, M.A.

HIGH MASTER OF THE MANCHESTER GRAMMAR SCHOOL
ENGLAND

First published 1980 by
THE MACMILLAN PRESS LTD
London and Basingstoke
Associated companies in Delhi Dublin
Hong Kong Johannesburg Lagos Melbourne
New York Singapore and Tokyo

Printed in Great Britain by
Lowe & Brydone Printers Ltd, Thetford, Norfolk

British Library Cataloguing in Publication Data

Maland, David
  Europe at war, 1600–1650.
  1. Europe – History – 17th century
  2. Europe – History, Military
  I. Title
  940.2′3   D247

  ISBN 0-333-23445-6
  ISBN 0-333-22446-4 Pbk

Contents

List of Maps

Foreword

This is very much an exercise in story-telling. No one with a school to run, and only a modest repertory of languages, could hope to offer original research in so wide a field as the Thirty Years War; but, by going over the story each year with my pupils, and by reflecting upon it at unwonted leisure throughout the Michaelmas Term of 1975 – thanks to the generosity of the Warden and Fellows of Merton College, Oxford, the Provost and Fellows of the Midland Division of the Woodard Corporation and the Custos and School Council of Denstone College – I believe that the story may gain by being retold with a different emphasis.

I am profoundly grateful to Bartle Frere, who read the manuscript and was unfailingly helpful in his advice and encouragement.

Introduction

Spain, the Netherlands and Europe

In the course of his reign, Philip II of Spain had dominated Europe, championed the Counter-Reformation and defended Christendom against the Osmanli Turks. At the end, however, bankruptcy and military stalemate took their toll of his ambitions. Obliged to come to terms with the sultan, each recognising the other's sphere of influence in the Mediterranean, he then withdrew from France and acknowledged the accession of his old enemy, Henry IV. Finally, in 1604, his successor, Philip III, ended the twenty-year-old conflict with England (see p. 32). These settlements, which in other circumstances might have brought peace to western Europe, were consented to by Spain for the sole purpose of prosecuting more effectively the war against her rebellious subjects in the Netherlands.

William of Orange, the leader of the Dutch revolt, had failed in his original intention of uniting the whole of the Spanish Netherlands against Philip II. Outraged by the intransigence of William's Calvinist supporters and by the success of their missionaries in fomenting social revolution in the cities, the nobility of the southern provinces combined together in the Union of Arras in 1579, and made peace with Spain in order to preserve their political authority and their Roman Catholic faith. William accordingly put pressure on Utrecht and the north-eastern Catholic provinces of Groningen, Friesland, Gelderland and Overijssel to accept the military leadership of the Calvinists of Holland and Zeeland in the Union of Utrecht. It was an uneasy alliance held together only by respect for William himself and by fear of the penalties to be endured should Spain prove to be victorious.

The fate of the United Provinces swayed in the balance when William was murdered in 1584, and the Spanish army crossed the Rhine and the Maas to isolate the north-eastern provinces from

Holland and Zeeland. They were saved not by local determination, nor even by the assistance offered by France and England, but by Philip II himself, who decided that at that moment the conquest of England and the defeat of Henry of Navarre were matters of greater importance. For this reason, his commander in the Netherlands, the duke of Parma, was required to concentrate his troops along the Channel coast throughout 1587 and 1588 to await the arrival of the Armada. Subsequently, in 1590, he was ordered into France to save Paris from Henry and in 1591 to relieve Rouen – in which campaign he received the wounds from which he died in the following year.

The United Provinces, meanwhile, were given the respite they needed. In Jan van Oldenbarneveldt, the advocate of Holland, the Dutch discovered an able administrator, well skilled in manipulating the members of the regent class – the urban patriciate to which he himself belonged. By placing his allies in positions of importance, he secured a measure of uniformity in the government of Holland and persuaded the delegates of the other provinces to follow Holland's lead in the States-General.

To strengthen the common cause he brought forward Maurice of Nassau, William of Orange's son, who at the age of twenty was already demonstrating the skills which were to make him the finest soldier of his age. Maurice had been elected stadtholder of Holland and Zeeland in succession to his father, and it was Oldenbarneveldt who persuaded the other provinces to appoint him captain-general. Under his leadership the Dutch seized Breda in 1590, undertook a spectacular offensive through Zutphen and Deventer in 1591 to restore communications with the north-eastern provinces and had cleared Gelderland and Overijssel of Spanish troops before Parma's death in 1592. As a result the Dutch were in possession of all land north of the river-line, and from Breda Maurice was well placed to counter-attack through Brabant and Flanders.

To make matters worse for Spain, expenditure on the Army of Flanders had to be reduced from 14 million florins a year to 4·5 million, and, since the troops went unpaid, mutinies broke out with sufficient regularity to guarantee the Dutch security behind the river-line. With the bankruptcy of Philip II in 1598 and his death in the following year, the Spanish campaign ground to a halt. Although it could make no headway in the north, however, the Army of Flanders could still defend the 'Obedient Provinces' of the south. Maurice led several invasions from Breda, and in 1597 won a brilliant cavalry victory at Turnhout,

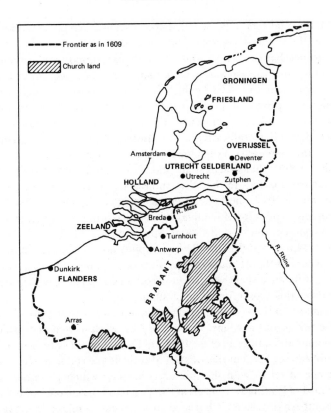

1. The Dutch revolt

but to no lasting effect and the war settled down to a form of stalemate, with the Dutch secure above the river-line and the Spaniards safe below it.

It was a stalemate which neither side could bring itself to accept. The Dutch were self-consciously proud that they were the only successful rebels of the sixteenth century, and having directed their own affairs for several decades they were resolved on nothing less than outright independence. This intransigence was reinforced by the Calvinists, who from the very beginning had played an important role in the revolutionary struggle against Philip II. Though they were in the minority their political influence had grown out of all proportion to their numbers. Since it went without saying that every success of the rebels was interpreted by them as God's intervention on behalf of his

Elect, the ministers could be relied upon to rouse their congregations to fury at the slightest suggestion of a negotiated peace.

The merchants, Catholic and Calvinist alike, supported the ministers in this because the war was making them rich. The *handel op dem vijand*, the trade with the enemy which horrified devotees of mercantilist economics, produced profits which none were prepared to forgo; Antwerp, the former entrepôt of trade in the Netherlands, was blockaded and its traffic diverted to Amsterdam; moreover, the Dutch, unlike the merchants of the Obedient Provinces of the Union of Arras, could exploit their belligerent status to break into Spanish and Portuguese markets in the West Indies, South America and the Far East, and in 1602 the States-General founded the Dutch East India Company. The ships of Holland outnumbered the combined mercantile marines of England, Scotland, Spain and France, and the Bank of Amsterdam controlled the flow of capital not only in the northern provinces but throughout northern Europe. No one, therefore, with an eye to a balance sheet wanted to negotiate a settlement which might endanger this prosperous state of affairs.

In addition there were the personal ambitions of Maurice of Nassau to be taken into account. It was only by warfare that the princely splendour and authority of the House of Orange could be preserved in a republican society, but this was not Maurice's sole concern. He refused to come to terms with the military stalemate which pertained, and dreamed of leading the one great campaign to liberate once and for all the southern provinces. What such an achievement might do to disrupt the expanding economy of the north, none of Maurice's supporters paused to consider – nor the effect which integration with the wholly Catholic population of the south might have on the Calvinist minority in Holland and Zeeland. For the time being, ministers and merchants thought only of continuing the war, and in Maurice they had a general who could claim to prosecute it with success. In their train there followed the nobles who sought employment in the army; at their heels the Calvinist immigrants from the south, who wanted to launch a West India Company to challenge Spain for the control of the seas and enlarge the conflict to resolve the destiny not merely of the Spanish Netherlands but of the whole Spanish empire.

Spanish attitudes to the conflict were more complex than those of the Dutch, partly because what the Spanish government believed to be its reasons for prolonging the struggle were not always correctly thought out. It was for example a point of faith with Philip II that the

Netherlands were of vital importance to the Spanish economy as a provider of essential services. Antwerp had been the market for most of Spain's silver and more than half her exports of wool, and an invaluable centre for raising government loans. Even when Antwerp was blockaded by the rebels, and the Spanish government had gone to Genoa for its loans, the Netherlands were still the best market in which Spain might purchase the Baltic naval stores necessary for her fleets; the weapons, textiles and other manufactured goods which she was unable to produce for herself and for her colonies; Polish grain, the staple of the Dutch Baltic trade, which Spain needed in greater quantity every year to compensate for dwindling imports from Sicily. What was in doubt was not the value of the Netherlands but Spanish logic. Since the Dutch were essentially a trading nation, trading even with their enemy, it was misguided of Philip II to insist upon reconquest. All that was needed was a truce.

In similar fashion the strategic importance of the Netherlands to Spain was made a reason for refusing to treat with the Dutch. Charles V's advisers had described the Netherlands as 'a citadel of steel, a shield which enabled him to receive the blows of England, France and Germany far away from the head of the *monarchia*', a sentiment echoed by the council of state in 1600, which advised Philip III that 'if that shield failed your enemies would fall on Your Majesty and his kingdoms in several parts, giving rise to greater expenses and dangers'. By 1600, however, Spain's enemies had demonstrated their readiness to attack wherever they imagined her defences to be most vulnerable, although this did not prevent the unquestioning repetition of the principle. Even as late as 1626, Philip IV pretended that, had Spain not continued its war against the Dutch, 'it is certain that we would have had war in Spain or somewhere nearer'.

The value of the Netherlands as an offensive base, or, as the council in 1600 expressed it, 'as a bridle which restrains and curbs the English and the French', was more evident. It was recognised that England was vulnerable to whichever major power controlled the Netherlands, and that possession of the provinces not only completed the encirclement of France but also gave Spain a military base only eighty miles north of Paris. Philip II was in the right when he wrote, 'it is from the Netherlands that the king of France can best be attacked and forced into peace', and as France had been Spain's enemy for most of the sixteenth century the strategic importance of the Netherlands was not in question. What Philip overlooked, however, was the fact that, in order to guarantee the security of the Obedient Provinces of the south, all he had to do was to negotiate a truce with the Dutch.

The rulers of Spain might more speedily have recognised that the advantages which they sought to secure by fighting the Dutch could have been achieved by restoring peace had not other issues clouded their judgement – a potent one being the association of Calvinism with the rebellion. Philip II believed that the mantle of the Holy Roman Empire had passed to him, that as the son of Charles V he had inherited a particular responsibility to defend Christendom against both infidels and heretics; moreover, it was his duty, as he conceived it, to answer to God for the spiritual welfare of his own subjects. Hence, he could reassure the pope in 1566 that if necessary he would take arms against the Calvinists in the Netherlands, 'and neither danger to myself nor the ruin of these states, nor of all the others which are left to me, will prevent me from doing what a Christian God-fearing prince ought to do'. It was almost a prophetic utterance, and whatever may be said of the political and religious elements which were often intertwined in Philip's policies there is no doubt that his persistent refusal to be the king of heretics put an end to all negotiations initiated during his reign. The Cortes of Castile, appalled at the high cost of seeking the salvation of the Dutch, petitioned Philip in 1593 to abandon the crusade and to leave the matter more economically and more efficiently to God. As for the heretics, 'if they want to be damned, let them be'.

Spain in fact was able when necessary to come to terms with both heretics and Moslems, but the Dutch were rebels. To make a truce with them might be politic. To grant them independence was anathema. There was also the fear that rebellion when successful might prove contagious, a fear very evident in the reports of the viceroys of Milan and Naples, who repeatedly urged the government to suppress the Dutch revolt.

Another consideration was the pride evinced by Spain in her overseas empire and her determination to exclude from it the merchants of other nations. To this end it was believed that peace in the Netherlands would be more damaging than war, that unless the Dutch were fully engaged in their own territory they would rampage through South America and the West Indies. Certainly it was the issue of Dutch trade which proved to be the sticking point in many attempts at negotiation in the seventeenth century.

In the last analysis, the determination to prosecute the war at all costs must be traced to two irrational but potent sources. One was the persistent delusion that one more campaign, one more major effort, would somehow turn the tide and settle matters once and for all. Associated with this was the fundamental reluctance to accept the humiliation of defeat. 'I cannot refrain from pointing out to Your Majesty', wrote one of Philip III's captain-generals, 'that it will appear good neither to God nor to the world if Your Majesty goes about begging for peace with his rebels.' As one justification of the war after another was exposed for its irrelevance or, futility, there remained the requirement to preserve Spain's *reputación* by nothing less than total victory.

The pursuit of total victory by each side could not but prejudice the peace of Europe. Since France still suffered in 1600 from the effects of her civil wars, the conflict of Spain and the United Provinces was in effect a struggle between the two most powerful, most highly organised and most wealthy states in western Europe.

It was a conflict, moreover, which polarised many of the irreconcilable tensions in European politics. On the one hand a monarchy, autocratic with moribund representative institutions; on the other a republic whose Estates-General wholly depended upon the decisions of vigorous provincial Estates and town councils. Spain was Catholic, aristocratic, medieval in spirit, pastoral in its economy – a static society dominated by landowners, monks and soldiers. The United Provinces were a new creation, Calvinist, bourgeois and dynamic, brilliantly successful in commercial enterprises. The one gloried in *limpieza de sangre*, the purity of the race; the other in its vocation to be God's elect.

The contrasts are effective provided that the polarities are not exaggerated. It is of course true that most Dutchmen were still Roman Catholic, the north-eastern provinces of Friesland, Overijssel, Groningen and Gelderland remained aristocratic and pastoral, and the attachment of many citizens to the House of Orange demonstrated the strength of the princely connection within the republic. Yet the model of two rival, irreconcilable cultures is sufficiently valid to account for the fact that Spain and the United Provinces each represented what the other most hated, feared or suspected. Moreover, each was looked to and appealed to for aid by the enemies of the other. In consequence, many local disputes which might, at any other period, have gone unnoticed acquired an international significance because the governments in Madrid and The Hague were invited, or found it expedient, to intervene.

Spanish lines of communication and supply, upon which the

outcome of the war in the Netherlands might depend, stretched across
Europe like a web, whose delicate filaments were susceptible to
disturbance by political, dynastic or religious changes in any one of a
dozen minor states. Since Spain was perpetually concerned to protect
her routes, and the Dutch to disrupt them, incidents of apparently local
significance could be transformed into crises of European magnitude.

A route vital to the outcome of the war was the so-called Spanish
Road. Recruits from Castile, Sicily, Naples and Albania made their
rendezvous in the harbours of the Ligurian coast to march north from

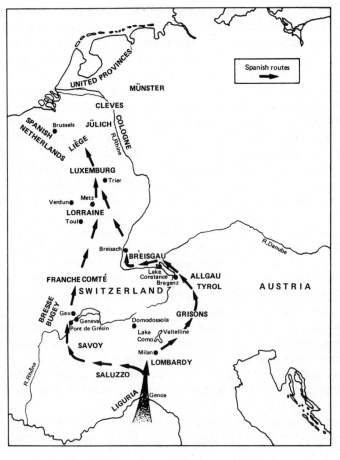

2. *Spanish lines of communication to the Netherlands*

Genoa, a city whose fortunes were closely bound with those of Spain, into the Spanish possession of Lombardy. From there, the Road followed a variety of routes across Savoy into Franche Comté, the heart of the old Burgundian inheritance of Charles V and still administered from Brussels. Thereafter the dukes of Lorraine allowed free passage to the troops of all nations provided that they spent no more than two nights in one place, and Spanish commanders had simply to avoid the French garrisons in Metz, Toul and Verdun (established there by the Treaty of Câteau-Cambrésis, 1559) in order to bring their men safely to the Spanish duchy of Luxemburg. From there it was an easy march across the diocese of Liège, whose bishops relied upon Spain to protect them from the Dutch. In addition, the prince–archbishops of Münster, Cologne and Trier, who had good cause to fear the spread of heresy from the Dutch Republic, allowed the Spanish government both to recruit and to march through their territories, which were strategically of great importance in the lower Rhineland. Trier, moreover, lay conveniently adjacent to Luxemburg, and free passage from Münster and Cologne to Flanders was assured by a long-standing alliance between Spain and the Roman Catholic dukes of Jülich–Cleves (see map 7).

The weakest stage of the Road lay through Savoy, because of the unreliability of its dukes. Accordingly the Spanish viceroys in Milan had tried for many years to find routes to by-pass the duchy. One proposal, explored in 1587, was to cross Switzerland from Domodossola to the Breisgau through the territories of the Catholic cantons. More promising was the agreement made with the Protestant Grisons (the Grey Lords) in 1593 after nearly thirteen years of negotiation, by which troops might go from Como to Nauders in the Tyrol by two separate routes (see map 5). The first went through the Adda Valley (the Valtelline) to Bormio and the Stelvio Pass leading to Nauders; the second by way of Chiavenna and the Maljola Pass.

Thereafter, the route lay through the Tyrol to Bregenz in the Allgau. This was the established rendezvous for the troops recruited in Austria and the Tyrol for service in the Army of Flanders, and the route to Brussels was already well defined. It ran along the northern shore of Lake Constance to enter the Breisgau and then followed the north bank of the Rhine as it flowed eastwards to Basel. There the troops would have embarked to complete their journey in relative comfort, had it not been for the implacable hostility of the elector Palatine, who controlled the middle Rhine; instead, they crossed the Rhine at Breisach, passed through Alsace, which was largely under the control of the Austrian Habsburgs, and gained Lorraine by the Bonhomme Pass.

Communication with the Netherlands by sea from any one of a number of good Atlantic and Biscayan ports offered many advantages over the Rhineland route and the Spanish Road, but, apart from the very real hazard of storms, it had become increasingly difficult to operate successfully in wartime. Privateers from England and La Rochelle, not to mention Dutch warships, waged a successful and wide-ranging war on Spanish shipping in the Channel and its approaches. Parma's recovery of Dunkirk in 1583 did not change matters significantly, because for much of the time the Dutch blockaded it with ruthless indifference to casualties, ready to lose ten ships to sink the one that might otherwise get away. Moreover, the line of sandbanks from Dunkirk to the Scheldt made it dangerous to Spanish shipping to enter Dunkirk, Gravelines or Mardyk except by sailing in close under the guns of Calais, recovered by the French in 1558. After 1570 almost every attempt to reinforce the Army of Flanders by sea ended in disaster. The expedition of 1572 landed 1200 men but only by running the ships aground on the sands of Blankenberge, and, though the great Armada arrived safely off the coast, it could not make contact with Parma. Only after the peace of Vervins was it possible to despatch 4000 men and supplies without mishap.

The wide-ranging extent of Spain's lines of communication made the outcome of the war in the Netherlands appear to be contingent upon the alliance of a duke of Savoy or the death of a duke of Jülich–Cleves, upon the direction of English foreign policy, the security of the Austrian Habsburgs or the result of a debate among the Swiss cantons. In reality, of course, the process was double-edged, and the survival of local rulers or the dénouement of local crises was often contingent upon action taken by Spain or Holland. Because of this, and because the war between Spain and Holland seemed to polarise the most serious rivalries of the age, Europe could not remain aloof. This is not to suggest that all the events which are usually narrated with reference to the histories of Italy, France, Germany and the Baltic in the first half of the seventeenth century were caused by the Spanish–Dutch wars, but many of them were critically affected and their importance exaggerated because the two principal antagonists of the day intervened, directly or indirectly, to save their own particular interests and to make of each specific event a microcosm of their own antagonism. Of all the complex and varied issues, therefore, which led to conflict in this period, the one which imparts a particular measure of coherence to the story, and whose importance has not always been given its full value, was the war between Spain and the United Provinces, which continued unabated after the death of Philip II in 1599.

I

Areas of Conflict 1590–1609

The Holy Roman Empire

The Peace of Augsburg, negotiated by war-weary enemies in the aftermath of Charles V's abdication in 1555, recognised that the Lutheran Church was firmly established in the Holy Roman Empire, and that the princes, Catholic and Lutheran alike, were too strong to be overawed by Imperial authority. The principle of *cuius regio, eius religio*, adopted at Augsburg, established that the inhabitants of Germany were to accept the religious views not of their emperor but of their local ruler. For most of the princes who had fought each other for a generation or more, the peace represented a practical compromise which sanctioned an existing state of affairs: it was not designed to withstand the vigorous, disruptive forces which were subsequently unleashed by the Counter-Reformation, on the one hand, and the Calvinist Church of Geneva, on the other.

The Council of Trent, meeting at various intervals between 1545 and 1563, reaffirmed the beliefs which Luther had challenged, and thereby ensured that every Catholic should be able to distinguish true doctrine from heresy. By rejecting compromise with Lutheranism, the council strengthened both the will to resist it and the missionary impulse to overcome it. Many German Catholic princes, therefore, who might well have sat on the fence with their Lutheran neighbours, were urged by their confessors to become more active and aggressive in the Catholic cause.

The Lutherans meanwhile lost the initiative to the Calvinists, who had not been recognised at Augsburg. Strengthened by the coherence of their doctrine and secure in the assurance of predestined salvation, they were better fitted than the Lutherans to oppose the militancy of the Counter-Reformation. In defeat they withstood persecution, in victory they offered no toleration.

Under the pressure of these new forces, the Augsburg settlement could offer no sure ground for future peace. Nor could it withstand the territorial expansion of Protestantism. The Diet of Augsburg had been silent on the matter, but the emperor, of his own authority, while confirming the secularisation of all church property confiscated before 1552, had prohibited it for the future. The Lutheran, however, would not permit the rich enclaves of a rival religion to exist within his frontiers and he sought by one device or another to acquire them. The Catholic, on the other hand, became increasingly alarmed as more and more church land fell into the hands of heretics.

In 1577, for example, the archbishop-elector of Cologne announced his conversion to Lutheranism and his intention to retain the electoral title, marry a nun, secularise the diocese and make it an hereditary possession. If he were allowed to succeed in this, the archbishop-electors of Trier and Mainz might one day follow his example, and conclude the affair by electing a Lutheran emperor. In the event the Catholic princes succeeded in forestalling the archbishop's plan, but over the years they could do nothing to prevent the less dramatic transfer of such wealthy and important bishoprics as Magdeburg, Bremen and Halberstadt to Lutheran control.

The Spanish government observed these developments with great anxiety, not simply out of family concern for the problems confronting its Austrian cousins, nor entirely because of its self-appointed rôle as champion of the Counter-Reformation. Its interest was provoked by the pressure of the Dutch war. Since a condition of stalemate in the Netherlands left neither side room to manoeuvre, each looked for opportunities to outflank the other in the lower Rhineland. Spain, moreover, was anxious to safeguard the free movement of her troops along the western frontiers of the Empire, and afraid that the Dutch might encourage crises within the Empire in order to divert the full force of Spain's armies from the Netherlands.

It was not just a matter of preventing an archbishop of Cologne from becoming a Protestant. It was vital to Spain's interest that the office of Holy Roman Emperor be denied to any one other than a member of the Austrian Habsburg family. In a memorandum widely circulated among European governments in 1617, Charles Emmanuel I of Savoy wrote that the Spaniards 'will be in constant anxiety lest the transfer of the Empire from Austria may be the means of losing them Flanders', and the reasons were not hard to find. The emperor, for example, could determine the succession to vacant or disputed fiefs, many of them adjacent to, or an integral part of, Spain's transcontinental routes. The 1617 memorandum was not blind to the fact that an emperor independent of the Habsburgs could 'claim the state of Milan as well as . . . other fiefs of the Empire which have been unjustly usurped', and the decisions of emperors were to be indispensible to Spain's interests in Jülich–Cleves (1609), the Palatinate (1621) and Mantua (1628). (See pp. 40, 77 and 120, respectively.)

The emperor, moreover, could still on occasions influence the outcome of a crisis. He had intervened in Cologne, for example, in 1577, and in 1598 he commissioned Spanish troops from the Netherlands to restore Roman Catholic control of the town council of Aachen, on the grounds that Protestantism had established itself in the city after the Peace of Augsburg. His actions therefore could be of major importance to Spain in protecting her routes to the Netherlands, and for this, if for no other reason, it was necessary to Spain that Imperial authority be exercised by a reliable ally.

Both the method of electing an emperor and the constitution of the Empire were enshrined in the Golden Bull of 1356. This entrusted the election to seven princes – the palatine of the Rhine, the margrave of Brandenburg, the duke of Saxony, the king of Bohemia and the archbishops of Mainz, Trier and Cologne. The constitutional assembly of the Empire was the *Reichstag* or Diet, which comprised the college of the seven electoral princes, the college of the other feudal and ecclesiastical princes and a college in which the so-called Free Cities were represented. As an institution it was rarely able to arrive at, let alone enforce, major decisions, and was little more than a convention of independent princes whose power to obstruct decisions they disliked denied the emperor the opportunity to impose his policies upon Germany.

The strength of an emperor's authority depended less upon the constitution than on his personality, the degree of unanimity he could achieve by persuasion and the extent of his personal territories, since what could not be done by an emperor might sometimes be brought about by the resolute action of a duke of Austria. The emperor since 1576 was Rudolf II, hereditary duke of Austria and elected monarch of Bohemia and Hungary (see p. 60). Although on occasion he could act resolutely, as in Cologne and Aachen, he suffered from morbidity and occasional insanity, so that in the end he hid himself away in the Hradschin palace in Prague. Without direction from the emperor, the Diet and other Imperial institutions could not withstand the tensions growing within the Empire and, as a result, the initiative in political affairs passed into the hands of the princely families, and in particular to the Bavarian Wittelsbachs, to their cousins of the Palatinate and to the Wettins of Saxony.

The Bavarian Wittelsbachs, securely based in the Upper Danube valley around Munich, had formerly held the Imperial crown and were, after the Habsburgs, with whom they were closely related by marriage, the most powerful of the German families. Duke Albrecht V (1559–79) had decided that the family estates, instead of being divided among all the children, should be concentrated in the hands of the eldest, and that the family should stay Roman Catholic. In return the pope allowed him powers over the church not very different from those appropriated by Lutheran princes, and promoted the twelve-year-old Prince Ernest to the see of Freising, a useful enclave within Bavaria. Ernest had no vocation for the episcopal life, but the family ruling on primogeniture had left him no other career and he pursued it with vigour. To Freising he added Hildesheim, and then Liège, which made him a close associate of the Spanish government in Brussels (see p. 9). Subsequently, after the intervention of Spanish troops to defeat his rival, he became archbishop-elector of Cologne.

As a result the dukes of Bavaria could exert influence in the lower Rhineland as well as on the upper Danube. Maximilian I (1597–1651) was a zealous champion of the Counter-Reformation and, initially at least, was ready to act in concert with the Habsburgs of Austria and Spain. In 1606 he played a decisive role in the affair at Donauwörth, a town of strategic importance on the upper Danube in which the Catholic monastery perpetually challenged the authority of the Protestant town council. After a riot in 1606, Rudolf, in a rare demonstration of Imperial authority, invited Maximilian to intervene. Peace was restored, a Roman Catholic majority was created in the council, the town was transferred to the Bavarian Circle, of which Maximilian was the director, and Maximilian himself was authorised to occupy it until the emperor was able to repay him the costs of the operation.

The action taken by the emperor and Maximilian provoked a hostile reaction throughout much of Germany, not least in Calvinist Heidelberg, where Maximilian's cousin, Frederick IV, ruled as the elector Palatine. The ally of the United Provinces and an implacable opponent of the Habsburgs, Frederick was well placed to be of service to the one and troublesome to the other: his Rhenish Palatinate controlled

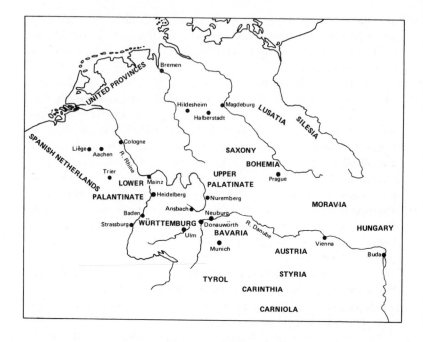

3. The Holy Roman Empire before 1609

the traffic of the middle Rhine, while the Upper Palatinate shared a common frontier with Bohemia. Heidelberg, moreover, was the European centre of the Protestant printing industry. From its presses there poured a flood of pamphlets to alert the rest of Europe to the activities, real and imagined, of Rome, Madrid and Vienna.

Heidelberg was, too, a centre of the Rosicrucian movement – a mystic society of Protestant reformers with a passion for the occult. Though few in number, its members were men of considerable learning, often influential in court circles, whose secret correspondence extended from Bohemia to England. Their prophecies and interpretation of the Cabbala pointed to the Triumph of God's Elect and the downfall of the Habsburgs, and thus reinforced the expectations of their more orthodox Protestant brethren.

The propaganda was supplemented by the diplomatic activity of Frederick's chancellor, Christian of Anhalt. A cultivated and charming counsellor, his self-appointed mission was to create a network of allies capable of thwarting the ambitions of the Habsburgs and of the

Counter-Reformation. He corresponded throughout Europe with every government and individual whose services might be harnessed to this cause – with Dutch Calvinists, French Huguenots, English Puritans and Protestant leaders in Bohemia, Austria and Hungary, and also with Henry IV, Charles Emmanuel I of Savoy, the Republic of Venice and other Catholic powers whose hostility to Spain made them, in his view, 'honorary Protestants'. He was at this date deep in schemes with Henry IV and the Dutch to deny Spain access to Jülich–Cleves (see p. 40), and, on hearing of the Catholic triumph at Donauwörth, Christian immediately persuaded a number of German Protestants to defend their interests by forming an Evangelical Union.

In addition to the elector Palatine, the Union included the dukes of Württemburg and Neuburg, the margraves of Baden and Ansbach and the cities of Strassburg, Ulm and Nuremberg. Its patron was Henry IV of France. It was not a stable alliance. The princes talked expansively of military undertakings, but not in front of their paymasters, the merchants of the southern cities, who counselled caution and economy. The Union was, moreover, almost exclusively Calvinist in character and thereby alienated the Lutherans. 'The Calvinist dragon is pregant with the horrors of Mohammedanism', wrote one Lutheran prince, and the others, despite their alarm over Donauwörth, believed that to ally with members of a sect which had no legal standing under the Peace of Augsburg would only discredit the Protestant movement as a whole.

No one believed this more firmly than Christian II, elector of Saxony and head of the princely house of Wettin. Lutheran enough to hate Calvinists, conservative enough to be shocked by the association of Calvinism and revolution, powerful enough to be lulled into a false sense of security, he kept out of intrigue and refused point blank to join the Evangelical Union. He alone recognised that, whatever their inadequacies, it was only the time-honoured institutions of the Empire which stood between the Germans and anarchy. He was also very shrewd. Bohemia lay on the Saxon frontier, and the family of the Albertine Wettins could not overlook the fact that the electoral title they enjoyed had been transferred to them from their Ernestine cousins by imperial decree in 1547; they had no wish to antagonise so powerful a neighbour nor jeopardise so recently acquired a title. Moreover, Christian mistrusted the motives of Henry IV in associating with the Evangelical Union, and, wisely, foresaw that the formation of a Protestant alliance would merely provoke the Roman Catholics to mobilise their forces in similar fashion.

By July 1609 this had happened. The anxieties of the Spanish government over the security of its Rhineland routes prompted Balthasar de Zuñiga, the ambassador in Vienna (see p. 21), to negotiate the formation of a Catholic League with Maximilian, his immediate neighbours, the Rhineland bishoprics controlled by his family, and the city of Aachen. It did not include Austria, because Maximilian, though respectful of Imperial authority and on good terms with the Austrian Habsburgs, was aware that their interests were not always his own. The League none the less accepted the subsidies promised on behalf of Philip III of Spain, who made it a condition of his support that the League's policies be acceptable to the emperor.

The 'hereditary lands': Austria, Hungary and Bohemia

Spain's interest in central Europe was not confined to matters relating to the emperor, the Catholic League and the Rhineland dioceses. In addition she observed with close attention the hereditary lands of the Austrian Habsburgs, which included the duchies of Upper and Lower Austria; the Tyrol; Carinthia, Carniola and Styria; the kingdom of Hungary and the kingdom of Bohemia, with its attendant provinces of Silesia, Lusatia and Moravia (see map 3). Not all of these were ruled by the head of the family and not all were, strictly speaking, hereditary. Many in terms of language, race and religion were very different from each other, and each was constitutionally self-regarding: 'What does it matter to the Tyrolese what happens in Bohemia, Moravia and other states?', wrote Count Lodron of the Tyrol. 'The Tyrolese have their own sovereign, their own rights, their own constitution and their own territory. If their monarch also rules over other states, that is pure accident.' The government of Spain could not be so disinterested. Alsace, the Breisgau and the Tyrol lay adjacent to, or were an integral part of, her lines of communication with the Netherlands, and, since the 'hereditary lands' as a whole constituted a massive bulwark across central Europe, abutting the three great powers of Bavaria, Saxony and the Upper Palatinate, it was necessary to ensure that they should not fall into the hands of any family other than the Austrian Habsburgs.

In Hungary the immediate challenge came from the Osmanli Turks, who had occupied more than two-thirds of the kingdom since their retreat from the siege of Vienna in 1529. To some extent the Osmanli lines of communication were too severely stretched to sustain a prolonged offensive into Austria, and the Habsburgs had strengthened their frontier fortresses, constructed minor forts at river crossings and at the approaches to the main cities, and established Hungarian refugees and Germans in a defence system of marcher lordships stretching from the Adriatic to the upper reaches of the Sava and the Drava. Their strategy, though expensive in that it absorbed almost entirely the revenues of Carniola, Carinthia and Styria, was well conceived. Since it took ninety days to supply an Osmanli army by camel trains from the Balkans, the season for campaigning was reduced to several months: the Habsburgs, therefore, relied on their new defence works to halt or at least to delay the invading army until the season was over. In the event, the line of effective Osmanli occupation lay midway between Vienna and Buda, allowing Rudolf a strip of Hungary varying in depth from forty to eighty miles, for which he paid an annual tribute to the sultan.

Rudolf found this too humiliating to endure and in 1593 declared war on the Turks and asked Philip II for aid. To defend Habsburg lands was one thing; to divert resources in a Balkan campaign was another; and Spain contributed only 300,000 florins and a small force of Sicilian levies. The conduct of the war was complicated by disputes among Rudolf's allies in Transylvania and Wallachia, and by Rudolf himself, who outraged the Hungarian nobility by an inopportune attempt to persecute the Protestants. With Hungary on the brink of rebellion and the sultan victorious at Keresztés, Rudolf's brother, the archduke Matthias, summoned a family council which compelled Rudolf to delegate authority to him in Hungary. Fortunately for Matthias, the decision coincided with a Persian attack on the eastern frontier of the Osmanli empire, and the sultan agreed to negotiate peace at Zsitva Torok in 1606. The treaty recognised the existing frontier and required only one, final payment of tribute to establish Habsburg Hungary as an independent kingdom.

The value of the terms was compromised in the eyes of the Spanish ambassador, St Clemente, by the guarantees of religious toleration given by Matthias to placate the Hungarian nobility. Matthias believed that the Osmanli Turks presented the most urgent problem of the day: to meet it he was prepared to give way on all other matters. St Clemente, on the other hand, was concerned only to preserve stability within the Empire until the Dutch had been defeated. He was therefore alarmed that heresy was on the increase in Hungary as in Bohemia, and that, because of the elective nature of the throne in both countries, an enemy of Spain, even an ally of the Dutch, might succeed Rudolf.

In his efforts to prevent this, St Clemente based himself at Prague, the

Bohemian capital, to which Rudolf had withdrawn. There he cultivated a group of important families who were intelligently aware of the
issues at stake in the Netherlands and whose sons served in the Army of
Flanders. *La facción española*, as it was nicknamed, was not of St
Clemente's founding. It had begun with Vratislav Pernštýn, who had
accompanied Maximilian II as a young prince to Valladolid, married a
Spaniard and served in Brussels before the rebellion. His sons fought
under Parma, and his daughter Polyxena married Lobkowitz, who had
served in Spain before becoming chancellor of Bohemia – an appointment of critical importance were there to be a disputed election for the
throne.

St Clemente and his colleagues disapproved of Matthias. He had
intervened inopportunely and ineptly in the Netherlands to try to
arbitrate between Spain and the rebels in 1577, and was equally suspect
for his concessions to the Hungarian Protestants; but, because it was
necessary for the Habsburgs to pretend that the Bohemain monarchy
embodied the hereditary principle, no other successor to Rudolf could
be proposed. Matthias himself was not prepared to wait very long.

In 1607 the Moravian Estates demanded political and religious
guarantees similar to those granted in Hungary. Their leader, Karl
Žerotin, had a foot in both camps. As one of the Bohemian Brethren he
inclined towards the Protestants; he was none the less contemptuous of
Henry IV, for whom he had fought, and in international affairs
supported Spain – for which reason he was closely associated with St
Clemente's 'faction'. In 1607, however, he followed a clear sectarian
line, maintaining close touch with Christian of Anhalt in the Upper
Palatinate and with George Tschernembl and Richard Starhemberg,
the leaders of the Austrian Protestants.

Matthias seized his opportunity. He persuaded the Estates of Austria
and Hungary to support his plan to depose Rudolf, marched on Prague
and was joined by Žerotin and the Moravian levies. Rudolf, for all his
voluntary withdrawal from affairs of state, was not prepared to be
hustled from them altogether, and fortified Prague, while Matthias
Thurn and other leaders of the German immigrant Lutherans secured
support for him from the Estates of Bohemia and Silesia. Matthias's
coup failed, and since he did not want to fight a civil war he withdrew in
June 1608 on advantageous terms: Rudolf was left to govern Bohemia
and Silesia, but Matthias's sovereignty was established in Austria,
Hungary and Moravia, and the reversion to Bohemia and Silesia was
assured on Rudolf's death.

Both princes had now to reward their allies. Matthias appointed Žerotin *hejtman* of Moravia, a title of distinction and power, and allowed to the nobility of Austria and Moravia greater independence in matters of religion and politics. Rudolf, to satisfy Thurn and his colleagues, published in 1609 a *Letter of Majesty* which established the terms on which Protestants and Catholics were to coexist in Bohemia and Silesia. Both were to elect their own diets, which in turn would appoint 'defenders' with clearly defined obligations and powers. Each diet guaranteed the churches, the worship and the properties of the other, with the special provision that Protestants might build churches on royal estates and in royal boroughs.

St Clemente and his colleagues were appalled. Matthias had been guaranteed the succession to Rudolf, but the consequences filled the Spanish–Catholic party with alarm, and, since Matthias was already an old man, the problem of the succession had merely been postponed by a few years. At this stage St Clemente died, to be followed by Balthasar de Zuñiga, an experienced diplomat who had spent five years in Paris and had served in the Spanish Netherlands and in the Armada. That a man of such quality was chosen to succeed St Clemente evinced the Spanish government's concern about affairs in Bohemia. With careful tact Zuñiga won new members of the 'Spanish faction'; he showed himself to be unusually perspicacious about future trends by cultivating both Ferdinand of Styria and Maximilian of Bavaria, and he played a significant role in the formation of the Catholic League. His great fear was that Rudolf in his dotage might go over to the Protestants: in that case, no matter what the consequences, Spain would have to intervene – and in the August of 1609 Philip III decided to assemble troops in Naples and Lombardy in case of need in central Europe.

Poland and Sweden

St Clemente's interests in Bohemia and Hungary extended also to their great northern neighbour, Poland, established along with Lithuania, Latvia, Byelorussia, the Ukraine, East Prussia and Danzig by the Union of Lublin in 1569. Lutheranism had initially made considerable inroads here, but the missionaries of the Counter-Reformation had made substantial recoveries which ensured a Catholic government within a tolerant tradition. Economically the country was thriving. Poland, with eastern Germany, lay in a different weather area from the rest of Europe, so that grain was often produced when harvests elsewhere were ruined. Encouraged by the merchants of the Hanseatic League, who could offer an efficient means of collection and delivery, the nobility ran vast estates on commercial lines to provide cereals for export, and the Polish ports along the Baltic coast grew rich from their customs duties.

St Clemente's interests centred on Danzig, where annual exports of cereals had increased from 28,000 tons in 1555 to 200,000 in 1600, because it was on Danzig that the Dutch Baltic trade largely depended. Although the city was a member of the Hanseatic League, its merchants refused to keep their stocks lying on the wharves if Hanseatic ships were not immediately available, and the Dutch had made such free use of the port that, significantly, they referred to it as their 'bread-basket'. A Polish government influenced by Spain might therefore strike a blow at the Dutch where they were most vulnerable, and St Clemente had, in the election for the throne in 1586, urged the candidature of Rudolf's younger brother, Maximilian – with the support of 200,000 florins readily supplied by the government in Madrid. In the event Maximilian suffered humiliating defeat and capture at the hands of Sigismund Vasa of Sweden, who reigned as Sigismund III of Poland from 1587 to 1631.

In the event Sigismund proved to be no enemy to the Habsburgs. Although the cause of Swedish independence against Denmark had been indissolubly bound by his grandfather with that of the Reformation (Sigismund's grandfather, Gustav Ericksson, led the Swedes in a successful rebellion against Denmark in 1521), Sigismund had been brought up by his Polish mother as a Roman Catholic. Consequently, the devotion to Catholicism which had helped him to win the throne of Poland lost him that of Sweden, where he was deposed by his uncle Karl in 1592. Poland and Sweden were thus at war.

Sweden was ill equipped for such a contest. The southern provinces of Blekinge, Skåne and Halland remained under Danish occupation, and her one Atlantic port, Älvsborg (Gothenburg), was easily blockaded and almost impossible to defend. Denmark's subsequent conversion to Lutheranism had in no way eased relations between the two countries, and the Danes awaited an opportune moment to intervene in the war between Karl and Sigismund. The Russians too were at odds with Sweden, over the loss of Estonia in 1583, but they were too preoccupied with civil war to take advantage of Sweden's difficulties.

Sweden was thus exposed to dangerous enemies, yet even more dangerous were the symptoms of internal dissension. The nobles considered themselves the natural leaders of Sweden, and their

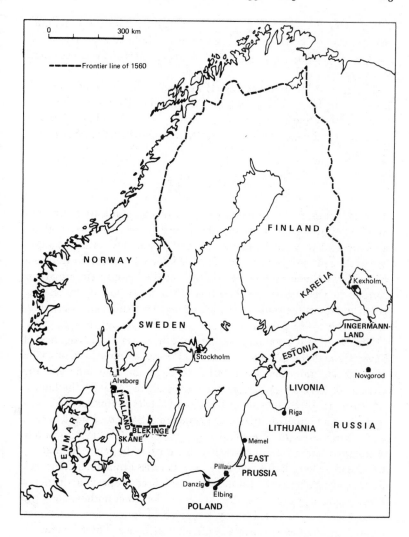

4. The Baltic powers

representatives sat by right of birth in the royal council, the *rad*.
Affronted by Gustav Ericksson's assumption of royalty in 1523, they
argued that the monarchy should be elective – and the subsequent
deposition of Sigismund gave practical force to their theory. As
disaffection increased, many nobles returned to their Danish allegiance,

others elected to serve Sigismund in Poland, while the remainder decided that on Karl's death they would withhold allegiance from his son Gustav Adolf unless he gave them a greater share in the government of the Kingdom.

The Spanish ambassador to the Holy Roman Empire could therefore hold out the hope to his masters in Madrid that Gustav Adolf would be defeated by Sigismund of Poland. Spain, as an ally of Poland, might then look for the use of Älvsborg as a base from which to attack Dutch shipping.

Northern Italy

The importance to Spain of her lines of communication through northern Italy did not escape the notice of her enemies, and an anonymous Savoy official prepared a brilliant analysis of the situation early in the seventeenth century. Having referred to northern Italy as a strong buckle holding together the belt of the Spanish empire across Europe, he went on to show how Spain 'has always found it necessary, either to possess the countries which lie between Milan and Germany, or, if unable to usurp them, to ensure at least free passage through them. Of the two main routes, one lies through the states of His Highness of Savoy through the County of Burgundy [Franche Comté] and on to the Netherlands; the other from Milan through the Valtelline and the Grisons to Germany and from there once again to the Netherlands.'

During the French Wars of Religion, Charles Emmanuel of Savoy had seized his opportunity to take possession of Saluzzo, a small French enclave in the Piedmontese Alps. In 1598 Henry IV, having securely established himself, demanded that the territory be returned, and, by the Treaty of Paris in the following year, Charles Emmanuel undertook to surrender Saluzzo or, as a substitute, the French-speaking district of Bresse on Savoy's frontier with France. In 1600, since nothing had been done, Henry IV invaded Savoy, occupied the duchy and summoned Charles Emmanuel to a peace conference at Lyons. There he made it clear that, if Saluzzo were not returned to France, he would claim not only Bresse but also Bugey and Gex, which together comprised all the land under Savoyard occupation beyond the river Rhône (see map 2).

Charles Emmanuel realised that with the accession of Henry IV he had little hope of expanding his duchy further to the west: Saluzzo, however, would be of prime importance were he to cast his eyes instead on Montferrat and the minor states of the Ligurian coast of northern

Italy, and he decided to retain it. This threw the Spanish government into alarm, since the surrender of Bresse, Bugey and Gex removed from the duke's jurisdiction the last stages of the Spanish Road through Savoy (see p. 8). The other north Italian and Swiss states represented at the conference recognised Spain's anxiety and proposed that the Swiss Confederation guarantee to Spain the use of a route via Simplon, Brig, Martigny and Lausanne to Pontarlier in Franche Comté. Unfortunately for Spain, the proposal foundered on the violent opposition of Geneva, a Calvinist city which had always regarded Spain with mingled fear and detestation, and could not agree that Spanish troops should march along her undefended eastern boundary. Spain's assurance that she set more store by the defeat of the Dutch rebels than the destruction of Geneva fell on deaf ears, and by the Treaty of Lyons, 1601, she had to make do with the Val de Chézery. This was a narrow defile between Savoy and Franche Comté, which, though it lay close to Geneva, was separated from its defended western frontier by a mountain range.

Troops passing through the Val de Chézery, however, would have to cross the Rhône at the Pont de Grésin (see map 2), and since this could easily be closed by French troops in adjoining Gex it was immediately clear to the count of Fuentes, governor of Milan, that the Spanish Road would have to be abandoned whenever Spain and France were in conflict. As a former military commander in Flanders, he realised the consequences of this and, being both daring and resourceful, did not choose to await the arrival of instructions from Madrid. He seized control of the petty Ligurian lordships of Piombino, Finale and Monaco in order to safeguard the sea route along the coast to Genoa, and negotiated in 1604 a treaty with the Roman Catholic cantons to allow Spain rights of passage through Brig, Schwyz, Zug and Waldshut, provided that the troops marched in small parties and had their weapons transported separately. This valuable concession was secured by the payment of subsidies worth over 82,500 florins a year to the leaders of the cantons, and the diversion along this route of trans-Alpine caravans of merchandise from Milan so that the cantons should enjoy more income from their tolls. As a result Fuentes was able to send 2000 infantry through to Alsace in 1604, and nearly 3000 in 1605, but after his death in 1610 the subsidies were withdrawn and the French, by paying them instead, closed the route permanently to Spain.

Spain's inattention to the Swiss cantons is explained partly by the inadequacy of Fuentes's successor, partly by Fuentes's own actions in

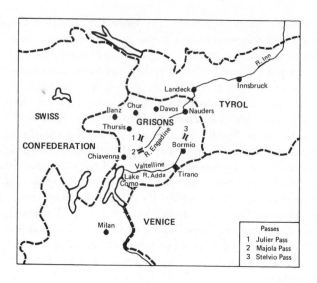

5. The Valtelline

developing the route opened up in 1593 through the commonwealth of
the Grisons. The commonwealth, whose authority extended more or
less within the present-day canton of Graubünden, comprised three
leagues; the Upper or Grey League at Chur, the so-called Ten
Jurisdictions at Davos, and God's House at Ilanz. Since they controlled
the Valtelline and the upper reaches of the Engadine Valley, their
importance to Spain in securing a safe route from Milan to the Tyrol
was considerable.

There were, however, serious complications. The inhabitants of the
Valtelline were Italian and Roman Catholic, while the Grisons were
Protestants and in association with the Swiss Confederation. There was
therefore a long history of conflict between the Grisons and their
subjects, a conflict exacerbated by family feuds and by international
intrigue. France wanted access to its ally Venice, but its route from
Chur, via the Julier Pass, to Tirano cut across the lines of communication allowed to Spain. Local families supported the rival
powers – the Plantas, for example, working in the Spanish interest, the
Salis in the French. All routes therefore led through Tirano, and the
inhabitants both of the valleys and of the mountains could not escape
involvement in the rivalries of Spain, France, Germany, Venice and the
Netherlands.

As a result of local family intrigues, France and Venice were granted access to the Valtelline in 1602 and 1603 respectively. Fuentes retaliated by building a fortress at the entry to the valley, near Lake Como, in order to be able to mass troops for an invasion if necessary and to prevent traders from passing through. The Grisons and the valley dwellers therefore lost not only their revenue from customs duties but also the supplies of grain and salt they needed from Milan. As a result, when Venice asked permission in 1607 for troops recruited in Lorraine to pass through to strengthen her in a dispute with the pope, the Spanish faction carried the day and the request was turned down. In the volatile and violent politics of the Valtelline, however, there was no guarantee against swift and unexpected reversals of fortune.

The Netherlands

Philip II was unhappily aware that the laborious task of directing the highly centralised structure of the Spanish monarchy and of mobilising its resources to defeat the Dutch rebels was beyond the capacity of his son and successor, Philip III: 'God, who has given me so many kingdoms to govern,' he complained, 'has not given me a son fit to govern them.' A talented minister might have compensated for the deficiencies of the master, but the duke of Lerma was not the man. Despite the reforming endeavours of several *juntas de reformación*, the economy deteriorated, government finance was bungled and administrative inefficiency went unchecked.

In the conduct of external affairs, however, Lerma was assisted by a number of extremely able ambassadors and soldiers, whose services he was sensible enough to retain. He benefited above all from Philip II's prescience in assigning the government of the Netherlands to the infanta Isabella and her Austrian husband, the archduke Albert. Isabella's keen discernment in political affairs had won her father's respect and confidence to such an extent that, when the unexpected birth of the future Philip III deprived her of the opportunity to inherit the throne of Spain, Philip II, by a special decree of 6 May 1598, appointed her and Albert independent sovereigns of the Netherlands.

The appointment of the archdukes, as Isabella and Albert were known, was welcomed throughout the Spanish Netherlands, since it marked the restoration of authority to the three 'collateral councils' in Brussels – the council of state, the council of finance and the privy council – and to the States-General and the provincial Estates. The archdukes' court, moreover, had all the trappings of an independent government, with foreign embassies accredited to it and its own ambassadors recognised throughout Europe. The tone of their correspondence revealed the confident assumption of sovereignty by the archdukes, and Albert's adviser Pecquius reported to him that he had corrected the sieur de Préaux, who had spoken slightingly of the archduke's dependence upon Spain by affirming, 'Your Highness is as much the master in his own country as other princes are in theirs.'

Yet the sieur de Préaux had not been deceived. Behind the appearances of autonomy the puppet strings led back to Madrid, since without Spanish troops and Spanish subsidies the Spanish Netherlands could not survive. The privy council had no jurisdiction over Spanish soldiers; the council of finance was denied access to the subsidies which were administered by Spain, and the council of state was unable to determine matters of war and peace. This was the prerogative of the 'Spanish Ministry', composed of men such as the archdukes' confessor, Inigo de Brizuela, and other Spaniards, appointed not by the archdukes but by Philip III, with whom they were required to correspond collectively and as individuals. The reason was clear. Not only were the archdukes unlikely to have children, in which case the Netherlands reverted to Spain, but in addition the anxieties of the Spanish government to safeguard the Obedient Provinces and to destroy the rebels were so pressing that they could not be delegated. Hence the creation of parallel departments of state in Brussels and the inefficiency of a dual administration.

Meanwhile the war continued. The Peace of Vervins released the Army of Flanders from its commitment in France, but the desperate shortage of funds led to widespread mutinies, which jeopardised the success of every campaign. In 1598 an attempt to outflank the Dutch lines of defence by establishing bridgeheads across the Rhine in Cleves came to grief because of mutinies in Ghent and Antwerp. In 1599 the capture of Rheinberg and Wesel was compromised by mutineers on the Bommelerwaard, an island between the Maas and the Waal, who sold their fortresses to the Dutch in return for their arrears of pay.

One means of breaking the military stalemate was proposed by Federigo Spinola, a Genoese sailor of influence and wealth, who persuaded the government in Madrid that a fleet of galleys, because of their shallow draught, could make better use of the Belgian ports and the inland waterways than the galleons, which had so far proved largely ineffectual. 'We could thus cut off the supplies which reach them [the

Dutch] from abroad and furnish them their ordinary means of support',
he claimed, 'and deprive them of the profits from the fisheries, trade and
cattle with which they have enriched themselves and sustained the
charges of the war for so many years past.' It was also part of his plan
that the galleys could undertake an invasion of England. As a result he
was sent to Sluys and commissioned to build galleys there, which, in
conjunction with the privateers of Dunkirk, began to attack Dutch
shipping in 1599 with such success that Oldenbarneveldt insisted that
Dutch troops be sent along the coast to destroy the Spanish bases.

Maurice of Nassau had little faith in the scheme, and still less in the
States-General's pious hope that his appearance in Flanders would
inspire the population to rise against the archdukes, but he was a man
under orders and set off along the coast in 1600 with 3000 cavalry and
12,000 men. He began the siege of Nieuwpoort and sent forward
detachments along the beach to Dunkirk, but there were no indications
of a general rising. Indeed, Spanish mutineers at Diest responded to a
personal appeal from Isabella and Albert and marched out to intercept
the invaders. The Dutch were taken aback; 2000 troops, sent to hold the
bridge at Leffingen against the Spaniards, arrived too late and, when
attacked, panicked and ran, with the loss of 900 lives. Maurice,
meanwhile, drew up the rest of his army near Nieuwpoort, and the
Spaniards, physically weakened by one engagement on the soft sand,
were not in good condition for a second. Maurice had been training his
pikemen and musketeers to work together in units of ten ranks, each
rank, after firing at the enemy, retiring under cover of the pikes to
reload while the next rank took its place. As the Spanish faltered under
the continuous fire, the Dutch cavalry closed in upon them from both
flanks, the front broke in disarray, and Albert was lucky to escape
capture. Maurice, delighted though he was by the victory, recognised
nonetheless that he was fortunate to survive and, sending for the
Zeeland fleet to join him at Ostend, embarked there and sailed for
home.

Maurice's embarkation at Ostend drew the archdukes' attention to
the fact that this was too dangerous a base to leave in Dutch hands, lying
as it did between Dunkirk and Sluys and affording a foothold in
Flanders behind the Spanish front line. In 1601 they launched an attack
upon the town. Siege warfare, however, had been revolutionised by the
general adoption in the late sixteenth century of defence works so
formidable that towns rarely fell to a direct assault. To blockade them
into submission, therefore, was a long business, requiring such excep-

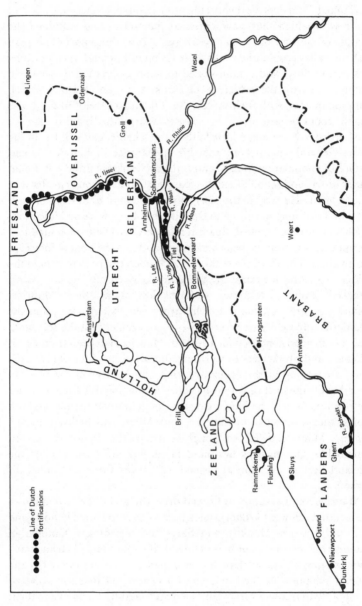

6. *The war in the Netherlands 1600–09 (1609 boundaries)*

tional skills of organisation and supply that, as William Davison put it to Burghley, 'one good towne well defended sufficeth to ruyn a mightie army'. This was very nearly the outcome of the siege of Ostend.

The first requirement of siege warfare was to muster sufficient men to prepare, and subsequently to defend, the siege works, and this could not be met when thousands of troops were mutinying for lack of pay. The special payment of the mutineers of Diest in 1601 and those of Weert in 1602 only sparked off other mutinies, and by the end of 1602 over 3000 men had abandoned their units and marched to set up an independent camp on the Spanish–Dutch frontier at Hoogstraten.

The situation was changed by the arrival in Flanders of Spinola's brother Ambrosio. Because the house of Doria had hitherto outshone that of Spinola in the affairs of Genoa, Ambrosio was determined to exploit his family's considerable fortune to make its name famous throughout Europe. Learning of Federigo's plans to invade England, therefore, he set out in 1602 with his own troops in order to join the enterprise, but ran into difficulties as the first victim of the Treaty of Lyons. Henry IV, who pretended that Spinola was marching through Savoy to assist the Huguenot rebel Biron, denied him access to the Pont de Grésin until Biron had been executed. When Spinola arrived in Flanders it was to learn that his brother had been killed in a galley raid on Ostend, and that despite Philip III's orders the archdukes were resolved to do nothing about England until Ostend had fallen. Spinola reluctantly agreed that the capture of Ostend would make the invasion easier to carry out and undertook to see to it himself, making his own fortune available for the purpose provided that he were given sole command of the operation. His ability to raise money enabled the army to be paid and sustained until, after a long war of attrition, which reduced the town to a pile of rubble, Ostend finally fell to his troops in September 1604.

It was in many respects a Pyrrhic victory, because Maurice in May 1604 had led his troops against Sluys. What began as a diversionary raid to lure Spain from Ostend developed into a properly conducted siege, and, since neither side would take the risk of interfering with the other's siege works, the fall of Ostend was balanced by the fall of Sluys – which, it could be argued, was more useful than Ostend to the United Provinces. Nonetheless, the capture of Ostend established Spinola's reputation as a commander and as a money-raiser, and he was well thought of both in Brussels and in Madrid.

In the meantime, however, his intention of leading an invasion fleet across the Channel was thwarted by the conclusion of a peace with James I. Spain's hopes of stirring up the Irish against Elizabeth had proved illusory by 1602, with the surrender of Spanish troops at Kinsale, and the exiles' stories of the civil war which was bound to follow upon Elizabeth's death were confounded by the peaceful accession of James I. Albert wasted no time in sending his ambassador Arenberg to negotiate a truce, and urged Philip III to follow suit. The government in Madrid, taken aback by the speed and independence of Albert's action, nonetheless agreed that to take England out of the war would make it easier to defeat the Dutch, and that the Channel route would be much safer if English ports were to be made available as refuges from bad weather or Dutch men of war. The Dutch and their allies the French knew this only too well, and Arenberg was dismayed at the influence they seemed to exert at the English court. Oldenbarneveldt went in person, as did the duke of Sully, to congratulate James on his accession and to solicit aid for Ostend, resulting in the Treaty of Hampton Court, by which the Dutch were to raise troops in England to be paid for by James and Henry IV. To make matters more tense for Arenberg, the constable of Castile, appointed by Philip III to represent Spain, made but slow progress to England and fell ill in Flanders, but at last, in August 1604, a month before the fall of Ostend, the Treaty of London was signed.

Under the terms of the treaty the English appeared to have things all their own way. They could continue to trade with the Dutch, their traders in Spanish ports were guaranteed protection from the Inquisition provided that they did not cause a public scandal, and English garrisons in the so-called Cautionary Towns of Brill, Flushing and Rammekens were to be treated by Spain as neutrals. As for the recruitment of levies to serve in the United Provinces, the terms were left deliberately vague: 'His Majesty', wrote Cecil to Winwood, 'promised neither to punish nor to stay but only that he will not consent, – a word of which you know the latitude as well as I', and English troops continued to serve the Dutch Republic for several decades. Nonetheless, the Treaty of London was harmful to the Dutch and it was significant that the city of London, fiercely Protestant and hostile to Spain, celebrated the capture of Sluys rather than the peace treaty. Spain no longer had to deal with England as an enemy and had access to English ports, while James I gave little official support to the Dutch, even claiming that the Treaty of Hampton Court had been made invalid by the Treaty of London. Moreover, the Dutch were alarmed lest the Cautionary Towns be handed over to Spain.

In Brussels morale was high. The Army of Flanders could take the field again, reinforcements could sail up the Channel, and Spinola's reputation inspired confidence. Isabella wrote fervently to Lerma in November 1604 that the issue might well be resolved at last by one final, well directed campaign, but the mood in Madrid was markedly different from hers. Most of the dissatisfaction was directed against Albert. His lack of military success, his appointment of Spinola, the loss of Sluys and his over-eager despatch of Arenberg to treat with James I were strongly criticised, and a *junta* of April 1604 had already advised that he be relieved of military authority in Flanders as *maestre de campo general* and as head of the *junta de hacienda*.

Philip III agreed and set about the issue with elephantine tact. He urged Albert to consider that his life was too precious to be risked in battle, as at Nieuwpoort, adding that he could scarcely sleep for worry about the dangers to which Albert was daily exposed. Albert hotly contested the point, declaring that the proposal humiliated the Spanish Netherlands as well as himself, and Isabella told Lerma that it was the lack of Spanish subsidies which lay at the root of Albert's difficulties and that God would protect him as he had done her father and grandfather. It was to no avail; Albert was compelled to resign his military appointments. The choice of his successor led to further dispute. Spinola was Albert's nominee, but the Genoese was regarded with great suspicion by the government in Madrid, which identified him not with the capture of Ostend but with the loss of Sluys. Opinions changed after his visit to Madrid in the winter of 1604–5. Though none of the debts he had incurred in Spain's service was paid, he was invited to approve a plan by which he should command 10,000 men against Sluys while the main army of 22,000 invaded the United Provinces. He refused outright and threatened that unless he were given the supreme command he would return to private life in Genoa. Spinola's ability to raise 5 million florins on his own account carried the day, and he returned to Flanders as head of the *junta de hacienda* and *maestre de campo general*.

Any direct assault on the Dutch position from the south involved crossing the Maas, the Waal, the Linge and the Lek. In 1605, therefore, Spinola left a force under Henri van der Bergh to hold Flanders against any surprise move by Maurice, and, by crossing the Maas and the Waal alone, led the main army into Cleves, from where he was able to threaten the Dutch frontier at its weakest point, in Overijssel. It was a successful campaign in that Oldenzaal and Lingen fell to him, and by autumn his troops were well placed to press on in the following year into Friesland, where, wrote Isabella to Lerma, the substantial Roman Catholic majority would welcome the restoration of Spanish rule. But neither Isabella's optimism nor a personal visit by Spinola to Madrid could conceal from Philip III that the 1605 campaign had failed to destroy Dutch resistance and was simply the prelude to yet more expense. So little money was available that Spinola had to return via Genoa to raise a personal loan of 650,000 florins. His visit, however, did much to improve his personal standing with Philip III, whose greatest anxiety was that, if Albert and Isabella were to die suddenly, the Spanish Netherlands might declare their independence. In consequence he had prepared the most detailed, confidential instructions about the administration of oaths of allegiance and other matters, and these he entrusted to the safe-keeping of Spinola.

Meanwhile Maurice consolidated his lines of defence. In addition to the fortresses already established on banks and islands in the Rhine delta, he built a chain of blockhouses linked by an earth rampart along the entire western bank of the Ijssel to Arnheim, up the west bank of the lower Rhine to Schenkenschans, and finally along the north bank of the Waal to Tiel. Consequently, when Spinola took the field in 1606, his task was more difficult than he had anticipated. Advancing as before through Jülich–Cleves, he recovered Rheinberg, lost in 1601, and advanced into Overijssel, where he captured Groll. The States-General of the United Provinces was seriously alarmed by his advance and openly criticised Maurice for failing to take the war to the enemy, but Maurice's defensive line held firm and the Spanish army was no better placed by the autumn that it had been the previous year. To add to Spinola's problems, the lack of money once again led to unrest among the troops. By December 4000 mutineers had set up an independent command in Diest and demanded their arrears of pay.

Negotiating the Twelve Years Truce

News of the mutiny at Diest caused dismay in Madrid, because Philip III and his advisers knew that no more money was available to prosecute the war in the Netherlands. The financial situation had deteriorated rapidly since the bankruptcy of 1596, and, despite the beneficial effects of the peace settlement with France and England, the burden of the Dutch war had become intolerable. The government's income was less than 10 million ducats a year, of which 6 million came from Castilian taxes and 2 from bullion imports: against this, the campaigns of 1605 and 1606, from which so much had been antici- pated, had each cost 4 million ducats, leaving only a fraction of what was required to pay the annual interest charges on the government's accumulated debts, maintain the administration and provide garrisons in Naples, Sicily and Milan. In consequence, Philip III refused to let Spinola visit Madrid in the winter of 1606–7, because he knew that his demands for subsidies could no longer be met. Instead, in a session of historic importance, the council met on 14 December 1606 to review the progress of the war, and decided, after permitting itself some token recrimination about the inadequacy of the archdukes, that the annual provision for the Army of Flanders was to be reduced to 1·5 million ducats. Since this was barely enough to keep the army on a defensive footing, the council was tacitly abandoning, for the time being, the notion of war, and its one concern was to find ways and means to persuade both the archdukes and the Dutch to agree to a truce.

Ironically, the decision preceded by a few weeks the receipt of despatches from Spinola reporting that the Dutch had asked for an armistice, that the archdukes had agreed and that it was hoped that Philip III would allow negotiations to take place.

The Dutch too were finding the war a great burden. Olden- barneveldt wrote to Aerssens, the ambassador in Paris, that the government was overspending by 200,000 florins a month (the equivalent of nearly a million ducats a year) and urged him to persuade Henry IV that 'the present condition of our affairs requires more aid in counsel and money than before'. This was not merely a ploy to put pressure on Henry. Some provinces were recalcitrant in paying their contributions to the Union and it was well known that large numbers of Roman Catholics in Groningen, Gelderland and Overijssel, the provinces most recently invaded by Spinola, were anxious to bring the war to an end. Division between the provinces was nothing new, and Oldenbarneveldt had always believed that it was only by the war with Spain that the separate elements of the Union of Utrecht were held together. By 1606 he had changed his mind. The war had become expensive, and, since Maurice was unable to make further inroads into Flanders, Oldenbarneveldt proposed a truce. In seventeenth-century terms it was a common-enough device to suspend hostilities for a short time on the chance of gaining some advantage over the enemy. It was by no means a sure preliminary to a peace settlement, and Oldenbarneveldt was concerned simply to discover whether or not the

archdukes could swallow their pride sufficiently to treat with the United
Provinces, 'taking them for free lands, provinces and towns against
which they claim nothing'.

The move was nonetheless opposed by a powerful war party led not
so much by Maurice of Nassau as by those in his entourage, such as the
impetuous Brederode, whose mistrust of Roman Catholics was not
confined to those in the Obedient Provinces. Like many other Calvinists
elsewhere, he believed implicitly in an international conspiracy
hatched in Madrid and Rome, and wrote perceptively 'of those who in
Styria, Carinthia and Croatia have usurped absolute power in the
interests of Spanish tyranny by destroying the very privileges and
ancient liberties of the Estates of these provinces, which at their
accession they had confirmed by oath' (see p. 61). His suspicion of
Habsburg intentions was echoed by Christian of Anhalt, who learned
with alarm of the preliminary negotiations and warned Maurice's
brother that these 'were stratagems to provide a little tranquillity to lull
the Estates into sleep'.

Brederode also suggested that Spain was in a more desperate
condition than the United Provinces, and that during a respite from
war it might be easier for an absolute monarchy than for a republic,
dependent upon the support of the provincial Estates, to raise money to
recruit and to re-equip new armies. Maurice himself was more cautious
in his views. He was not happy to purchase French aid at the price of
accepting Henry IV as sovereign, but did not see how otherwise the war
might be prosecuted. The signing of the armistice in March 1607,
however, gave him something positive to criticise and he condemned it
for being undertaken simply to satisfy 'the provinces nearest to the
enemy'.

To demonstrate to captious critics that he was not prepared to truckle
to the enemy, Oldenbarneveldt demanded that negotiations should be
conducted directly with Philip III rather than with the archdukes
alone. The Spanish government objected strongly. It was one thing to
negotiate by proxy, quite another to meet rebels in the open, and Philip
was already embarrassed by the complaints of Spaniards serving in
Flanders, who, in their ignorance, imagined that the whole affair was an
ill considered manoeuvre by the archdukes. But 1607 proved to be a bad
year for saving face. A Spanish fleet waiting in Gibraltar to intercept
Dutch interlopers returning from a profitable expedition to the East
Indies was taken unawares by a Dutch squadron and utterly destroyed.
Fast on the heels of this humiliation came the government's admission of

bankruptcy in December 1607. As a result Philip III had no choice but to agree in the following January that his personal representative should join those of the archdukes in negotiating with the Dutch.

It was tacitly agreed that Spain would renounce its sovereignty over the United Provinces, but negotiations foundered on two long-term issues regarded as vital by both sides. The Dutch refused to offer satisfactory guarantees of the rights of Roman Catholics within the republic; nor would they accept the exclusion of their merchants from the Spanish colonial empire, since the East India Company was declaring such handsome dividends from its illicit operations that many merchants were demanding the formation of a West India Company too. As a result the truce was extended in May 1608 for a further six months to afford Philip III an opportunity to revise his demands. In the meantime his government did its best to undermine Dutch solidarity by suggesting to the inland provinces that their interests would no longer be served by fighting simply for the commercial advantage of Holland and Zeeland, and by attempting to mollify the latter by offering the substantial concession of free trade with Spanish ports.

It was all to no avail. The colonial trade was too lucrative to be renounced, the Calvinists were too determined that nothing should prevent the elimination of Roman Catholicism within the Dutch Republic, and both merchants and clergy were supported by influential groups of refugees from the south whose bitterness could not be assuaged and whose demand for the liberation of the Obedient Provinces could not, with safety, be repudiated by the States-General. Moreover, both France and England had agreed to guarantee military assistance to the United Provinces should Spain prove obdurate and the negotiations fail. As a result, when Philip III declared in September 1608 that he could not abandon the interests of the Dutch Roman Catholics nor allow free trade within his empire, the Zeeland representative declared in the States-General that to support the truce any longer was tantamount to treason against the republic.

The prospect of war alarmed the French government, since Henry IV was not at all anxious to fulfil his obligations to subsidise Dutch campaigns, and his minister Jeannin hastily intervened to suggest that, if a peace treaty could not be agreed upon, a prolonged truce, perhaps for a period of twelve years, might be acceptable provided that Philip, for the period of the truce alone, withdrew his demands about colonial trade and the Dutch Roman Catholics. Oldenbarneveldt agreed, since in practice it gave the Dutch what they wanted, albeit for a limited period. It also allowed him to shelve the delicate problem of the Scheldt by ensuring that the Dutch blockade, which benefited Amsterdam's trade at the expense of Antwerp, could therefore be maintained pending a final peace settlement. Maurice too agreed. He did not wish to lose the power and the patronage he enjoyed as commander-in-chief, but a truce was less of a blow than a peace treaty and he was promised compensations in the way of a substantial pension. With his acquiescence and with Oldenbarneveldt's active support, coupled with a threat of resignation if the truce were not approved, the measure was finally agreed to by the States-General despite the Calvinist clergy, the exiles and the champions of a West India Company – which could not be founded with official backing during the suspension of hostilities.

The archdukes supported the proposal because without money Spinola could not even defend the Obedient Provinces let alone invade the north. Philip III, naturally enough, was reluctant to withdraw his terms, no matter for how short a period, but he was impressed by the fact that it was now the 'Spanish Ministry' in Brussels which unanimously urged him to concede. Most influential of all was Inigo de Brizuela, former confessor to the archdukes and regarded by Philip as his particular watchdog in the Netherlands. He drove home the argument that an offensive war would cost 300,000 ducats a month, and that a defensive war not only was a waste of time but also might endanger the provinces. 'Half measures', he wrote, 'will not gain Holland. They will lose Belgium', and, striking Philip III at his most sensitive point, 'you must consider that, if the Obedient Provinces are lost, the Catholic religion, which is now well established and accepted there, will be lost too'. Philip capitulated and the Twelve Years Truce was ratified on 9 April 1609.

The effect of admitting defeat, if only for a period of twelve years, was traumatic both for the Spanish government and for the people, who seemed unable to reconcile themselves to the turn of events without demanding a scapegoat. They found one in the Morisco population, the baptised descendants of the Moors who had overrun Spain in the fifteenth century. Denied civil equality with the Spaniards, barred from the professions and forbidden to own land, the 500,000 Moriscos, living mainly in Valencia, formed a separate, underprivileged and unpopular community amidst the 7 or 8 million inhabitants of Spain. The Valencian landowners, from whose class came Lerma, regarded them with jealousy and hatred. Whatever they did was criticised:.their tradition of early marriages and large families betrayed improvidence their frugality a desire to cheat the government of its purchase taxes, and their capacity for unremitting toil the fruits of avarice. Not even the high rents they paid for their land could reconcile the Spaniards to so nonconformist a group. In an age which set such store by uniformity, they were hated simply for being different.

To persecute the Moriscos was to seek a welcome distraction from unpalatable truths about the Dutch war. Those of Valencia were deported in 1609 and the remainder followed in 1610. For these last the expulsion was particularly cruel. Being few in numbers they had been more easily assimilated into the Spanish population and were generally practising Christians; to expose them to the Moslems of North Africa was a crime, mitigated only by the inefficiency of the administration to expel them all. In this unhappy manner, by scattering the descendants of those who had once threatened to engulf Spain in the world of Islam, a weak government disguised the humiliating fact that it had had to treat with heretics and rebels.

2

Europe during the Twelve Years Truce 1609–21

The Problem of Jülich–Cleves 1609–14

The duchies of Jülich, Cleves, Mark, Berg and Ravensberg, ruled by one family, were of great strategic importance in the lower Rhineland. Their territories, interlinked with those of Cologne, provided Spinola in 1605 and 1606 with a most valuable base from which to attack the United Provinces through Overijssel and Friesland. Similarly, the Dutch, if able to control these territories, could sever communications between Flanders and Cologne and launch an invasion across the Maas against the undefended flank of the Army of Flanders. Both Spain and

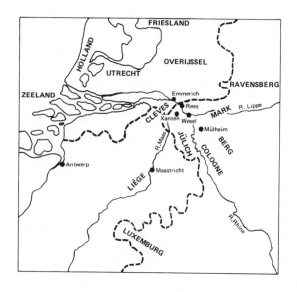

7. *Jülich–Cleves*

the United Provinces, therefore, observed with unabated interest the fortunes of the ruling family of Jülich–Cleves.

Duke William (1539–92) had flirted with heresy in his youth and married his daughters to Lutheran princes – one to Philipp Ludwig, count Palatine of Neuburg, and another to the duke of Prussia, whose daughter in due course married Johann Sigismund, the elector of Brandenburg. In the event William himself remained Roman Catholic, as did his son and successor, John William, who, though feeble-minded to the point of insanity, was kept in the faith, and out of the clutches of the Dutch Republic, by two successive Roman Catholic wives. When he died without children in 1609, the duchies were claimed by the elector of Brandenburg, who sent his brother Ernest as his proxy, and by the count Palatine of Neuburg, who sent his son Wolfgang Wilhelm.

The emperor Rudolf declared the duchies to be 'fiefs escheated to the Empire in default of male heirs', and entrusted their administration, pending his final adjudication, to his younger brother Leopold, bishop of Passau and of Strassburg. Ernest and Wolfgang Wilhelm, meanwhile, had already arrived in the duchies and agreed by the Treaty of Dortmund in June 1609 that they would hold them in common pending adjudication by the members of the Evangelical Union. A month later Leopold seized Jülich by force. The Union was uncertain how to react. It accepted that the matter was properly within the emperor's jurisdiction, but took its revenge on Leopold in March 1610 by invading his diocese of Strassburg. This in turn provoked the Catholic League to mobilise its members and the situation grew critical.

Nonetheless, both League and Union behaved with circumspection, since neither Spain nor the United Provinces, though vitally concerned about the outcome in Jülich–Cleves, was anxious to break the Twelve Years Truce which had just been negotiated with such difficulty. At a session of the Evangelical Union at Halle in January 1610, the Dutch offered 8000 men to serve under its command, thereby preserving the truce, and James I of England was shamed into pledging the 4000 English troops in Dutch service.

Henry meanwhile pursued a variety of hares. He declared his support for the Treaty of Dortmund and told the Dutch he understood only too well that the loss of Jülich–Cleves to Spain 'would cause the loss of the Spanish Netherlands'. He listened sympathetically to Charles Emmanuel of Savoy, who wanted to attack Milan and Genoa, and proposed a marriage between his daughter and the duke's son; he also proposed that the dauphin marry the heiress of Lorraine and thereby close the Spanish Road for good. Simultaneously, he discussed the possibility of a Spanish match for his daughter in return for the French-speaking provinces of the Spanish Netherlands. Suddenly, in April 1610, his purposes hardened, his belligerency became more pronounced, as he began to talk no longer of raising 8000 French troops but of raising 30,000 or more, and of his determination to settle the fate not only of Jülich–Cleves but also of the archdukes and the Spanish Netherlands.

The explanation was to be found, unexpectedly, in his passion for the seventeen-year-old Charlotte de Montmorency. Two years earlier she had come to court and attracted Henry's attention. Intending to make her his mistress, he married her to the gauche young prince of Condé, but discovered to his anger that Condé rejected the role of complaisant husband and fled to Brussels dragging Charlotte unwillingly behind him. The archdukes were in a quandary. They could not refuse to look after the princess while the prince, to spite Henry IV, went off to join the Spanish garrison in Milan, but they recognised that Henry's threats of war were seriously intended. 'I don't suppose anything like this was ever seen or heard of before,' wrote Isabella to Lerma, 'for should war break out we are caressing and entertaining the cause of it here…and yet get but poor thanks for our pains.'

There is little doubt that Henry was not play-acting. His attempt to recover Charlotte not only forfeited James I's support but also meant that he now contemplated a major war with Spain. 31,000 troops were to invade Jülich and Flanders, 14,000 more were to cross the Pyrenees and, by a treaty made at Brussolo, another 14,000 were to join Savoy's 13,000 in Lombardy. Moreover, in marked contrast to the impoverished condition of the Spanish government, France had sufficient funds to finance a major war. Henry's assassination by a Catholic fanatic in May 1610 as he left Paris to take command of his army was, therefore, interpreted aright by Spain as one of the saving miracles of the House of Habsburg.

Henry IV's death did not altogether prevent military operations going ahead in Jülich–Cleves. Maurice of Nassau with the support of English troops in Dutch service and of a token force sent by Henry IV's widow, Marie de Medici, led the Dutch into Jülich and expelled Leopold from the duchies. The archdukes, however, made no move. So relieved were they at the turn of events, so anxious not to precipitate a general conflict, that they did nothing to save Jülich, nor to prevent the passage of French troops across Luxemburg and Liège. Events were

EUROPE DURING THE TWELVE YEARS TRUCE 1609-21   43

beginning to move their way. The death of Frederick IV, elector Palatine and leader of the Evangelical Union, left its members uncertain what to do, the Dutch were evidently resolved to preserve the truce if possible by avoiding encounter with Spanish troops, and James I was backing out fast: 'I only wish', he told Salisbury, 'that I may handsomely wind myself out of this quarrel wherein the principal parties do so little for themselves.'

Most important of all was the diplomatic revolution achieved in France by Cardenas, the Spanish ambassador, in alliance with the *dévots*, influential Roman Catholics who disapproved of alliances with Protestants and believed that France should cultivate the friendship of the champion of the Counter-Reformation. Between them they persuaded Marie de Medici to withdraw from Jülich–Cleves and to abandon the Treaty of Brussolo with Savoy. In return Cardenas secured the marriage of her daughter Elizabeth to the future Philip IV of Spain and of her son Louis XIII to the infanta Anne of Austria.

Philip III and the archdukes were thus spared a major war, and the Catholic League, prompted by Zuñiga, profited from the occasion to drive the Evangelical Union's troops from the diocese of Strassburg. There yet remained the serious challenge of a Lutheran condominium in Jülich–Cleves, and the fact that with Dutch help the two claimants had fortified Mülheim across the river from Cologne. The resolution of the problem in 1614 was as swift as it was unexpected. Ernest died leaving the initiative with the elector of Brandenburg, who had passed his youth in Heidelberg and had subsequently become a Calvinist: meanwhile, Wolfgang Wilhelm, after many months of secret negotiation, at last declared himself a Roman Catholic and was married to the sister of Maximilian of Bavaria. The elector of Brandenburg promptly expelled him from the duchies and appealed to the Evangelical Union and to the United Provinces for support. Wolfgang Wilhelm, for his part, invoked the aid of the Catholic League, of Spain and of the emperor.

Matthias, who had succeeded Rudolf as emperor in 1612 commissioned the archudukes and the archbishop–elector of Cologne to act on his behalf in Mülheim and in Jülich–Cleves. As an imperial commissioner, rather than as commander of the Army of Flanders, Spinola could therefore risk an encounter with Dutch troops without jeopardising the truce, although, in the event, he acted with such speed that the Dutch were taken wholly by surprise. Leaving Maastricht with 18,000 men and 3000 cavalry, he razed the fortifications of Mülheim and concluded his campaign triumphantly by forcing the surrender of Wesel.

Wesel was a prize of great consequence. Described by the English ambassador Carleton as 'a nursing mother of religion, and a retreat and refuge for all those who for their conscience have been exiled', it was the stronghold of Calvinism in the lower Rhineland, the Rhenish Geneva, and a close ally of the United Provinces. It was, moreover, of considerable strategic importance, sited at the junction of the Rhine and the Lippe: 'the most important place on the Rhine', reported the Spanish ambassador, 'and one which could become the chief military station for all the armies of Flanders to assemble in at any moment'. The Dutch were crestfallen. They had urged the town to accept a Dutch garrison, but Wesel had chosen to rely for protection on its status as an imperial city. Once occupied by Spinola, it could not be recovered by Maurice without prejudicing the truce, and, were war to be renewed, Maurice feared that, given the prevailing attitudes of Marie de Medici and James I, the Dutch might suffer badly at the hands of Spain. All Maurice could do, therefore, was to reinforce Jülich and to steal a march on Spinola by occupying Emmerich and Rees on the Rhine below Wesel.

At Xanten in November 1614 the parties agreed to a compromise. Jülich and Berg were assigned to Wolfgang Wilhelm, and Cleves, Mark and Ravensberg to the elector of Brandenburg; but, since neither side could trust the other to withdraw according to the treaty, Jülich remained for the time being in Dutch hands and Wesel in Spain's. It was a settlement which afforded Spain more advantage than she could possibly have hoped for at any time since the death of Duke John in 1609, while the Dutch, who had hoped for much more than they gained, were glad to compromise, because a domestic crisis of some magnitude was beginning to break.

Trade, religion and politics in the United Provinces

The foundations of Dutch prosperity were laid at the end of the fifteenth century, when they wrested control of the North Sea herring fisheries from the Hanseatic League. The League, comprising nearly eighty ports around the Baltic and the north Atlantic coasts, had been catching, salting and distributing up to 13,000 tons of herring each year, but it could no longer compete with the initiative and hard work of the Dutch seamen. Recognising that the herring live in shoals near the surface in order to feed upon the plankton, they invented a drift net 350 feet long which they towed at night, when the luminous surface shoals were easily detectable. In addition they designed a new type of boat, the *buizen* or *busses*, which revolutionised the industry. Unlike the open boats they replaced, the *buizen* were decked vessels of up to 100 tons carrying coopers and salters, so that the catch could be processed at sea and exported immediately the fleets returned to port. By the time of the Twelve Years Truce, nearly a thousand *buizen* were at work, producing over 300,000 tons of salted herrings annually, more than enough to justify the States-General's reference to the North Sea as, 'one of the most important mines of the United Provinces'.

As they became wealthy from their herring fisheries, the Dutch put their money into commercial ventures. Unlike the merchants of Flanders and Brabant, however, whose industrial hinterland and long-established fairs allowed them to wait for trade to come to them, those of Holland and Zeeland had to sail out on their own initiative to find cargoes to carry – even those belonging to the enemy – and to undercut their competitor's prices. This they did by underpaying their crews, by borrowing money cheaply on the Antwerp Bourse – later, from the Bank of Amsterdam – and by stringent economy in shipbuilding. Bulk purchases of timber were made; fir was used whenever possible, in place of oak; and the shipyards were equipped with wind-driven sawmills and other labour-saving devices. The Dutch also designed a new type of freight carrier, the *fluyt*, which was virtually a long floating container with enormous holds. Its great length, often six times its beam, created longitudinal stress, but this was compensated for at the expense of the crew's quarters by reducing the superstructure fore and aft. Each *fluyt* was designed for its appropriate trade. Shallow drafts were needed for the silted estuaries of the Baltic, deeper drafts for the Atlantic, and the holds were specially modified for the timber and grain trades.

The first area to attract Dutch attention was the Baltic, where the Hanseatic League had forfeited its monopoly of the carrying trade as it lost its cohesion, its members preferring to exploit the short-term advantages of trading independently. The Dutch began in a humble way as contractors for the League and ended by taking over most of the grain trade from Poland, which became the staple of their commerce. In addition they acquired a major share of the valuable exports of the forest regions – amber, furs, wax, potash and the indispensible naval stores of pitch, hemp and timber. As a result the records of the Danish Sound dues, recording the payments made by ships passing in and out of the Baltic, revealed an increase in the annual number of Dutch payments from 1300 in 1500 to 5000 in 1600.

Once established in the Baltic, the Dutch found it prudent to cultivate whenever possible the alliance of the Hanseatic towns, and in particular to act with them to oppose the expansion of Danish influence and trade. They sent troops in 1617 to help Brunswick defend itself against the Danes, and with the Hanse they opposed increases in the Sound dues levied by Denmark. In addition they kept a watchful eye on Spanish diplomacy in the Baltic, which sought to win the alliance of Hanse towns against the Dutch by offering them special privileges in Spanish ports, and to disrupt the grain trade with Danzig. For this reason the Dutch made treaties of their own with the League and gave assistance to Sweden, not only to keep Denmark in check but also, as reported by Carleton, the English ambassador at The Hague, to restrain Poland in order 'to preserve those seas from molestation, where they are jealous the king of Spain doth serve himself of the king of Poland as an instrument to interrupt their trade, which is the seal of their commonwealth' (see p. 22).

From the Baltic the Dutch swept down along the Atlantic coast, and, despite the long years of warfare with Spain, the Atlantic trade never slackened. Spain could not do without grain, fish, metal goods and textiles for herself and for her colonies. She also needed timber for her oceanic fleets. There was oak in the interior but it was difficult to transport it to the coast and the expanding iron industry at Vizcaya competed with the shipbuilding yards of Bilbao for what was available. From 1570, therefore, Baltic timber was imported. In return the Iberian merchants needed Dutch vessels to transport Castilian wool and soap to the textile manufacturers of England and the Netherlands, salt from Setubal to the Dutch fisheries, and fruits from the Mediterranean, wines from Seville and the Canaries, spices from India and silver from America to the markets of northern Europe. In addition, shortages of raw materials in the Mediterranean, and in particular a dearth of corn after a succession of bad harvests in the 1590s, gave the Dutch a golden opportunity to slip past Gibraltar and tap the rich markets of Barcelona, Marseilles, Naples and Leghorn. Their reputation as enemies of Spain, moreover, helped the Dutch to secure concessions from the Venetians and from the Osmanli Turks.

Their most recent venture was the penetration of the Spanish–Portuguese empire. Though vastly less valuable to their economy than the herring fisheries and the Baltic trade, it had nonetheless caught the imagination of individual Dutch merchants, who by 1600 were to be found regularly sailing to the Far East. So great were the difficulties of raising sufficient capital to finance voyages lasting up to three years, and so great the danger of losing it, that Oldenbarneveldt persuaded the free-trading Dutch that the colonial trade was one area in which cut-throat competition and indiscriminate rivalry might be harmful. In 1602 the East India Company was founded with capital of 6.5 million florins, of which nearly half was supplied by the States-General. The directors' aims were commercial rather than colonial, and their agents were ordered 'to keep in view the necessity of peaceful trade throughout Asia, from which is derived the smoke in the kitchens here at home'. Neverthless, the company could not neglect to defend itself against other interlopers, native rulers and, of course, the Spanish government.

The truce of 1609 was therefore of importance to the East India Company, since it was tacitly granted temporary access to the Far East by the admission that it might trade 'in the countries of all other princes, potentates and peoples who may wish to permit them to do so'. The princes and potentates, being subject to Spanish rule, would not in fact be allowed to permit the Dutch to trade, but so inadequate was Spanish naval power in Far Eastern waters that there was no way by which this could be prevented. In the West Indies, on the other hand, Spain increased her expenditure on fortifications and convoys so that Dutch interference in the islands' trade was kept to a minimum throughout the Twelve Years Truce.

Paradoxically, the Dutch were on better commercial terms with their enemy Spain than with England their ally. The English of course had Baltic, Levant and East India companies of their own, and complained that it was the *buizen* and not English ships which took advantage of the annual migration of the herring shoals along the east coast of Scotland and England. 'His Majesty's seas', wrote Tobias Gentleman in *England's Way to Win Wealth*, 'is their chiefest, principal and only rich treasury whereby they have so long maintained their wars and have so greatly prospered and enriched themselves. . . . O slothful England and careless countrymen! Look but on these fellows that we call the plump Hollanders, behold their diligence in fishing and our own careless negligence.' Since English sloth and negligence were not to be replaced overnight by positive action, James I acted as dog in the manger in 1607 by denying the *buizen* access to his territorial waters. Oldenbarneveldt, whose valuation of the North Sea fisheries was no less than Tobias Gentleman's, immediately sent his brother Elias to placate the English government, and by cleverly confusing the issue with those involved in the Jülich–Cleves crisis succeeded in gaining a few years delay in the execution of the proclamation.

With the fishing dispute temporarily shelved, the two governments finally settled the matter of the Cautionary Towns, Brill, Flushing and Rammekens, held by England as pledges for loans made by Elizabeth. So great was the influence at the English court of Gondomar (see p. 56), Philip III's shrewd and extremely able ambassador, that Oldenbarneveldt was ever anxious that James I might make these available to Spain. In 1615, therefore, the United Provinces offered to settle their debts. James claimed that these amounted to £600,000, but finally accepted Oldenbarneveldt's offer of £100,000 down with three further payments of £50,000 at six-monthly intervals. Afterwards he convinced himself that he had been tricked and in 1616 retaliated by ordering tolls to be levied on all *buizen* in his waters. The Dutch, so vital was the issue, resolved to give nothing away. They ordered the arrest of admiralty agents sent to collect the tolls, and though they eventually released them with an apology they refused to recognise any English rights over their herring fleets.

Other disputes arose over cod in the North Atlantic and whales off Spitzbergen, and armed conflict broke out in the Far East, so that the two countries seemed to be on the brink of war. The privy councillor Winwood, an ardent enemy of Spain and an advocate of the Protestant alliance, was driven to remark bitterly that 'only the Spaniards have cause to triumph and to make bonfires of joy and gladness', and Gondomar's reports to Madrid recorded his satisfaction at the turn of events. Nonetheless, the Protestant alliance held, since James remained, in the very marrow of his being, a contentious but essentially Protestant theologian, and it was in this role that he intervened to preserve, as he imagined it, the true faith within the United Provinces.

The theological controversy which attracted James' attention revived in a Calvinist setting the old problem of free will. Calvin had taught that God had predestined the fate of all men, and his followers comforted themselves with the assurance that they alone were destined for eternal bliss. Arminius, a Calvinist theologian of remarkably liberal and humane views, questioned whether God would predestine a man's soul to the horrors of hell. This, he argued, conflicted with the notion of a merciful God and paradoxically made God the author of sin. At Leyden, where he had held the chair of theology since 1602, he was challenged by Francis Gomarus, whose exile from Bruges in the

Catholic south had made him an embittered champion of Calvinist orthodoxy: 'An eternal and divine decree', he thundered, 'has established which men were to be saved and which were to be damned.' When Arminius died in 1609 his followers drew up a remonstrance, setting out their views and asking for official protection from the attacks of Gomarus. Oldenbarneveldt was sympathetic. He had always hoped to see a state church established on broad foundations, and Arminianism, in his eyes, was an opportune development, since it glossed over some of the differences between the Calvinist and Catholic faiths. Moreover, the regent class, which dominated the Estates of Holland, was anxious to assert its authority over the Calvinist clergy and to this end gave formal support to the remonstrance. Gomarus retorted by publishing a counter-remonstrance, to which most of the clergy subscribed, and the Estates, embarrassed by the hornet's nest they had stirred up, appealed for restraint 'in these lofty and mysterious questions which are, God help it, all too much in dispute'.

James I could not be denied the opportunity to intrude his theological expertise. Oldenbarneveldt tried to persuade him that the counter-remonstrants were contentious and unruly Puritans, 'endeavouring in ecclesiastical matters at least to usurp an extraordinary authority, against which his Majesty with very weighty reasons has so many times declared his opinions founded upon God's Word and upon all the laws and principles of justice'. The ploy failed. James declared his support for Gomarus, and Winwood threatened that if a remonstrant were appointed to Arminius's chair at Leyden 'to brave or despite his Majesty, the king has the means if it pleases him to use them, and that without drawing sword, to range them to reason, and to make the magistrates on their knees demand his pardon'.

What precisely James intended to do, Oldenbarneveldt did not know. In any case, he had more urgent opposition to face at home. The root cause was not so much Arminianism as the existence of a Roman Catholic majority. Spinola had persuaded Philip III not to let the truce negotiations founder on the issue of protecting the Dutch Roman Catholics, because he believed that once the pressures of war were removed the Calvinist government would relax its attitude and permit them a greater measure of freedom. In the event he was wrong. The Dutch Calvinists, watching with tense anxiety the events in Jülich–Cleves, along with those of Bohemia and northern Italy (see pp. 57, 60), remained convinced that Madrid and Rome threatened their faith and their independence at every turn. Consequently they regarded their own Roman Catholics with greater suspicion than before. The action of Oldenbarneveldt and the Estates of Holland in endorsing the remonstrance was interpreted as an attempt to water down the pure doctrine of Calvinism and to weaken the power of the Calvinist clergy within the republic. Moreover, the belief of the remonstrants that there was no predestined company of the Elect, and that Catholics and Calvinists alike were offered opportunities of salvation, was held to be not only heresy but treason.

Every Calvinist congregation became a centre of disaffection, from every pulpit Oldenbarneveldt was denounced, and, oblivious to the fact that the southern provinces had deliberately chosen to remain Catholic rather than ally with the Dutch, a war of liberation was demanded to release them from the yoke of the Spanish Inquisition. The truce, so beneficial in its effect, was condemned as a compact with the forces of evil, the war extolled as a crusade untimely thwarted in its course by Arminian heretics in the pay of Spain. As the conflict expanded from the question of free will to embrace the issues of war and peace, the quick minds of the Amsterdam merchants awoke to the opportunity for profits which war with Spain might afford. With appetites enlarged by the success of the East India Company, they dreamed of yet greater profits to be derived from the creation of a West India Company to promote piracy and trade among the Spanish islands. As a result the city espoused the counter-remonstrance and demanded the dismissal of Oldenbarneveldt and an end to the truce.

To make matters worse for Oldenbarneveldt, his determination to preserve the French alliance, despite the rapprochement between Henry IV's successor and Spain, only confirmed the suspicions of the counter-remonstrants. Under the treaty of 1609, the Dutch were bound, when requested, to send 4000 men to the French king's aid, and Calvinist sentiment was outraged when in 1616 Oldenbarneveldt agreed to help Louis XIII against his Huguenot rebels, who included the duke of Bouillon, brother-in-law to Maurice of Nassau.

Until this time Maurice had carefully avoided public dispute with Oldenbarneveldt. He chafed under the burden of inactivity imposed by the truce, but he bided his time, knowing well that though the Dutch admired him for his military exploits they remained republican at heart. A campaign to establish the leadership of the House of Orange would have failed had not Oldenbarneveldt by his handling of the Arminius affair provided him with powerful allies. His cousin William Louis, stadtholder of Friesland and a staunch supporter of Gomarus, urged him to intervene, reminding him 'how valiantly and constantly you have fought for the preservation of this country, and for the reformed religion which is its life-blood, indeed its very heart'. The letter furnished the patriotic theme which Maurice was well able to exploit. Indifferent to the theological subtleties of the counter-remonstrants and disdainful of the profit-hungry merchants of Amsterdam, Maurice realised their value as enemies of the advocate and of the truce. To their side he added the weight of his own authority, his personal connections with the Huguenots and the support of the petty nobility of the inland provinces who served in his army.

Within months Oldenbarneveldt was outnumbered in the States-General by enemies who extolled the House of Orange as the sole guardian of true religion. In Holland, however, despite the opposition of Amsterdam, he retained his supremacy and took steps to defend the province against Maurice's army. The Estates were persuaded in December 1616 to enlist a force of militia, the waardgelders, responsible solely to the advocate and his fellow regents, and orders were given to all regular troops stationed in Holland to co-operate in its defence.

Maurice retaliated in the following months in a scene brilliantly stage-managed to create the maximum effect throughout the United Provinces. Summoned by the Holland representatives in the States-General to advise them about the dispute, he called, in Carleton's vivid account of the proceedings, 'for the register book, wherein his oath was set down, which he took in the year '86; at which time he entered into the charge he now holds for the service of the state; which being read in all their presences, and there in this article noted in particular, that both he and the states do mutually bind themselves, even to the last drop of blood, for the defence of the reformed religion, which was the first ground of their quarrel, and for which his father lost his life. This oath (said he) will I keep whilst I live, and this religion will I defend.'

Some months later Maurice went to Brill, a Calvinist stronghold and which in 1572 had been the first town in Holland to have called upon his father's leadership. It was a private visit, the captain-general reviewing one of his garrisons, but it had its effect on the town council, which decided not to enlist waardgelders. Encouraged by this, Maurice began a royal progress with his army through Gelderland and Overijssel, provinces jealous of Holland's predominance within the Union. Each town in turn made open declarations of loyalty to him and dismissed all regents suspected of Arminianism. In August 1618 he ventured into Holland itself and the separate towns disbanded their waardgelders as he approached. Oldenbarneveldt alone refused to submit, remaining at The Hague until taken prisoner by the prince's bodyguard.

Maurice was not the enemy of the regents as a class: he wanted not to destroy their privileged position but to make them subservient to his directions. Just as Catholics had been replaced by Calvinists during the revolt, so the supporters of Arminius and Oldenbarneveldt were replaced by the protagonists of the counter-remonstrance and the House of Orange; but both new and old were of the same class as before. The high hopes of the Calvinist congregations for innovations in the urban constitutions were disappointed. They were allowed, however, to summon a national synod at Dordrecht in 1618 to draw up a new confession of faith from which all taint of Arminianism was removed, and to secure the dismissal of remonstrant clergy from their livings and university posts. As for Oldenbarneveldt, he was found guilty of opposing Maurice's assumption of sovereignty, of fostering Arminianism and of favouring the East India Company at the expense of others. Maurice sought his submission not his death, and would have spared him had he sued for a reprieve, but Oldenbarneveldt was resolved to make no move that could be interpreted as an admission of guilt. Rather than acknowledge the authority of the House of Orange, he chose to accept death by execution.

Sweden, Denmark, Russia and Poland

The years which saw the settlement of Jülich–Cleves and the downfall of Oldenbarneveldt were also of importance in the history of Sweden. The kingdom in 1609 was hard-pressed to survive (see p. 22). Sigismund of Poland had intervened in the Russian civil war to establish his own son Wladislau as tsar in 1610, thus strengthening his position on Sweden's eastern frontier, while the Danes seized the occasion to invade Sweden from the south west. With Karl's death in October 1611 the defence of the beleaguered country passed into the hands of his sixteen-year-old son.

Fortunately for himself and for his country, Gustav II Adolf immediately came to terms with the leading noble families. He recognised that Sweden was too small a country to withstand the secession from public life of so important a section of the community, and he respected the nobles' desire to be employed in positions of importance. He disarmed them entirely by conceding straightway to the demands presented on their behalf by Axel Oxenstierna. They were given employment beyond their expectation in a civil service organised into five colleges, or departments, under a chancellor, a marshal, a high steward, a treasurer and an admiral. The nomenclature was that of medieval government and so were the sources of revenue, since the administration was maintained by the produce of crown lands assigned to the separate colleges; but because of the co-operation established between Gustav and his nobles the system worked admirably, withstanding the burdens of maintaining perpetual warfare, of assimilating conquered territories and of governing in the absence of a king whose reign was spent with the army.

Since the nobles thus gained responsibility and power, their privileges, especially their exemption from taxation, were not, as in France and Spain, the residue of an anachronistic tradition, but the reward for service genuinely undertaken in the service of the state. Being trusted, the majority proved trustworthy, and in Axel Oxenstierna the best qualities of public service were personified. He was an admirable foil to the volatile king, being practical, cautious, diplomatic and a gifted bureaucrat: when Gustav complained, 'If we were all as cold as you we should freeze', he retorted, 'If we were all as hot as Your Majesty we should burn.' Gustav appointed him chancellor, responsible for co-ordinating the work of the other colleges, and since two of the other four senior offices were held by his relatives he was able to supervise the administration to good effect for the next thirty years.

Gustav's concessions pacified the nobles and released him from the performance of duties for which had no aptitude. The violent energy and fiery personality of his grandfather Gustav Ericksson, who had led the revolt against Denmark, were evident in him, making him careless of administration but incomparable as a leader of men. A big clumsy youth with tawny beard and hair – *il re d'oro* to the Italian mercenaries – immensely strong, with the fierce temper, the easy manner and the blunt directness of an infantry officer, he inspired others with his boundless self-confidence. 'He thinks the ship cannot sink that carries him', wrote the English ambassador, and this, in 1611, with Sweden's enemies closing in on all sides, was a commendable virtue.

The Danes presented the most immediate and most dangerous threat. Christian IV was a popular and resourceful king, determined to restore his country's greatness after the loss of Sweden and the period of rebellion which had then ensued. Since his accession in 1588 he had done much to re-establish royal authority and to encourage trade and industry. He exploited his power to levy dues on all traffic in the Sound, and alarmed the Hanse by seeking to extend his influence in northern Germany, between the Elbe and the Weser, where the Hanse operated its overland trade route by way of Lübeck and Bremen. As a duke of Holstein, Christian was already a prince of the Lower Saxon Circle, the secularised diocese of Schwerin being administered by his brother and that of Verden by his son. Nonetheless, it was in Sweden that his principal ambition lay, and in 1611 he believed that his time had come. Älvsborg, Sweden's only Atlantic port, isolated among the Danish-held provinces on the west coast, was taken and his armies were poised to strike at the heart of the kingdom. While Gustav mobilised what troops he could, Oxenstierna tried to persuade Christian to make peace. Christian, who lacked neither energy nor courage, was unaware of the true weakness of the Swedish army, was finding it difficult to finance his campaign, and his troops around Älvsborg were disconcerted by the bitter resistance maintained by the local peasantry. The conquest of Sweden, though conceivably within his grasp, appeared to involve a prolonged war of attrition, too expensive to sustain, and he settled instead for the retention of Älvsborg.

By the Treaty of Knäred (1613) Älvsborg was assigned to Denmark until it could be redeemed at a price well beyond the Swedish king's resources. This saved the day for Sweden. The Danes' success, moreover, had brought the Dutch upon the scene, anxious to re-establish Sweden as a counterweight to Danish power in the Baltic. With the help of Dutch loans Älvsborg was redeemed by 1619. In addition the Dutch supplied the capital, the engineers and the mining experts to exploit Sweden's reserves of high-grade iron ore and copper. Iron production rose to 5000 tons a year by 1620 – to 20,000 by 1630 – but it was the copper which transformed the royal revenues. In the Stora Kopperburg Sweden enjoyed possession of the largest deposit of copper in Europe, at a time when every government needed copper urgently for the manufacture of coinage and artillery. Gustav appropriated the mine in 1613, partly to raise money for the redemption of Älvsborg, and from then until its exhaustion, after 1650, the annual production of 3000 tons of copper gave Sweden a particular advantage over her enemies, since it enabled her to procure in Amsterdam a constant supply of foreign exchange to pay her continental armies.

In the meantime affairs had improved for Sweden on the Russian front. Wladislau had proved to be unpopular as tsar and a general rising took place in 1612. In the confusion Swedish troops seized Novgorod and claimed the throne for Gustav's brother, but the Russians had had their fill of foreigners. Feodor Romanov, a great noble who had been compelled by a previous tsar to take monks' vows under the name of Filaret, had offered the throne to Wladislau in 1610, but on terms unacceptable to the Poles, who took him prisoner. As opposition to Wladislau grew, Filaret's name became a rallying cry and in 1613 his son Michael Romanov was acclaimed tsar. Gustav II Adolf, once the Danish war was over, landed in Russia to defend Novgorod against both sides and advanced his power so successfully that in 1617 Michael came to terms at Stolbova. Gustav evacuated Novgorod and renounced his brother's claims to the throne; in return he kept Ingria, Karelia, Ingermannland – the land bridge between Finland and Estonia – and the isle of Kexholm (see map 4). This deprived Russia of her access to the Baltic and made Sweden controller of her Baltic trade.

In the following year, after Wladislau had led his troops to the gates of Moscow in 1617 without gaining entry, Poland and Russia agreed to an armistice. The agreement, signed at Deulino in 1618, was to last fourteen years: Russia ceded Smolensk for the period of the truce and the Poles released Filaret, who returned to become patriarch of the Russian Church and adviser to his son Michael.

As for Sweden, a series of short-term truces were agreed upon with Poland until Gustav, attracted by the valuable customs duties to be collected at the mouths of the Polish rivers, invaded Livonia in 1621 and laid siege to Riga. Standing at the mouth of the Dvina and controlling one third of Poland's exports, Riga was one of the great cities of the Baltic: it was also a great fortress, and it was the measure of Gustav's success that within ten years he had brought his kingdom so successfully from the brink of defeat that he could now believe that so great a prize might lie within his grasp.

Spanish lines of communication

If Riga were to fall to Sweden, the governments of Europe would have to take account of Gustav Adolf in their calculations of the balance of power between the Habsburgs and their enemies; and Poland, for many years the great north-eastern bastion of the Habsburgs' network of alliances, would need to be strengthened. In the meantime the pressing concern of the Spanish government was to preserve its lines of communication after its relative success in the dispute over Jülich–Cleves.

The security of the sea route to the Netherlands depended upon the goodwill of James I, and nothing could have caused Philip III more anxiety than the marriage in 1613 of James's daughter, Elizabeth, to Frederick V, the new elector Palatine. Frederick, like his father (see p. 15), was a Calvinist, an ally of the United Provinces and leader of the Evangelical Union: for many decades his fortress at Heidelberg had denied the Spaniards access to the waterway of the middle Rhine. Most Englishmen interpreted the marriage as a missionary enterprise to strengthen continental Protestantism, and the celebrations in London evoked many public demonstrations of hostility to Rome and Madrid. Afterwards, and the significance was not lost on Philip III, the couple left for an official reception by Maurice of Nassau at The Hague.

James I saw things differently. Salisbury and Henry, prince of Wales, who had to some extent embodied the Elizabethan tradition of hostility to Spain, had died in 1612. Raleigh was in the Tower, and James cast himself not merely as defender of the faith but as arbiter of Christendom. Having brought together the leaders of the Protestant alliance through the marriage of Elizabeth to Frederick, he then planned to reconcile them with the Catholics by the marriage of his son Charles to a princess of Spain. To Philip III's great relief, it became clear that Dover was not to become another Heidelberg, and that his convoys to Flanders were still to pass safely through the Channel. To safeguard this favourable situation, he sent to London Don Diego Sarmiento de Acuna, later to be known as count of Gondomar, a brilliant ambassador who swiftly established considerable influence over the king.

Gondomar's ability was first put to the test when Raleigh persuaded James to release him from the Tower to find gold in the region of the Orinoco. Since this meant the intrusion of English ships in Spanish-American waters, Gondomar made his protest, and was rewarded not only with assurances that there would be no interference with Spanish settlements but also with details of Raleigh's itinerary. Yet Gondomar knew that James was hedging his bets. If Raleigh succeeded in finding gold, Spain's protests would go unheard and the alliance be jeopardised. Moreover, as the English ambassador in Madrid put it, the Spanish government was concerned 'that Sir W. Raleigh, failing of the gold he pretends to find may (considering his strength) prove a dangerous infestor of the coast of their Indies, where doubtless he shall find very poor resistance'.

In the event Raleigh failed dismally and returned to face humiliation and execution, and James's public apology for the wrongs done to Philip III angered his subjects in the same measure as they gave satisfaction to Spain. The matter was presented as a Dutch conspiracy to endanger good relations between Spain and England, and Gondomar improved the occasion by renewing the matter of the Spanish match for Charles, with enticing hints of the dowry to be furnished by Philip III's munificence. It was consequently the turn of the Dutch to become alarmed – 'there being nothing more prejudicial to the good correspondence betwixt his majesty and this state', wrote Carleton to Winwood from The Hague, 'than the belief of matching our prince with Spain, which I advertised to your honour in my last was no small cross to my negotiations with this state'.

While the Channel route was being safeguarded, Spanish troops were denied access to the Spanish Road through Savoy. Charles Emmanuel had recognised the lesson of the Treaty of Lyons that so far as Savoy was concerned France was a more dangerous enemy than Spain, and he redirected his territorial ambitions from the Rhône valley to Lombardy and the Ligurian coast. Writing to the Venetian ambassador in 1607, he had confided his new policy: 'When it comes down to it I am essentially an Italian, and I believe we have every reason to come to an understanding, because it is not for our own good that these foreigners assume friendship towards us but only to take from us what we own and compel us to serve their purposes.' In 1609 he expelled the Spanish garrisons appointed to protect the Road, and in the following year, by the Treaty of Brussolo (see p. 42) with Henry IV, agreed to invade Lombardy with the aid of 14,000 French troops. News of Henry's assassination recalled him to the path of prudent neutrality, but not for long.

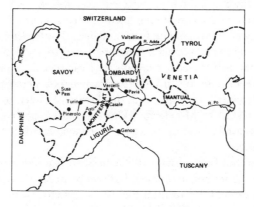

8. Savoy and northern Italy

Francis IV of Mantua, to whom also belonged the fortresses of
Montferrat and Casale, which flanked the Spanish route from Genoa to
Milan, died without immediate heirs in 1612, giving Charles
Emmanuel an opportunity to test his strength in northern Italy by
making himself master of Montferrat. 'It is time to throw off the yoke
which the Spaniards wish to impose on us', he wrote to Venice; 'this is
the opportunity we must not let slip for we shall never have a better
one'. The regency administration in France was in alliance with Spain
(see p. 43), but the proud and independent governor of Dauphiné, the
Huguenot Lesdiguières, agreed to cross the Alps in support of Charles
Emmanuel, whose ambassador in London reported many schemes
afoot to send a fleet to the Mediterranean and an army from the
Evangelical Union. Inojoso, governor of Milan, did not wait upon
events but marched against Savoy in 1614. Finding himself without
allies, Charles Emmanuel agreed at Asti in the following year to
withdraw his troops and to submit his claim to Montferrat to Imperial
arbitration. Carleton, who attended the negotiations at Asti, after being
in correspondence with those in Venice, France, England, Germany
and the United Provinces who had offered help to Savoy wrote
mournfully that their troops 'were but in project when they should have
been in action'.

Carleton also noted that 'Spain takes exception against the form of
the peace as too much to the honour and advantage of the duke of
Savoy'. Since the Treaty of Brussolo in fact, Spain had been nursing its
grievances against Charles Emmanuel, and Inojoso was recalled in
disgrace for not securing better terms. His successor, the marquis of
Villafranca, was soon given an opportunity to remedy matters. Charles
Emmanuel, finding himself unexpectedly reinforced by Lesdiguières
with 7000 men, and an additional 4000 Germans sent by Christian of
Anhalt, renewed the campaign but was defeated at Apertola. In 1617
the States-General of the United Provinces voted 50,000 florins to raise
troops for Charles and tried to persuade the Evangelical Union to follow
suit, but it was too late. When Villafranca's men took Vercelli by storm,
Charles surrendered and agreed, in the Treaty of Pavia, to renounce
entirely his claims to Montferrat. Thus chastened, he reopened the
Road for Spanish use and in 1620 a force of 8500 passed through on its
way to Flanders.

Venice had not been unsympathetic to Savoy's attempt to dislodge
the Spaniards from northern Italy, but was preoccupied with its own
conflict with Philip III's Austrian cousins, in particular with Ferdinand
of Styria. For some time Ferdinand had been employing Bosnian and

Albanian pirates, the uskoks, to harass Venetian shipping in the Adriatic, and by 1615 was at war with the republic because of a longstanding dispute over the border fortress of Gradisca. When Habsburg troops seized the fortress and fortified the line of the river Isonzo, the area became the object of intense international interest. Zuñiga, Spain's ambassador to the Empire, raised troops for Ferdinand with funds sent from Spain to finance the Catholic League; Albert released Dampierre and other officers from the Army of Flanders; and a young Bohemian noble, Waldstein, won Ferdinand's gratitude by arriving at the Isonzo with a detachment of 200 cavalry raised at his own expense. The Venetians had the advantages of greater wealth and interior lines of communication, but they nonetheless applied to the Dutch for aid. The States-General, preoccupied with the Arminian crisis as well as with the war in Savoy and the fishing dispute with England, could not agree on a policy, but the representatives of Zeeland and Gelderland met the Venetian agent privately and suggested that Venice should first offer the Dutch a formal alliance against the Habsburgs. In the meantime, 4000 troops, led by Maurice's cousin Jan Ernst of Nassau, joined the Venetian camp in 1616.

Zuñiga was recalled to Spain in 1617, but his successor, the count of Oñate, was no less active in mobilising help for Ferdinand against the Venetians. He raised troops in Alsace and, without reference to Madrid, persuaded Osuna, the viceroy in Naples, to provide naval assistance in the Adriatic – which led to Dutch complaints about attacks on their own shipping. When the French mediated a peace between the belligerents at Wiener Neustadt in 1618, Osuna refused to let the matter rest, and, in a rash and unauthorised conspiracy with Bedmar, the Spanish ambassador in Venice, attempted to organise a coup. It was a grim failure. Two mutilated corpses, supposed agents of Osuna, were publicly displayed, followed five days later by a third, and this without further comment was sufficient to advertise that the city fathers remained firmly in control.

Throughout their conflict with Ferdinand the Venetians had been active in the Valtelline in order to recruit troops, but their efforts had been thwarted because the entente between France and Spain ensured that the Spanish faction was temporarily dominant in the valley. In 1617 the Planta family complained of the Venetian efforts to raise troops and urged the acceptance of proposals which would guarantee access to France and Spain alone, provided that Fuentes's fortress was dismantled (see p. 27). The full assembly of the Grisons, however, rejected this and, by way of retaliation, launched along the valleys a combined missionary and military operation directed against all Roman Catholics and supporters of Spain. Jorg Jenatsch, the Calvinist pastor who led the campaign, established something of a reign of terror from August 1618 to January 1619: the Roman Catholic bishop of Chur was deposed and over 150 victims were executed, tortured or exiled by self-styled 'peoples' courts' at Thursis and Davos on charges of conspiring with Spain. In the process many old scores were settled, and when Jenatsch's men swept down across the floor of the Valtelline they tortured to death the old Roman priest in Sondrio and opened a new Protestant church. Most dangerous of all for Spain, because it demonstrated their acute awareness of events outside the valley, they declared their support for the Protestant rebellion which had just broken out in Bohemia.

Bohemia, Hungary and Austria 1609–18

The emperor Rudolf in his dotage made one final attempt to recover some of the power he had lost in 1608. In January 1611, his favourite nephew, Leopold, who had acted as his agent in Jülich–Cleves, raised nearly 10,000 men and cavalry in Alsace and marched on Bohemia, via the Upper Austrian territories of Matthias. His unexpected arrival with so great a force at the gates of Prague caused immediate panic, especially as no one could fathom his precise intentions, but the inhabitants succeeded in holding the city centre against him. Rudolf in fact had no clear idea what his raiders were to achieve, and after several weeks of fruitless occupation of the suburbs they began to get out of hand. Because the security of Bohemia was of importance to Spain, Zuñiga, the Spanish ambassador, lent Rudolf 40,000 florins to pay off and disperse his troops, and, with the arrival of Matthias at the invitation of the Bohemian Estates, peace was restored and the crown transferred from Rudolf to Matthias. In the following year, on Rudolf's death, Matthias was elected Holy Roman Emperor.

Philip III had always feared that Rudolf might go over to the Protestants and was not greatly reassured by the election of his successor, since Matthias had already demonstrated that to preserve a united front against the Osmanli Turks he was ready to grant substantial religious and constitutional privileges to his subjects (see p. 19). Matthias, however, was already an old man, without legitimate children, and Zuñiga's choice fell on Ferdinand of Styria, a younger member of the Habsburg family who had already proved his abilities as a reliable Catholic prince. In private life a man of great good humour and kindness, he was capable of ruthless cruelty in the defence of his authority and his faith. Where his father Charles had made concessions to the Protestants, Ferdinand on his accession debarred them from public office, closed their churches and schools and gave all but those of noble birth three weeks in which to conform or to leave the country. It was a calculated gamble which few other rulers in Ferdinand's position would have chosen to take, but, although 10,000 of his subjects chose exile, his authority in Styria was established beyond doubt.

Zuñiga reported to Philip III in 1613 that the archduke was eager to succeed Matthias and would trade Alsace for Spanish support. The government in Brussels, however, advised against the deal: though the possession of Alsace would be of immense strategic importance to Spain, Spinola pointed out that it would unhappily provoke the jealous fears of all the Catholic powers in the Rhineland, upon whose co-operation Spanish communications depended. Without official sanction therefore, Zuñiga and his successor Oñate continued their negotiations with Ferdinand, concluding a formal treaty at Graz in 1617. In return for Spanish support, Ferdinand was to consider marrying the infanta Maria – currently being offered by Gondomar to the prince of Wales – and would grant to Spain the Sundgau in Alsace, along with Piombino and other Imperial fiefs in northern Italy, as they fell vacant. Territorial considerations apart, Oñate was satisfied that, if Ferdinand were to succeed to all Matthias's lands and titles, closer relations would be established between the emperor and the king of Spain than had pertained for many years.

Fortunately for Spain, Matthias agreed that no other member of the family could rival Ferdinand's political skill and determination. The Habsburgs of Spain and Austria therefore were united in their objective. The first step to achieving it was to secure Ferdinand's election as Matthias's successor in Bohemia, not an easy task in view of the influence exercised by Count Andreas Schlick, Matthias von Thurn and other Protestant champions of the *Letter of Majesty*. Thurn had already expressed his anxieties about Ferdinand to Christian of Anhalt – it had even been discussed with James I at the elector Palatine's wedding in London – but there was no agreement about an alternative candidate. Moreover, it was not at all clear from past precedents if the process of election was a genuine privilege or simply the solemn ratification of the hereditary candidate.

The chancellor Lobkowitz, the key figure of the Spanish party in

Bohemia, handled the matter consummately well. Following a brief illness of Matthias, he called an emergency session of the Bohemian Estates in 1617. Beforehand, at a private meeting of the leading nobles, he pretended to assume that Ferdinand's nomination was a matter of course, that opposition to the hereditary candidate would only be futile and offensive, and that the *Letter of Majesty*, which was so highly prized, would be unconditionally guaranteed by the new king. Schlick, the most exalted Protestant in the company, put no faith in Lobkowitz's assurances, but since there was such confusion about the procedure, and no agreed rival candidate to propose, he fell in with Lobkowitz's plans. The following day the Estates met with full pomp in the presence of Matthias, who declared his wish that Ferdinand be nominated his successor. Lobkowitz so arranged it that the vote was given in order of seniority, beginning with those whose support had already been elicited. Thurn and his colleagues, who had been anticipating a lively debate, sat in horrified amazement as the greatest nobles of Bohemia, including Schlick, declared their support for Ferdinand, so that when the time came for them to vote there was nothing to do but tamely follow suit.

Subsequently there was much recrimination among the Protestants, who awaited the chance to win allies against Lobkowitz among the Catholic supporters of the *Letter of Majesty*. Their opportunity came in December 1617, when Matthias and the chancellor left for Austria and Hungary to arrange the succession, leaving a council of ten regents to govern the kingdom. Regency government was unpopular in Bohemia – it had been Rudolf's principal virtue in his final years that he preferred Prague to Vienna or Pressburg – and the composition of the council gave offence. Seven members were Roman Catholic, including two, Martinitz and Slavata, who had never signed their assent to the *Letter*, and Thurn was not only excluded but also compelled to give up a lucrative office for a less profitable one. To those prejudiced against them, the regents seemed to waste no time in showing their hand, by inquiring if Protestant churches at Braunau and Klostergrab were built on church land, which was an illegal act, or on royal land protected by the *Letter*.

When a deputation from Klostergrab was arrested, the Protestants claimed their rights under the *Letter of Majesty*, summoned a diet and elected defenders to write in protest to Mathias. From Vienna Lobkowitz replied that the defenders had exceeded their powers, because the churches stood on church land, but so swift was the reply that the Protestant diet refused to belive that it was anything but a fabrication by the regents to justify their actions. In defiance of the regents' order to disperse the diet, Thurn and his colleagues marched on the Hradschin palace to accuse the regents of forgery. Once inside, they picked upon Martinitz and Slavata, inquired of the crowd outside if they were guilty of high treason and, receiving the verdict by acclamation, threw them from the window. The two victims, along with an unfortunate clerk thrown after them, by chance survived their execution, their fall being broken by a mound of rubbish, and, as they limped away with the mob at their heels, they were rescued, appropriately enough, by Polyxena Lobkowitz, who gave them refuge in her house.

The defenestration of Prague at this time was no accident, the chance consequence of an angry moment. It was planned and carried out in deliberate imitation of the event which precipitated the Hussite rebellion of the fifteenth century, and was intended by Thurn as an act of defiance, not necessarily against Matthias but against all who challenged the *Letter of Majesty*. The Protestant diet proceeded to elect thirty-six directors in Matthias's name to replace the regents, and Thurn was appointed commander-in-chief.

Matthias was too old and too ill to act for himself and Ferdinand had yet no authority to act on his own. The day was saved by Oñate. In a series of remarkably high-handed and historically important acts, he not only strengthened the will of the Austrian Habsburgs to fight in Bohemia, but also made that will effective, by providing the men, money and arms. He ordered Dampierre and the Spanish troops still stationed on the Isonozo river to advance to Vienna, persuaded Matthias to ask Albert to send over Buquoy, one of the best commanders in the Army of Flanders, appealed to the viceroys in Milan and Naples for troops, and raised a fortune on his own account – to such good effect that by the end of August 1618, when Buquoy arrived, nearly 12,000 men had been mustered and Oñate himself was in debt for 130,000 florins.

News of the defenestration and of Oñate's vigorous responses were alike received with consternation in Madrid. 'The stirs in Bohemia were speedily advertised hither', reported Sir Francis Cottington to his government in London, 'and with it they are here not a little troubled; as they already groan under the excessive charges and expense which they are daily at for the subsistence of those princes of Austria and especially this king of Bohemia.' Lerma wanted to countermand

Oñate's arrangements, until Zuñiga, drawing upon his experience of Germany, persuaded him of the importance of denying Bohemia to potential enemies of Spain and of the advantages to be derived from the Treaty of Graz. In the council debate, however, Count Salazar explained that, since the government's regular income was insufficient to meet the interest charges on its debts, 'the royal finances cannot provide such sums at the present time'. At this moment, one of the most decisive in the history of European conflict in the early seventeenth century, Philip III himself took a hand, declaring that, notwithstanding Salazar's good counsel, 'these measures are so urgent that the council of finance must find a way. *Germany simply cannot be lost.*'

The situation in Bohemia by the autumn of 1618 gave much encouragement to the Habsburgs. The Protestant diet had drawn up plans for a national militia, comprising every fifth townsman and every tenth peasant; but, though several of the directors pledged their estates to pay their own detachments, there was not enough money available for the remainder. As a result taxes were raised, loans contracted and the first spoliations made of property belonging to Roman Catholics. Several Roman Catholics fled for refuge, not to Austria, which they considered to be in as dangerous a state as Bohemia, but to Bavaria; many Bohemians held aloof or declared their wish for an accommodation with Matthias, the important cities of Budweiss and Pilsen declared against the directors, while Moravia, though claiming to be neutral, allowed free passage to Buquoy's army on its way to invade Bohemia in September.

9. The Bohemian revolt

With the coming of winter, Buquoy, who had advanced as far as Čáslav, withdrew to quarters in eastern Bohemia, and, though this left unguarded the route to Vienna, Thurn, who made a swift thrust in that direction, was stopped by bad weather. His one crumb of comfort, the one unexpected gesture of international support, came at the very end of the year with the arrival of 2000 Germans led by Mansfeld. Ernst Mansfeld, a former officer in the Army of Flanders, had been taken prisoner in Leopold's service at Jülich and when no one chose to ransom him offered himself to the Evangelical Union. Christian of Anhalt had sent him with 4000 men to aid Charles Emmanuel and he was returning after the Treaty of Pavia when news came of the defenestration. Charles Emmanuel, who knew better than most the importance of the Empire to Spain, decided to send Mansfeld with half his force to embarrass the Spanish cause in Bohemia. Anhalt agreed, delighted that Charles Emmanuel chose to pay Mansfeld anonymously and to allow the credit for the operation to go to the elector Palatine. Arriving in Bohemia, Mansfeld restored the rebels' morale by a successful surprise attack on Pilsen.

From the death of Matthias (1619) to the Treaty of Ulm (1620)

Matthias died in March 1619. In Heidelberg there was jubilation. 'Now we have in our hands the means of overturning the world', proclaimed Christian of Anhalt. In his imagination the Dutch, the English and the Huguenots were to supply men and money for the cause; Savoy and Venice would block the Alpine routes, while the Evangelical Union confined the Army of Flanders within Flanders; Žerotin in Moravia and Tschernembl in Austria would lead their Estates to unite with Bohemia in rebellion against the Habsburgs, and the elector Palatine would not only become king of Bohemia but also ensure the election of a Protestant emperor. The intoxicating prospect of all things conspiring for good was further reinforced by Rosicrucian pamphlets prophesying the downfall of Antichrist in 1620.

Frederick V wrote carefully at Anhalt's instruction to win the support of his father-in-law, urging England's Defender of the Faith to agree that 'these Bohemian Estates should not be oppressed nor despoiled of their liberty and the exercise of their religion'. It was an artful appeal, but James I did not respond as Anhalt had intended. Little courage, less money, a genuine attachment to Spain and deep-seated horror of rebellion prompted him to reply to Frederick's ambassador, 'There are some of the princes in Germany who wish for war in order that they may aggrandise themselves. Your master is young and I am old. Let him follow my example.'

In order to maintain James in this opinion, Philip III, prompted by Gondomar, flattered his desire to become the arbiter of Christendom by inviting him to mediate in Bohemia. It was a shrewd ploy and ensured England's neutrality, even though it caused Spain some embarassment when James insisted on taking his role seriously and sent Lord Doncaster on a mission of investigation. An astonished Ferdinand refused to see him, explaining that mediation was a matter for the four lay electors and that 'His Majesty of Great Britain was not well informed how the Bohemians had behaved themselves.' Spanish agents moved swiftly to explain matters to their allies, but Doncaster was in no doubt that both he and his master had been taken for a ride.

The Dutch response to the news of Matthias's death was very guarded. Truce or no truce, they knew what was to be feared from any accession of Habsburg strength in Europe – and what might be gained by exploiting Habsburg weaknesses – but their reaction was less impassioned, less clear-cut, than Philip III's. The States-General wrote to the Evangelical Union that 'the Bohemian war will decide the fates of all of us', adding tamely, 'especially yours since you are the neighbour of the Bohemians. For the present we shall seek out all ways of bringing you help . . . though we have many difficulties to face.' Their first difficulty was that James I, instead of giving a lead to the Protestant cause for the sake of his son-in-law, continued to force a quarrel on the Dutch over the herring fisheries. Moreover, the Arminian crisis was not yet resolved. The month of Matthias's death was that of Oldenbarneveldt's trial, and the States-General was in cautious mood. In the event it recognised a Captain Frenck, one of Mansfeld's officers, as official representative of the Bohemian Estates, accredited him to recruit 1000 musketeers and agreed to provide a monthly subsidy of 50,000 florins.

Disappointed by the lack of any vigorous response from England or the United Provinces, Anhalt turned to Charles Emmanuel of Savoy, who offered in the Treaty of Rivoli to renew his subsidy to Mansfeld, but the duke was not to be deluded by proposals to nominate him for the Bohemian or Imperial throne. 'He suspects', wrote the English ambassador in Turin, 'the Princes of Germany do only serve themselves of him to beat the bush, and that they intend to keep the birds for themselves if any may be gotten.' His ambitions were centred less on

Germany than on northern Italy, and there he dared not challenge Spain without French support. France, however, still clung to the entente with Spain, and the news from Bohemia confirmed Louis XIII in his resolve. Since he identified the Protestants of Bohemia with his own rebellious Huguenots, he found the duke of Bouillon, a persistent rebel, an unsatisfactory advocate of the Bohemian cause. The arch-dukes in Brussels, on the other hand, had earned his gratitude by forbidding his subjects to recruit troops in Flanders, and he informed them graciously in May 1619 that he had no wish to see the Imperial crown pass from the Habsburg family. Better still, he sent the duke of Nevers to Ferdinand to offer him full diplomatic support.

Within its 'hereditary lands', however, the House of Austria ran into serious difficulties after Matthias's death. Lusatia and Silesia, led by the margrave of Jägerndorf, declared for the rebels; Moravia, after Karl Žerotin had been displaced by his cousin, did the same and opened the way for Thurn to march unchallenged into Lower Austria. In Upper Austria Tschernembl persuaded the Estates to repudiate Ferdinand and to make common cause against him with Bohemia, while Bethlen Gabor, prince of Transylvania, led the Hungarian nobility in revolt. Most critical of all was the situation in Lower Austria, where Ferdinand was in great personal danger. Thurn's army had reached the gates of Vienna, and within its walls the leaders of the Estates had seized arms and forced their way into the Hofburg, where, in scenes alarmingly reminiscent of the demonstration in the Hradscin, they confronted Ferdinand with their demands for an end to the war with Bohemia, more privileges for Protestants and more power for the Estates. At the height of the crisis, Dampierre with cavalry from Flanders charged through Thurn's camp, entered the city and burst into the Hofburg. His arrival, though coincidental, was an opportune symbol of the Spanish aid without which Ferdinand could not have survived. The leaders of the Estates, suspecting a counter-coup, fled for their lives, and Thurn, seeing the city reinforced, broke up the siege.

Spain's determination to save the House of Austria at all costs had never faltered since Philip III had settled the matter by decreeing that Germany could not be lost. 'If it be true that the Bohemians intend to depose Ferdinand and choose another king,' commented the archbishop–elector of Cologne, 'we may expect a war of twenty, thirty or forty years; for Spain and the House of Austria will stake all they hold in this world sooner than relinquish Bohemia.'

Spinola, anxiously holding the front line in Flanders as the Twelve

Years Truce began to near its end, endorsed the decision that the ultimate defeat of the Dutch depended upon the immediate defeat of the Bohemian rebels, and even reduced his own garrisons to release troops for this purpose. 'If we do not do so,' he advised Philip, 'it is quite possible that the House of Austria may be turned out of Germany bag and baggage. If the Protestants succeed in doing this they will then join the Dutch in an attack upon these provinces, not only as a return for the help which they are getting from them, but because they will imagine that whilst your Majesty's forces are here, they will not be left undisturbed in the enjoyment of their new possessions. If all the German and Dutch Protestants were to unite in attacking us after a victory in Germany it would be hopeless for us to attempt to resist them.' Anhalt himself could scarcely have interpreted more cogently the far-reaching consequences of the Bohemian revolt.

In July 1619, by a triumph of common interests over local differences, representatives from Bohemia and its associated kingdoms of Lusatia, Silesia and Moravia met to inaugurate a new constitution, a *Confederatio Bohemica* inspired in part by that of the United Provinces, though preserving the monarchy albeit in elective form. It was an ambitious undertaking, with provision, if the occasion arose, for the incorporation of Austria and Hungary, and in its essence it represented the repudiation of Lobkowitz's policies. The *Letter of Majesty* and the privileges of Protestants were enshrined as fundamental laws, and the power of the elected monarch was subjected to closer supervision than in the past. In addition, since all thoughts of negotiation with Ferdinand had been abandoned, crown lands and those belonging to the Roman Catholic Church were confiscated to pay for the Confederation's defence.

Meanwhile the processes for the election of an emperor were getting under way in Germany, but amid much confusion. The candidate most likely to succeed against Ferdinand was Maximilian of Bavaria, but he refused to stand and the elector Palatine could not expect support from his colleagues. Though it was clear that the Bohemian Estates intended to elect him king, thereby providing him with a second electoral vote, this had not yet been done; moreover, Bohemia's right to repudiate Ferdinand was not generally recognised. The three archbishops were likely to support Ferdinand; John George of Saxony, like his father, Christian II (see p. 17), disliked both Calvinism and rebellion and would not support Frederick, while John Sigismund of Brandenburg, having recently acquired East Prussia as a fief of the Polish crown, feared that any hostile act against the Habsburgs would result in Sigismund of Poland's taking action against him. Although the odds, therefore, were in Ferdinand's favour, the Spanish and Austrian governments fretted throughout the summer, reading volumes into any hint of correspondence between the electors, and Albert, for fear that a Protestant would be chosen, urged Philip III to increase the subsidies for Flanders to their wartime footing of 300,000 ducats a month. In the event, John George proposed that no vote be taken until the Bohemian crisis had been resolved, a device to strengthen his bargaining power with Ferdinand, but when the Palatine, to stop Ferdinand at all costs, proposed Maximilian once again, despite his refusal to stand, John George lost patience and ordered his representative to vote immediately for Ferdinand – as did the representatives of Brandenburg and the three archbishops. Ferdinand voted for himself, and the Palatine's representative, having ineptly failed to challenge Ferdinand's right to vote as king of Bohemia, ended up by voting for him himself.   •

The imperial election took place on 28 August 1619. Two days earlier in Prague, the Estates, unknown to the imperial electors, had formally appointed Frederick as their king. Schlick had wanted John George of Saxony, but he declined to be associated with rebellion, leaving Frederick the only acceptable candidate, The leaders of the Estates had of course long been in correspondence with Christian of Anhalt. They believed that it was Frederick who had sent Mansfeld to Pilsen and, more to the point, they believed that he could bring with him the support not only of the Evangelical Union, of which he was head, but also of England and the United Provinces. The strength of this belief, for which there was very little justification, was later evident at the coronation, when a Rosicrucian print represented Frederick accompanied by the four lions on whom he would rely – the two-tailed lion of Bohemia, the Palatinate lion, the lion of the Netherlands and the lion with drawn sword of Great Britain.

In one sense Frederick's acceptance of the Bohemian crown was a foregone conclusion. The Palatinate had been for over sixty years a declared enemy of the Habsburgs and of the Roman Catholic Church; with Anhalt at his shoulder Frederick was unlikely to forgo the occasion to strike a blow against both. To avert a major conflict, however, Maximilian of Bavaria wrote to him in urgent but conciliatory tones, assuring him that there was no international Catholic conspiracy as Anhalt imagined, and pointing out that his powers as king under the new Bohemian constitution were scarcely worth fighting for. Similar views were expressed by the council in Heidelberg, by Frederick's mother and by the Evangelical Union, which added that only with certain and substantial aid from England and the Dutch Republic could the venture be considered at all. Although most Englishmen echoed Archbishop Abbot's opinion that God had set the elector up and that Parliament should be called to support him, James I declared the Bohemians to be rebels, the election illegal and advised Frederick not to accept the crown. Only the Dutch approved the offer. Maurice indeed was angry at Frederick's hesitation, and told his agent that, with the truce about to expire, he wanted to see the Habsburgs challenged by strong enemies and hoped that Frederick would not lack vigour in defending his title.

When Frederick resolved his indecisions and accepted the Bohemian crown, the Dutch alone came forward to assist him, their concern admirably expressed by Carleton: 'If the Spaniard should dispossess the new king and make a prey of that kingdom, *l'appetit vient en mangeant* and they expect here no greater courtesy than Polyphemus promised Ulysses, he should be the last eaten of his companions.' At the coronation service in Prague the alliance was symbolised when Scultetus preached in High Dutch and Corvinus in Czech, and more substantial tokens of support soon followed. In addition to its monthly subsidy of 50,000 florins, the States-General guaranteed the Bohemian government a loan of 200,000 florins and declared it would make war on any prince who openly opposed Frederick's accession. This warning, as Albert reported to Philip III in November 1619, effectively ensured the neutrality of the Catholic League, whose members were not so devoted to the Habsburgs that they would risk the invasion of their own territories. In addition, the Dutch tried to force James I's hand, threatening to cancel their support for his son-in-law unless he too did something to help, but James steadfastly refused to be drawn.

While the western European powers debated their policies, events were moving fast within the hereditary kingdoms. In September 1619 the Estates of Upper and of Lower Austria both elected to join the Bohemian Confederation, while Bethlen Gabor, advancing with great speed across Hungary, took Pressburg, the capital, in October and drove the Habsburg troops in headlong flight up the Danube to Vienna. Buquoy, who had done little more than hold Budweiss in eastern Bohemia (see map 9), now withdrew to strengthen Vienna, while Thurn crossed Moravia to join the Hungarians, their combined armies numbering more than 25,000 men, though Bethlen was incensed with Thurn for bringing no money to pay them.

In The Hague it was believed, as Carleton recorded, that Bethlen would take Vienna by storm 'if he be not diverted by the Polac', and ambassadors were sent immediately to Gustav Adolf of Sweden to persuade him to keep Sigismund III in check, 'by threatening an invasion in his country in case he molests Transylvania'. They arrived too late to influence matters, but Sigismund was in any case unable to intervene directly, because too many of his subjects were Lutherans and sympathised with the Bohemian cause. All he could do was to allow the Habsburgs to recruit within his kingdom. The duke of Nevers, who far exceeded his brief from Louis XIII of France to give diplomatic aid to Ferdinand, commissioned the Lisowczycy, a force of irregular Cossacks, who by invading Transylvania compelled Bethlen to abandon the siege of Vienna and return home in haste. In January 1620 the disgruntled prince made a separate peace with Ferdinand, even though the Hungarian diet still remained officially in a state of rebellion.

Philip III complained that Bethlen had been let off too lightly and wrote sharply to Ferdinand demanding assurances that he would not make peace so easily with Frederick. He wanted no uncertainty about the outcome, since Spain's commitment to the emperor's cause was becoming greater with every month as a result of Oñate's tireless efforts. He had had 300,000 ducats credited to him from Madrid in February 1619 and a further 300,000 in May, though, the latter had to be delivered in cash because the bankers of Nuremburg and Frankfurt supported the elector Palatine and would not cash Oñate's bills. In November he received 150,000 ducats and 100,000 in January 1620. In addition, as the Spanish viceroys in Italy recruited troops for Flanders and Bohemia, sending 8000 through the Valtelline in June and 7000 more in November, Oñate intervened to commandeer them all and well deserved Ferdinand's grateful description of him as 'the man with whose friendly and open help all the affairs of the Habsburg family are being arranged'. By the early spring of 1620 he had secured both for Buquoy, then returned to Bohemia, and for Dampierre in Lower Austria over 12,000 troops each, all recruited, supplied and paid for by Spain.

Meanwhile, as part of its extraordinarily wide-ranging continental strategy, the Spanish government urged Sigismund to hold Poland firm against Gustav Adolf and to monitor the movements of Bethlen Gabor in Transylvania. Agents were sent to inquire of the Hanseatic towns if they would stand by the emperor or the elector Palatine, a fleet was despatched to Flanders in readiness for the expiry of the truce, the archduke Leopold in Alsace was sent 500 men to reinforce the vital Rhine bridgehead at Breisach, and plans were drawn up with the archdukes in Brussels for the occupation of the Palatinate. It was known that Maximilian of Bavaria, once his advice had been rejected by Frederick, had mét the emperor in October and declared his willingness, given favourable circumstances in the Rhineland, to use the army of the Catholic League in Bohemia provided that he was assured of at least the Upper Palatinate and its electoral title. Philip III was resolved that Spinola should therefore occupy the Lower Palatinate and, by making himself master of Heidelberg, guarantee Spanish lines of communication through the Rhineland. In January 1620 his government agreed to provide 100,000 ducats a month for the projected Palatinate campaign and the same for Oñate's activities in Austria and Bohemia.

Fear of a Spanish invasion of the Palatinate caused panic among members of the Evangelical Union, who made urgent appeals for guarantees of support from England and the United Provinces. Philip III had recognised that this might happen and summarised his anxieties in a letter to Albert in March 1620. 'The invasion of the Palatinate will give the English a fair pretext for openly interfering in Germany and for sending all their forces to the assistance of the Dutch. . . . You will thus be attacked by the combined forces of England and Holland, and then, if we are to take part in the Bohemian war, we shall be at the expense of maintaining two armies, and we shall have to fight with England, though a war with that power has always been held by us to be most impolitic. Its inconvenience at this time will be especially great on account of our poverty.'

Having reconciled himself to the worst, it was therefore a great delight for Philip to discover that Gondomar had steered James away from war by reviving the notion of the Spanish match, even suggesting some advance payments of the dowry. James was in fact so torn between his duty to Frederick as a relative threatened with the loss of his rightful electorate and his abhorrence of Frederick as the illegal sovereign of rebels that he was nearly at his wits' end. In the event the Evangelical Union was informed by James that he had it on Gondomar's authority that its members had nothing to fear from Spain and that therefore they had no need of his assistance. As a result, the Union's attempt to raise a loan of £100,000 in the city of London failed for lack of royal support.

The States-General was aggrieved beyond measure that James should so feebly fail to support his son-in-law and the Protestant cause. In Maurice's mind the matter would have been simply resolved once and for all by an English invasion of Flanders, which would make it quite impossible for Albert to spare any troops for an attack on the Palatinate. Unfortunately for the Dutch, they chose this very time to arrest four English ships which interfered in their fishing grounds. Gondomar so worked upon James's excitable nature that he succeeded in convincing him that, if the 8000 Englishmen in Dutch service could be persuaded to mutiny, the English fleet should then sail across to join them. Albert was very scornful of the scheme, but Gondomar had the truth of it when he reported to Philip that, 'if the treaties rarely turn out as beautiful as they are represented to be, that is no reason why one should not get all the good one can out of them'. Certainly the Dutch were left in no doubt that, even if Spain invaded the Palatinate, England would make no move, and it was left to the States-General alone to give the Evangelical Union the assurances it needed. The demands of maintaining its own defences, and of garrisoning re-monstrant towns to prevent civil disorder, meant that only 5000 troops could be spared if necessary, but a subsidy of 50,000 florins a month was offered to the Union to recruit more troops of its own.

The offer arrived too late. The troops of the Evangelical Union had been manoeuvring dangerously close to those of the Catholic League near Ulm when the duke of Angoulême offered on behalf of Louis XIII to negotiate between them. The Union readily agreed. Deserted by England and, as it thought, by the United Provinces, it had been further disconcerted to learn that John George of Saxony had promised to fight Frederick in return for Lusatia. Strassburg, moreover, had already withdrawn from the Union in order that its territory be guaranteed by Spinola. As for the Catholic League, its leader, Maximilian of Bavaria, wanted nothing better than a truce with the Union to release his army for service in Bohemia. Consequently, by the Treaty of Ulm in July 1620, each side agreed to respect the other's neutrality in Germany without prejudice to whatever action it might choose to take in Bohemia. Spinola complained that this still left the Evangelical princes free to oppose his invasion of the Palatinate, while denying him assistance from the League, but the overall result of the treaty was immeasurably to strengthen the Habsburgs' position in Bohemia.

In the meantime, before the campaigns began in Bohemia and the Rhineland, the Habsburgs were cheered by good news about their lines

of communication with northern Italy. The events of 1618–19 in the
Valtelline (see p. 60) had soon led to a reaction. The Plantas escaped to
the Tyrol and there, with the aid of the archduke Leopold, planned a
counter-stroke. Feria, viceroy in Milan, also intervened. Spanish troops
marched safely through the valley in midsummer 1619, and in 1620 the
Plantas returned to lead a rising by the Italian-speaking Catholic population. In Sondrio, the priest's murder was avenged by the death of
the Calvinist minister and 140 of his congregation; elsewhere the *sacro
macello*, the holy butchery, accounted for 600 Protestant lives. France
refused the Grisons' appeal for help, nor did Venice at this juncture dare
to risk direct confrontation with Feria. When the Grisons counter-
attacked at Bormio at the head of the valley, Feria, defeated them and
constructed a chain of forts to hold the Valtelline for the future. At the
same time the duke of Savoy dared not resist the demand for 8000
Spanish troops to make their way to join Spinola along the Spanish
Road.

10. The Palatinate campaign

Campaigns in the Rhineland and Bohemia 1620–1

Spinola was so well prepared for action by August 1620 that Carleton drew unfavourable comparisons with the Protestant governments, 'which begin commonly to consult, when the Spaniards have resolved; to levy, when they march; to move, when they are in possession'. Armed with the emperor's commission to act within the Holy Roman Empire, Spinola marched to Coblenz, where his army was reinforced from Franche Comté and northern Italy to make it 16,000 strong with 3000 cavalry. His campaign was brilliantly conceived and executed. Crossing the Rhine on a bridge of boats to Ehrenbreitstein, he advanced on Frankfurt and caused consternation among his enemies, who could not yet discern from his movements his ultimate destination. He could wheel back upon the Palatinate, go on to Bohemia, or turn north and from the right bank of the Rhine force a crossing of the Ijssel into the United Provinces. Maurice hastily moved men forward to stand guard nearer the Spanish garrison at Wesel; the Evangelical Union put some of its men in the Rhineland near Mainz and the remainder in the Hunsrück, a line of hills on the right bank of the Moselle between Trier and Coblenz. In the event Spinola turned back to Wiesbaden, crossed over to Mainz and took possession of Kreuznach and Oppenheim. If he had gone directly for the Palatinate without trailing his coat in this manner, he would have had to fight his way through the defiles of the Hunsrück, giving the Dutch time to send reinforcements up the Rhine into the Palatinate. As it was, by the end of September Spinola was master of the river from Coblenz to Mainz, the Dutch were kept at bay downstream, and the forces of the Evangelical Union, having failed to hold Oppenheim against him, had retired up river to Worms.

Within days of the Treaty of Ulm, Maximilian had marched into Upper Austria, where the Estates, overawed by his army of over 15,000, made their submission to him as the emperor's representative. Protestants were removed from office, many of their churches were closed and more troops were recruited before Maximilian moved on to Bohemia, where he joined forces with Buquoy at the end of September. Meanwhile John George of Saxony had made himself master of Lusatia, Mansfeld went unpaid and refused to leave his quarters in Pilsen, and the numbers under Thurn's command dwindled daily for lack of money and supplies. All the confiscation had not saved the government from bankruptcy, landowners and cities defaulted on their contributions, and, as the new queen's secretary noted, 'our friends here have no minds to dig wells until they grow athirst'.

But it was not only for its lack of finance and foresight that the government was in disarray. The inexperience and tactlessness demonstrated by Frederick and Elizabeth had alienated many citizens of Prague; the failure of all foreign governments save the Dutch to provide assistance sapped the rebels' morale; but the central fault was the inability of the leaders, in the months following the excitement of the defenestration, to inspire the mass of the people with the relevance and value of their cause. From the registers of the expropriations made after the revolt, it is clear that thousands of knights and burghers had willingly fought to defend the *Letter of Majesty* or the principle of an independent Bohemia, but the people at large were relatively unmoved by the call to defend privileges which meant little to them. At the time of the confederation between Austria and Bohemia, Tschernembl had demanded a more radical programme: 'Let the freedom of subjects be proclaimed in the land and villeinage abolished.' The liberation of the peasantry would have released dynamic forces, similar to those released in the Hussite war, against which Ferdinand and his allies might have struggled in vain. Instead, as the armies closed in on Prague, the rebel leaders, increasingly isolated from the people, had neither an effective policy to offer nor the means to carry it out.

During the night of 7 November, Maximilian and Buquoy came across the rebel army outside Prague on the plain known locally as the White Mountain. The rebels numbered between 16,000 and 20,000 and were unfortunate not to be in greater strength; Mansfeld was still in Pilsen, Frenck and the Dutch were in Southern Bohemia and 8000 Hungarian cavalry were crossing Moravia in too leisurely a fashion to be of use to Frederick in his moment of crisis. The army was dispirited and disorganised, but Christian of Anhalt took the initiative by manoeuvring it to a position rather stronger than the enemy's and prepared for battle. Maximilian and Buquoy had about the same number of troops between them, of whom nearly two-thirds came from Spanish territories, including 2000 from Spain itself. Those under Buquoy's command were becoming disorderly for lack of pay, but Maximilian's men were still well paid, well disciplined and imbued with the sense of a crusade. Buquoy and the League commander, Johan Tilly, counselled caution in view of Anhalt's position and suggested a feint attack on the capital, to bring the rebels down among them. Maximilian, more optimistic, believed that one firm assault would carry the day and, overriding his advisers, ordered an attack at dawn. Within two hours, as the rebels dispersed in headlong flight, he was proved to have been correct in his judgement.

The Battle of the White Mountain ended the Bohemian revolt. The citizens of Prague closed their gates against the survivors and submitted to Maximilian, while Frederick and Elizabeth fled the kingdom. They were urged to make a stand in Moravia, as yet untouched by the war, and join forces with Bethlen Gabor, but so dispiriting had been the experience of their short reign that they chose instead to abandon the cause and seek safety in the United Provinces. In Silesia Jägerndorf was joined by several leaders of the Estates and established himself with 12,000 men at Neisse near the Moravian frontier. There he was prepared to live off the land and offer his services to the highest bidder. Mansfeld in Pilsen did the same.

The emperor placed Frederick under the Imperial ban in January 1621, declaring that he had, 'by putting himself at the head of rebels, disobedient and untrue, shown himself both traitorous and injurious to the Imperial Highness and Majesty, and committed an offence against the peace of the Empire and other wholesome Imperial statutes'. As a result Maximilian was ordered to occupy the Palatinate, a move which did not altogether satisfy Philip III, who feared it might provoke too hostile a reaction among the Protestant states. He proposed instead that, if Frederick were to present himself suitably chastened before the emperor and undertake to renounce Bohemia, abandon the Evangelical Union and reimburse Spain the costs of the campaign, he might then be allowed to return to the Palatinate. This was not a suggestion that Ferdinand could accept. Maximilian was in occupation of Upper Austria and the only way to get him out was to honour the pledge to give him the Palatinate and the electoral title. Frederick, moreover, proved intransigent and from his exile in the Hague steadfastly refused to renounce the Bohemian throne.

In this emergency the Dutch tried to shame James I into helping his son-in-law. They sent a formal embassy to demonstrate how 50,000 florins a month had been paid to Bohemia for nineteen months and to the Evangelical Union for eleven, in addition to the cost of sending troops to Wesel, to the Rhineland and to Bohemia. In conclusion the embassy demanded to know what James was prepared to do. James was not to be caught out and asked the embassy what instructions it had received about the fishing disputes. Though the discussions lasted 454 days, they proved inconclusive.

The English government had nonetheless been alarmed by news of Frederick's defeat, and a benevolence of £30,000, collected several months earlier, was sent to pay the garrison of Worms. The council of war even considered the Dutch proposal that England should distract Spinola from the Palatinate by landing 25,000 men and 5000 cavalry at Sluys. It reckoned that it would cost £250,000 to prepare such an expedition and £900,000 to maintain it in the field, but, though James asked Parliament for only £500,000, the members turned him down. No matter how strongly they championed the elector and the Protestant cause, the measures they advocated were naval rather than military – harking back to wistful but misleading memories of the Elizabethan privateers – and the stricter enforcement of the laws against Roman Catholics. Their counter-proposals led to dispute with James over his prerogative to direct foreign affairs, and Gondomar was able to sit smugly by as tempers became so heated that James dared not allow Frederick and Elizabeth to come to London for fear of popular demonstrations against his government.

The Evangelical Union meanwhile held a diet at Heilbronn in January 1621 to debate the Imperial ban on Frederick and its anxiety about Spinola's occupation of Mainz, Kreuznach and Oppenheim. 'Those who were wont to be so ready on horseback in other men's quarrels do now so easily give way to this inundation of strangers', wrote Carleton scornfully as the diet threatened to abandon Frederick unless he renounced the Bohemian throne. In March several of the princes of the Lower Saxon Circle met Christian of Denmark at Segenberg to arrange joint military action in the Palatinate, but when this failed the Union was on the brink of collapse. Spinola completed the process by pretending to undertake a spring offensive in the Rhineland, knowing full well that if the truce expired he would not be able to sustain it, and his bluff succeeded in its purpose. At Mainz an *Accord* was drawn up with the princes of Ansbach and Württemburg by which they agreed to disband their forces if Spinola guaranteed their rights as neutrals. In May the Evangelical Union met to confirm this for all its members, and never met again.

The Spanish and Dutch debates on the ending of the truce

There is much to support the view, that, although several problems had yet to be resolved in the spring of 1621, peace might nonetheless have been restored throughout Europe. The most important problem was the fate of Frederick, who, having lost his kingdom and his electorate, still lived in a fool's paradise, putting his faith in dangerous adventurers such as Mansfeld and Jägerndorf. Philip III was ready to propose that he, or his infant son, might be restored to the Lower Palatinate and share the electoral title, turn and turn about, with Maximilian. A joint expedition, financed by all the interested parties, would then bring Mansfeld and Jägerndorf to heel. The difficulty was that Frederick was too stupid to compromise, and Maximilian too ambitious, but the problem was not insoluble. The Evangelical Union had disbanded, the Bohemian revolt was over, northern Italy had been settled, James I was neutral, and Louis XIII, plagued by Huguenot conspiracies and the rivalry of great nobles, was anxious to support an international settlement. Everything depended, therefore, upon the decisions of Spain and the United Provinces whether or not to renew the truce between them.

The truce had never been popular in Spain. It was attributed, unfairly, to the deficiencies of the Brussels administration and was bitterly criticised from time to time in the *consulta* prepared for the king. Evidence of Dutch encroachment in Mediterranean, West Indian and Far Eastern waters intensified the mood of general dissatisfaction, which was summed up in 1616 by the president of the *consejo de hacienda* (council of finance): 'the peace is worse than if we had continued the war'. In their exasperation Spaniards tended to forget that the truce had recognised a condition of military stalemate and financial insolvency for which peace had been the only remedy. Moreover, the fact that there was no more money to spend on warfare in 1609 did not mean that during the truce the treasury could magically and of itself begin to refill its coffers. Resentment at Spain's apparent inability to restore its reputation by a major war was therefore redirected against the truce itself.

It was the viceroys, governors and ambassadors working away from Madrid who formulated more aggressive policies and exploited their positions of authority to carry them out. Their actions have already been described – those of Zuñiga and Oñate in the Holy Roman Empire, of Fuentes, Villafranca and Feria in Milan, of Osuna in Naples, Bedmar in Venice, Gondomar in London and Cardenas in Paris. They blamed the truce, rather than the circumstances which had caused it, for Spain's decline in wealth and power, and throughout its course it had been their deliberate policy to prepare for the ultimate defeat of the Dutch by seizing every occasion to strengthen Habsburg influence in Europe and to safeguard the lines of communication with Flanders. Hence the Imperial title retained within the Habsburg family. Bohemia denied to a hostile power, Austria safeguarded, the Palatinate occupied, Venice restrained, Milan defended, the Spanish Road reopened, the Valtelline fortified and the rulers of France and England persuaded into benevolent neutrality.

Philip III applauded them on occasion and was personally responsible for the vital decision to intervene at all costs in Bohemia, but Lerma disapproved of their belligerence. Reluctant convert though he had been to the truce in 1609, he became even more reluctant to abandon it, and it was clear that while he remained in office the ambitions of the war party would be thwarted. His downfall was therefore as important in its way as that of Oldenbarneveldt in the United Provinces.

The administration of affairs had been disastrous. Since finance was the nub of the matter, it was Spain's tragedy that she had never learned the proper use of her bullion imports; as the Castilian Cortes complained to Philip III, 'the treasure immediately goes to foreign kingdoms leaving this one in extreme poverty'. If the royal share of bullion was sent abroad to pay the bankers, the rest soon followed to pay for the manufactured goods and even the foodstuffs which Spain was no longer able to produce. The Spaniards had fallen into the error of confusing wealth with bullion and of failing to understand that the true source of a nation's prosperity lay in industry and trade. The government of Philip III not only failed to encourage industry but also accelerated its decline by its fiscal policies. The taxes it doubled and redoubled bore most heavily on the peasantry, which therefore had little left to spend, while the commercial classes were handicapped by the *alcabala*, a sales tax of 10 per cent. Worst of all, the government tampered with the *vellon* currency, an amalgam of copper and silver. Finding the revenues for 1599 and 1600 pledged in advance, Philip removed the silver; in 1602 the weight of the copper in each coin was reduced by half; in the following year the debased coinage was called in to be stamped at double its value and the device was repeated in 1618.

An experienced minister, and there were many who had served Philip II, might possibly have saved the day, but Lerma was not the man to share authority with those more talented than himself. As he stood to Philip III, so Rodrigo Calderon stood to him, and the succession of parasites, each with its own family to cater for, grew to infinite proportions. With no understanding of the economic weaknesses of Spain and seduced into believing that everything could be covered by American bullion, Lerma set an example of extravagance and corruption which aggravated the collapse of the economy. Occasions for ostentatious display were exploited to the full, and the court became three times as expensive to maintain as in Philip II's day. Offices and titles were created by the king and sold to fill the pockets of his favourites, the currency was debased to procure a quick profit at the expense of trade and industry, and the resources of the state were ransacked in the attempt to satisfy insatiable appetites.

When popular protests at the unbridled corruption of the administration began to be noticed by the court, Lerma saved his own position by jettisoning some of his creatures. Several councillors of finance were arrested in 1609, and the house of one was so full of bullion that it took three days to transfer it all back to the treasury. So public a display of the profits to be derived from high office simply served to whet the appetites of the envious, who redoubled their intrigue to discredit Lerma with the king. Their success was finally owing to the count of Olivares, Zuñiga's nephew, who won the goodwill of the future Philip IV and of Lerma's own son, in whom greed was stronger than filial devotion. In 1614 the cabal secured the arrest of Calderon; in 1618 Lerma found it politic to accept a cardinal's hat and retire from court with a fortune rumoured at 44 million ducats.

Olivares was to be the outstanding statesman of seventeenth-century Spain. A restless bureaucrat, always in a rush about the court, his hat and pockets stuffed with papers, his voice booming down the corridors, his mind was as active as his body. Ebullient though easily dejected, shrewd yet on occasion gullible, his most remarkable characteristic was his breadth of vision. No man had so clear a notion of the unity of Spain; no man saw more clearly the map of Europe in relation to the war with the Dutch.

With such a man in power, Zuñiga was recalled to court and public criticism of the truce swiftly gathered momentum. When Philip III visited Portugal in 1619, he was taken aback by the complaints of the Council of Portugal that its Far Eastern empire could not survive another decade of Dutch encroachment under the terms of the truce. Only by the renewal of war, it claimed, would the Dutch be compelled to concentrate their efforts once again on the defence of their own provinces. Zuñiga pressed home the point: 'If the republic of these rebels goes on as it is, we shall succeed in losing first the two Indies, then the rest of Flanders, then the states of Italy and finally Spain itself.' As a result, on 25 December 1619 the council of state agreed in principle that the truce was not to be extended and that preparations be put in train for war.

The debate continued in Flanders, where Colonna, the governor of Cambrai, argued in June 1620 that, unless the Dutch agreed to abandon the Indies and open the Scheldt, the war would have to be resumed. He added that the times were propitious: 'one cannot but note that it looks as if God had permitted the troubles in Germany so that when in His Divine Mercy He uses the victorious arms of Your Majesty to bring them to an end, you may retain the prestige which is your due, whilst the Dutch rebels may be filled with a livelier apprehension of their own approaching doom, and His Imperial Majesty may be led to repay Your Majesty in the same coin with his armies and with his authority in the task of rooting out this new and pestilential republic'. The archdukes, however, were more cautious. They accepted all the criticisms of the truce but were afraid that Spain could not afford the costs of war. 'I see Your Majesty', wrote Albert in December 1620, 'entangled in Bohemia, in the Palatinate and, through the Valtelline affair, in Italy, and were you to take on your shoulders a war in these provinces with Holland this next summer you would find it a heavy piece of work'. In February 1621 he urged that the truce be prolonged, 'whilst we see how things turn out in Germany and the Palatinate, for it would be a bad business for us to have so many wars on our hands at once'.

Within the United Provinces the Arminian controversy had revealed how deep-rooted were the fears of Spain and of Catholicism, and it was to be expected that the tensions generated by Oldenbarneveldt's fall should have found release in an emotional desire to renew the war. In Holland and Zeeland there was also considerable enthusiasm for ending the truce, because from past experience making war was associated with making profits. In particular, while the East India Company was sufficiently well established to survive conditions of war and peace alike, it was only in time of war that a West India Company could be established to plunder the rich shipping lanes of the Caribbean and the south Atlantic; to prolong the truce was to delay the collection of dividends, while a permanent peace settlement would at best merely offer access to the Indies under licence, requiring the payment of dues to the Spanish and Portuguese governments. In the inland provinces, however, and especially in Gelderland and Overijssel, attention was concentrated less on commercial advantage than on the fear of invasion from the Spanish base at Wesel. Here, as Maurice noted, there was much support for a peace settlement, provided that the independence of the provinces was recognised by Spain.

Popular attitudes to the truce nonetheless reflected the general conviction that it had enabled Spain to steal a march on the United Provinces. Not only had the Spaniards taken Wesel and achieved military and diplomatic successes throughout Europe, culminating in the invasion of the Palatinate, but, it was firmly believed, they had been enabled by the truce to amass vast stores of American bullion. Anxieties of this nature were brought to a head in March 1621 by the arrival in The Hague of Frederick and Elizabeth. The Dutch Republic had been the only state to provide substantial aid for the Bohemians, not only out of sympathy for their cause but also to engage as many Spanish troops as possible far from the Dutch frontier; and, because of its fear about their survival, the States-General had debated the matter on no fewer than six separate occasions between November 1620 and January 1621. The exiled king and his attractive wife were therefore welcomed by Maurice and presented to the public as the victims of a Catholic and Habsburg conspiracy which could not go unavenged.

Maurice, of course, wanted war. His understanding of the financial and military difficulties to be anticipated was more realistic than that of his exuberant supporters, but he believed in his ability to outmanoeuvre Spinola and longed to strike the one great blow that might leave Flanders at his mercy. He played a cautious role nonetheless, letting the Calvinists and the merchants make the running.

A Madame de'Tscerclaes, the Catholic widow of a Brabanter exiled in Holland, regularly visited a married daughter in Brussels, and since she was known personally to both Albert and Maurice occasionally served as their go-between. In February 1621 she brought Maurice proposals which may or may not have sought to suborn him from his loyalty to the States-General, but which certainly led in the following month to a public request by Albert that the States-General should receive a mission led by Pecquius, his chancellor. Maurice publicly welcomed the proposal so strongly and encouraged such exaggerated expectations to be entertained of its outcome that, when Pecquius demanded as his initial bargaining point that the Dutch return to their allegiance to the archdukes, the sense of disappointment was so acute that it was swiftly transformed to anger. Only Maurice's efforts saved Pecquius from being lynched on his return journey, and he sent him home with the message that the archdukes were 'misinformed' if they looked for any recognition of their authority. It is possible that Maurice had intended to support Pecquius, until his maladroit introduction made any settlement impossible; it is probable that he exploited the mission to convince his countrymen that war was the only alternative to submission. This at any rate was the effect that was produced.

Philip III died on 30 March 1621 and his successor and his advisers were determined to resort to war. 'I can assure you that the truce with Holland will not be reviewed', wrote the French ambassador, Bassompierre, to Louis XIII, 'because de Zuñiga, who now controls things, is opposed to it.' In essence Bassompierre was correct, since there were few more consistent critics of the truce than Zuñiga, yet, though it did not affect official policies, Zuñiga himself at the very last minute betrayed a most uncharacteristic pessimism about the result. 'We cannot by force of arms reduce these provinces to their former obedience. Whoever looks at the matter correctly and without passion must be impressed by the great armed strength of these provinces both by land and by sea, their strong geographical position ringed by the sea and by great rivers, lying close to France, England and Germany. Furthermore, that state is at the very height of its grandeur, while ours is in disarray. To promise ourselves that we can conquer the Dutch is to seek the impossible, to delude ourselves.' It was a curious prophecy to be made by such a man, yet, though ultimately it was to be fulfilled, the events of the next seven years seemed to indicate how unjustified had been his fears.

3

The Seven Fat Years of the Habsburgs 1621–8

Summer 1621 to spring 1622

When Albert died in July 1621, Philip IV's advisers proposed that someone of authority be sent to offer formal consolation to Isabella, but in reality to establish closer control over the Brussels administration. In the event the choice fell on Bedmar, cardinal de la Cueva, who was already serving in Flanders as ambassador. Though Isabella as an able and determined woman was not to be excluded from policy-making, Cueva's authority superseded that of the council of state. He directed the administration through two separate juntas, one of Belgians, the other of Spaniards, and was himself responsible to the Council of Flanders in Madrid.

The correspondence between Madrid and Brussels reveals an almost total grasp of the nature and the significance of the actions of other European powers – an awareness of the concurrence of events in Germany, Italy, France and the Baltic which is often lost to later generations reading the separate accounts of individual national histories. The object of this and the following chapter therefore is to take the whole of Europe for a canvas and, by sketching in the principal events, to demonstrate coincidence and contemporaneity and to discern throughout the confusing movements of armies and diplomats the rise and fall of Habsburg fortunes.

After all the heated debates about the need to abandon the truce, the war renewed in a surprisingly half-hearted manner. The Dutch, for all their wealth, had insufficient funds to launch a major campaign; the council of state complained that provinces were in arrears with their contributions, and so great was the fear that Spinola might seize the initiative by crossing the river-line that Maurice was ordered to withdraw from his forward positions in Cleves at Emmerich and Rees. There was no hesitation, however, in establishing, no shortage of private funds to establish, a West India Company. Of the company's capital of just over 7 million florins, 3 million alone were contributed by Amsterdam, many of whose merchants, being Calvinist exiles from the southern provinces, welcomed the company's formation not only as a source of profit but also as a weapon of war to challenge Spain's colonial power and to threaten the flow of bullion from America to Spain.

The Brussels government was also slow to take action. Its correspondence with Madrid, far from reflecting enthusiasm for the war, echoed the very anxieties which had forced it to negotiate in 1609. 'If we go on with the war in the Lower Palatinate,' wrote Isabella, 'we shall have before us a struggle of the greatest difficulty. We shall be assailed by the whole force of the opposite party and the burden will fall with all its weight upon Spain. It will hardly be possible to bring together sufficient forces to meet the enemy.' Isabella was agitated that too many troops of the Army of Flanders were still serving as far afield as Hungary and Bohemia, and, though she secured permission to recall Spinola from the Rhineland, he was required to leave two-thirds of his men behind under the command of Gonsalvo de Córdoba. The autumn campaign was only moderately successful. An attack on Sluys achieved nothing, while Spinola, who planned to occupy Jülich, as the preliminary to the invasion of Overijssel, encountered unexpected resistence from the small Dutch garrison in the city, which did not fall until February 1622.

In the Rhineland the truce established early in 1621 in order to allow the Evangelical Union to disband was broken by Sir Horatio Vere, an English officer serving with English troops in the employment of the United Provinces. Without money or supplies and desperate to keep his small force in being, he staked everything on the reckless venture of invading the diocese of Speier. Vere's action was to be repeated endlessly throughout the next decades by other commanders. The poverty of European society which made it easy to recruit soldiers made it difficult for governments and commanders to maintain them. The only way to hold men together in these circumstances was to unleash them upon open country or against a town, no matter whether friend or foe, and, irrespective of strategic consideration or government policy, terrify the inhabitants into surrendering whatever was of value. The cost to the local population in goods and suffering was incalculable, the loss of discipline among the troops became only too evident, but the commander heeded neither of these provided that essential supplies were secured and loot acquired for distribution in lieu of pay.

By September 1621 Mansfeld was in much the same plight as Vere. The Bohemian war was over and the countryside impoverished, Maximilian had occupied the Upper Palatinate without difficulty, and it was only the chance visit of the English ambassador Digby which prevented Mansfeld from surrendering. Persuaded by him to continue the struggle on Frederick's behalf in the Lower Palatinate, and aware of the rich terrain to be exploited there, Mansfeld set off immediately, with Maximilian's general, Tilly, in hot pursuit. As the armies of Vere, Mansfeld, Córdoba and Tilly converged, two other commanders arrived to complicate the situation. Christian of Brunswick, Lutheran administrator of the diocese of Halberstadt, was a violent youth, intoxicated by cavalry warfare and quixotically romantic in his devotion to Frederick's wife Elizabeth. He persuaded the Dutch to help him to raise 11,000 men and rode off to do battle for his lady – 'For God and For Her' was his blazon – in the defence of her husband's electorate. There he was joined by a man of different nature, the fifty-year old prince of Baden-Durlach, a devout Protestant who had long maintained that the faith could be defended only by arms. Ashamed at the cowardice of the Evangelical Union, he too raised about 11,000 men with Dutch assistance and set out to challenge the Catholic powers of Spain and the League.

Vere, Mansfeld, Brunswick and Baden-Durlach, almost wholly dependent upon Dutch subsidies, might in combination have made a brave defence of the Lower Palatinate. The English garrisons held Heidelberg and Frankenthal on the Rhine and Mannheim on the Neckar (see map 10). All that was needed was a concerted attempt by the others to harass the movements of Córdoba and Tilly, separated from each other by rivers and by suspicion, but this was beyond the financial means of the commanders. As winter approached, Christian of Brunswick moved north into Westphalia, to quarter his troops in the dioceses of Münster and Paderborn and to ransack the area for the gold and silver he needed for the spring. Mansfeld, to the horror of the archduke Leopold, moved south-west for the winter and occupied Alsace.

James I, though unwilling to help Frederick in Bohemia, felt obliged to do so in the Palatinate, especially as the defence of Heidelberg was entrusted to English troops. When Digby visited the English garrisons and lent them £10,000 on his own account, the king in a momentary flush of enthusiasm for his son-in-law's cause repaid the debt and sent an additional £30,000 to Frederick in The Hague. Both Olivares and

Isabella had foreseen that the sea route to Flanders might be endangered if James took offence at the Palatinate campaign, and Olivares was anxiously contriving solutions to placate him. In the event Gondomar was charged to revive the Spanish match with a new sauce, offering the Palatinate as the infanta's dowry so that James might then return it to Frederick. Gondomar concealed the fact that neither Maximilian nor Frederick had been consulted, and with his accustomed skill tried to persuade the king that by no other means could the matter be settled without bloodshed. For once he met with failure. 'I like not to marry my son with a portion of my daughter's tears', said James with rare dignity, and the threat of war became very real.

Paradoxically, it was Frederick's allies who finally deflected the king from intervening. The Dutch, by blockading the Flemish coast since the end of the truce, interfered with English trade, and conflicts were coming to a head in the Far East between the agents of the rival East India companies, so that Caron, the Dutch ambassador, reported, 'I have seen the time when the friends of Spain were held here as open enemies, but the king's subjects are now so irritated by these East Indian disputes that they take part against us.' But it was those who most vociferously championed Frederick's cause in Parliament who did it the most harm, for their speeches in the autumn provoked a major crisis over Parliament's right to discuss foreign affairs at all. When the Commons refused to vote supplies unless the king intervened directly in the Palatinate, and John Pym spoke of 'the religion which is being martyred in Bohemia', James retorted by rebuking all who spoke ill of 'our dear brother the king of Spain'. Gondomar reaped a fine harvest. James gave him authority to recruit two regiments of English and Scottish Catholics for service in Flanders, and when Parliament was dissolved in January 1622 Gondomar reported, 'It is the best thing that has happened in the interests of Spain and the Catholic religion since Luther began to preach heresy a hundred years ago.'

Spain's success in keeping open the sea route was second only to her achievement in safeguarding the Valtelline. Once Feria had built his forts, he tried to secure agreements with the Grisons to recognise Roman Catholicism as the official religion of the valley and to protect Spain's right of passage. Catholics, however, objected that this still left them subject to the Grisons, and family feuds, endemic in this highland area and stimulated afresh by the Venetian–Protestant faction, broke out into civil war. The Protestant pastor Jenatsch led a descent upon the valley, and Pompeius Planta was executed along with other friends of

Spain. On this occasion the French intervened, not to challenge Spain, since the entente still held and the government was about to launch a campaign against the Huguenots of Saumur, but in an effort to provide a more permanent settlement. Spain would have preferred to settle the matter on her own by force, but under French pressure agreed in April 1621 to the Treaty of Madrid, which required her to dismantle her forts and guaranteed the Protestants' rights in the valley. Fortunately for Spain the treaty was wholly unacceptable to the Catholic population, which appealed for support both to Feria and to Archduke Leopold of the Tyrol, while Jenatsch was encouraged by the Venetians to launch another attack on the valley. Habsburg troops settled the matter. In January 1622 the Articles of Milan abolished the Grisons' sovereignty in Bormio and the valley, and assigned the protection of Davos and the Lower Engadine to Leopold.

11. Bohemia and its neighbours

Further to the east the Habsburgs survived a renewed onslaught by Bethlen Gabor and the Hungarian nobility. Buquoy led the Imperial armies in a successful assault on Pressburg, but was killed at the siege of Neuhäusel. This gave Bethlen his opportunity. His wild cavalry, though a powerful force, could not maintain a sustained campaign without infantry, but he made contact with Jägerndorf, who set out across Moravia to join him with 12,000 men. Buquoy's army was hustled back to Pressburg, but held out there until Jägerndorf had to abandon the siege to go marauding for supplies. Bethlen, an inconstant enemy, once again offered to negotiate, and with members of the Hungarian Estates met Ferdinand's representatives at Nikolsburg. Ferdinand welcomed any opportunity to purchase peace in the Danube while other matters pressed so heavily upon him, and by the Peace of Nikolsburg (January 1622) granted the Estates' demands for virtual autonomy and recompensed Bethlen with a pension of 50,000 florins for surrendering the crown of Hungary.

It was Bohemia, therefore, that occupied most of Ferdinand's attention. The revolt had been brought to an end on the White Mountain. Mansfeld had left for the Rhineland, a few isolated garrisons in Dutch pay surrendered during the winter of 1621–2, and only Jägerndorf still operated independently in Silesia. Liechtenstein, the new governor of Prague, set up courts to deal with those who had survived the fighting. Twenty-seven leaders were executed in June 1621, eighteen imprisoned and a further twenty-nine, including Thurn, sentenced in their absence. The working out of a religious and constitutional settlement to replace the *Letter of Majesty* was not completed until 1627 (see p. 111) but immediate measures were taken to establish a more conformist society. The Calvinists were proscribed, then the Bohemian Brethren, and finally, despite the promises made to John George of Saxony, the Lutherans. At the same time Liechtenstein created a civil service staffed no longer by members of the families traditionally represented in the Estates, but by new men whose self-interest lay in loyalty to Vienna and whose appointments were controlled from there. Instead of being called 'officers of the kingdom of Bohemia', which in the past had meant that they were servants of the Estates, they now bore the title 'royal officers in the kingdom of Bohemia', and Lobkowitz's work was brought to fruition.

The new administration began by confiscating the lands of those who had actively supported the rebellion, but by February 1622 the scope was widened to include all those who had not actively resisted it. The result was a land transfer of massive proportions. 486 of the 911 noble estates were confiscated; as for the lesser nobility, its share of the land fell from a third to a tenth, so that an important class, in touch with the peasantry and mainly Protestant, was much reduced in power. With well over half the land in the kingdom to redistribute, Ferdinand re-endowed the Catholic Church and rewarded the loyalists. The latter had to buy their estates, but prices were low and in many cases the government gave land to settle its debts. Among the beneficiaries were, predictably, Polyxena Lobkowitz, Liechtenstein, Martinitz, Slavata and many of the commanders recruited from Spain, Italy and Flanders.

The destruction wrought by the civil war, the plunder exacted by the army of occupation, followed by the punitive contributions levied by Liechtenstein on town and countryside, led to a general economic collapse in which the price of land fell sharply, especially since so many confiscated estates were up for sale by the government. The beneficiaries of the new regime therefore did not derive quite the rich rewards they had anticipated, and the more influential of them set out to remedy this by debasing the currency. At first they ran a profitable swindle by producing nineteen florins, then twenty-seven and subsequently thirty-nine and even forty-seven, from one eight-ounce mark of silver. Then, in February 1622, Liechtenstein and his associates, including Hans de Witte, a Dutch Calvinist financier who had been long established in Bohemia, lent the emperor 6 million florins in return for one year's profits from the mint. As a result they purchased all the silver available in the kingdom, forbade the import and circulation of foreign currencies, and issued florins at the rate of seventy-nine to the mark.

One of the most important beneficiaries was Albert Waldstein – Wallenstein, as he was later more generally known. Born into the lesser nobility in 1583 and brought up among the Bohemian Brethren, he first fought against the Turks in Hungary alongside Tilly and Thurn. Later, after becoming a Catholic, he determined on a career as a professional soldier in the service of the Habsburgs. He married a rich, elderly widow whose fortune allowed him to attract Ferdinand's attention by bringing reinforcements at his own expense to Gradisca (see p. 59). After the defenestration of Prague he appropriated the Moravian treasury for Ferdinand – though it was later returned to ransom several government servants in rebel hands – and raised three regiments of his own to take the field against Thurn and Mansfeld. In December 1621 he became military commander of Bohemia, his services rewarded with confiscated land, and joined Liechtenstein's consortium at the mint. With de Witte's assistance he raised 85,000 florins to lend to Ferdinand and secured as a pledge the vast estates of his relatives, the Smiricky family, who had elected to fight for Frederick. With these as a nucleus between the frontier towns of Friedland and Reichenberg (see map 11), he built up a private domain which was subsequently to provide him with the means to take Germany by storm.

While Wallenstein was laying the foundation of his military career, Gustav Adolf significantly advanced his own by an ambitious assault on the Polish port of Riga. His achievement in surviving the difficulties of his early years as king of Sweden had not yet attracted much international attention, but against so wealthy a city, protected by so formidable a fortress, his swift success established his reputation throughout Europe. It also provided him with a base from which he was able to overrun Livonia, and which in the course of time was to become the second capital of Sweden's Baltic empire.

By the spring of 1622, therefore, though the Habsburgs' ally Poland had suffered a grievous blow at the hands of Sweden, the Habsburgs themselves could be satisfied with the way things had gone. A new administration had been established in Brussels following Albert's death, the Dutch were on the defensive and the Palatinate seemed to be at the mercy of Tilly and Córdoba. England remained benevolently neutral, Spain had re-established control of the Valtelline, Hungary had been defended, Bohemia was being plundered – and, though no one could yet appreciate the significance of it for the Habsburgs, the career had been launched of Albert Wallenstein.

Spring 1622 to autumn 1624

The Rhineland was now to be settled. Mansfeld, who had wintered in Alsace until the spring of 1622, marched north to Speier. While governments sought to impose coherence upon the pattern of military events, adventurers such as Mansfeld, determined to stay in the game at all costs by keeping their armies in being, ignored the purposes for which they had been recruited and laid waste whole provinces. 'The bishopric of Speier is ours', recorded one of Mansfeld's men. 'We are plundering at our ease. Our general does not wish for a treaty or for peace. He laughs at the enemy. All his thoughts are fixed upon the collection of money, of soldiers and of provisions.'

Frederick, the refugee elector Palatine, decided that Mansfeld, by the very rogue-elephant quality of his conduct, was the man most capable of restoring him to power, and set out from The Hague disguised as a merchant in a reckless adventure to join him. Though captured by Habsburg troops, he succeeded in concealing his identity and escaped to join Mansfeld and Baden-Durlach. With the advantage of numbers they overwhelmed Tilly to the south of Wiesloch and drove him back to the Neckar. Córdoba recognised the danger and abandoned the siege of Frankenthal to bring the Spanish army to Tilly's aid, but Mansfeld, running short of supplies, withdrew with Frederick to

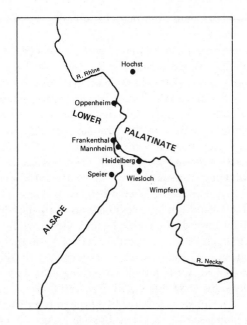

12. The Rhineland campaign

Oppenheim. Baden-Durlach courageously faced the Catholics alone; defeated at Wimpfen, he disbanded his troops and retired from the war.

Learning that Christian of Brunswick had acquired considerable treasure during his winter occupation of Westphalia, Mansfeld and Frederick moved north to join him. So too did Tilly and Córdoba, who intercepted and defeated Christian at the bridgehead of Hochst. Christian escaped with most of his treasure and joined Mansfeld at Mannheim, and when it became clear that the region could not support their combined forces they decided to abandon the Palatinate campaign and make their way to Alsace.

Frederick was totally disillusioned. Instead of marching in triumph to Heidelberg his capital, he faced the prospect of a long winter pillaging in Alsace in company which had become unendurable. 'As for this army it has committed great disorders. I think there are men in it who are possessed of the devil, and who take a pleasure in setting fire to everything. I should be glad to leave them. There ought to be some difference made between friend and foe but these people ruin both alike.' He nerved himself to escape. His uncle the duke of Bouillon gave him refuge in Sedan, and from there he wrote to James I agreeing to abandon the war.

Although their commissions were thereby cancelled, Mansfeld and Christian remained on the loose in Alsace. This caused great anxiety to Philip IV, who declared to Maximilian that Alsace was of greater consequence to Spain than the Palatinate and begged him to intervene. Unmoved by Philip's plea but afraid that the adventurers might forage across the Rhine into Bavaria, Maximilian sent Tilly to evict them. Thus harassed they moved north into Lorraine, by-passed Sedan, where Frederick cowered in his uncle's fortress, and then, in an unexpected and desperate manoeuvre, raced across Flanders to join an astonished Dutch army at the relief of Bergen-op-Zoom. Through lack of funds, Spinola had been late beginning his campaign that summer, and after a feint towards the Rhine he took the Dutch by surprise by marching on Bergen, only twenty miles north of Antwerp. He had been promised that the town major would surrender the town on his arrival, but as he was killed in the initial skirmishing Spinola was forced to conduct a siege for which he was ill prepared. Bergen, on the other hand, was well fortified, garrisoned by fourteen companies of English and Scots in Dutch service and well supplied by sea. Maurice did not take the siege too seriously at first, imagining that Spinola was trying to lure his men from the defence of the vulnerable north-eastern provinces, but when he realised what had happened he closed in on Spinola's lines and made it impossible for the Spaniards to forage freely. With the arrival of Mansfeld and Christian, Spinola decided to withdraw.

With no one of any substance left to oppose him in the Palatinate, Tilly forced the surrender of Heidelberg in September 1622, of Mannheim in November, and of Frankenthal in the following March. Maximilian meanwhile set about the expulsion of the Protestant clergy, despatched Frederick's library as a gift to the pope and demanded that Ferdinand appoint him elector. The secret agreement was already known across Europe, because of documents captured and published by Mansfeld, and, since it was obvious that a full Diet would never give its approval, Ferdinand summoned a diet of deputies to Regensburg. The deputies had no authority to pass imperial laws, but Ferdinand intended them to furnish as convincing an assembly as possible to authorise and witness the transfer of title from Frederick to Maximilian.

The strongest opposition came not from within the Empire but from Philip IV, who believed that Tilly's success against the English garrisons in the Palatinate, combined with the public recognition of

Maximilian as elector, could not fail to bring England into the war. He was also more than a little put out that he had not been fully consulted, and complained, as Zuñiga put it to the Imperial ambassador, that, 'His Imperial Majesty never considered for one second what Spain had done for him, and took it as a matter of course that the king should leave his own country and people to go to wrack and ruin and hasten to his help.'

There was a measure of play-acting in this exchange, intended to reassure the English ambassador of Philip's good faith, and Ferdinand was persuaded to agree that, if Frederick 'would but humble himself, deprecate his conduct and refrain from all other machinations', he might yield 'to the intercessions of princes friendly to him and restore him to grace'. But Frederick would not humble himself, and, with his reputation tarnished by association with Mansfeld's depredations, there was none to plead for him. The deputies met on several occasions in the winter of 1622-3 and in February the title was assigned to Maximilian for life, leaving it an open question who should acquire it on his death. Though there was nothing to be done to alter this, the representatives of the electors of Brandenburg and Saxony refused to attend the final ceremony; so too did the Spanish ambassador.

In the Valtelline the leaders of the Protestant-Venetian factions failed in an attempt to seize power, and the Articles of Milan (see p. 89), which they had hoped to repeal, were given general recognition at a conference held at Lindau on Lake Constance in September 1622. Unfortunately for Spain, the French government, as Louis XIII became more self-confident, began to revert to Henry IV's policy of maintaining French influence in the valley in alliance with Venice and the Grisons. This had been in abeyance for nearly a decade, because of the powerful influence exerted at court by the Catholic *dévots*. The government, moreover, had had to deal with a series of Huguenot rebellions, which made it reluctant and unable to interfere abroad. In October 1622, however, the Treaty of Montpellier put an end to civil war for the time being; in the following month Louis XIII met Charles Emmanuel of Savoy, and in the spring of 1623 France, Venice and Savoy signed the Treaty of Paris, which pledged them to restore the Grisons to their full sovereignty.

Olivares, in an ingenious riposte, persuaded the pope to take over the protection of the Valtelline Catholics, so that should French troops invade the valley they would have to fire on papal banners. The effect of this on the *dévots* could easily be imagined, and Olivares went one stage further in embarrassing the French government by proposing that France and Spain should both guarantee the rights of Roman Catholics in the valley, deny sovereignty to the Grisons and allow each other free right of passage. Louis XIII refused to be drawn; on the other hand, he did nothing to implement the Treaty of Paris. The Spanish government therefore had good cause to be satisfied with the course of events. The Valtelline remained open and the Rhenish Palatinate had been occupied by Spanish troops.

During the winter of 1622–3 the Brussels administration fortified the harbours at Ostend and Dunkirk and built light cruisers to co-operate with the Dunkirk privateers in preying upon North Sea shipping and raiding the Dutch herring fisheries. Philip IV and Spinola had hit upon this plan when the truce expired, and some of the Flanders cruisers had already proved their value, because the Dutch, with so many vessels at sea, found it impossible to protect them all. When more cruisers were launched, in 1623, the Dutch were compelled to organise convoys – a move which lowered morale and bred criticism of the conduct of the war. Dutch confidence suffered another blow in May when Spinola sent a flotilla of fourteen flat-bottomed boats to penetrate the canals and rivers of Zeeland. Walcheren was raided and thirty fishing boats were taken.

Even more alarming to the Dutch government was the action of the Catholic League. Throughout the winter Christian of Brunswick had occupied Lower Saxony, where he was well placed to attack Maximilian's brother in the dioceses of Cologne and Liège, or expel his brother-in-law, William of Neuberg, from Jülich. Tilly had therefore been ordered by Maximilian to move north from the Palatinate in order to contain Christian. In August 1623 he defeated him at Stadtlohn in Münster, only ten miles from the Dutch frontier, and Christian fled to The Hague for refuge.

Tilly, poised on the Dutch frontier, had only to join Spinola for the United Provinces to be in serious danger, but Maximilian refused to let him intervene. He had no wish to risk open war with the Dutch, lest they succeed one day, in alliance perhaps with England and France, in removing him from the Palatinate, a fear which haunted him until 1648. In any case, he had deep suspicions about Spain's future policy in the Rhineland. The memory of the Treaty of Graz still rankled, he could not but be vexed that the Spanish ambassador had refused to attend his installation as elector, and he had observed that, while Tilly had gone north in pursuit of Christian, Córdoba and the Spanish army had stayed behind in the Lower Palatinate. The Catholic League army, therefore, instead of helping Spinola to deliver what might have been the final blow to Dutch independence, hovered on the frontier, causing Maurice the most acute uneasiness, until it finally moved off into the secularised diocese of Osnabrück and restored it to Roman Catholic administration.

Ferdinand approved Maximilian's caution, not that he was in dispute with his Spanish cousin but because his own situation had suddenly deteriorated, making it impracticable, as he put it, 'to attack the Dutch with the forces of the Empire and the League'. The Vlachs, the so-called Wallachians of East Moravia, were wild tribes whom none could tame, though Comenius, the Czech patriot and Calvinist, understandably acclaimed them as courageous partisans who 'continued to resist with arms and could not be brought to deny their faith or offer submission'. By the summer of 1623 they had agreed to act in concert with Jägerndorf in Silesia, Christian of Brunswick and Bethlen Gabor. Thurn had been to Constantinople with Dutch assistance to secure Osmanli infantry for Bethlen's campaign and was now returned to serve under Jägerndorf.

It was a dangerous coalition for Ferdinand to encounter, especially since the Catholic League army was no longer in his neighbourhood. Nonetheless, it had served its turn at Stadtlohn by ensuring that Christian was removed from the scene, and while Bethlen awaited the Osmanli infantry Ferdinand had time to bring in Montenegro, a Neapolitan soldier, to organise with Wallenstein the defence of Moravia. They concentrated their troops around Göding (see map 11) at the junction of the Austrian, Hungarian and Moravian frontiers. Bethlen did not reach them until mid October, and then, to Wallenstein's disappointment, drew back rather than risk an attack on prepared defences. As both sides faced each other with neither making a move, Göding ran desperately short of supplies and Bethlen had only to await its collapse. In the event his Osmanli troops grew restive as the winter set in, and he himself, as he had so often done before, lost patience with everyone and abandoned the conflict. The Vlachs' leaders went to The Hague to solicit further support, but with Christian defeated and Bethlen discredited there was only Jägerndorf to stand by them – and with his death in the following March his army broke up in disorder.

Stadlohn, though it had not led, as Spain might have wished, to a major attack on the Dutch, had nonetheless served the Habsburg cause well by preventing Christian from intervening in Moravia. News of the battle had a different result in Madrid. Gondomar's advocacy of the Spanish match had proved to be unexpectedly successful, with the result that Prince Charles and the duke of Buckingham had arrived incognito in March 1623 to woo the infanta in person. Their appearance was initially welcomed as an indication that Charles was prepared to become a Catholic or at least to allow considerable freedom to English Catholics, and, although the manners of the English visitors offended Spanish protocol, negotiations were begun in real earnest. Charles convinced himself that he was in love, but by August, when news arrived of Stadlohn, it became clear that nothing Spain could do would restore the Palatinate or the electoral title to Frederick. In consequence Charles and Buckingham returned home humiliated and eager to be revenged.

It was as well for the Dutch that England was preparing to jettison the Spanish alliance, because after Stadtlohn and throughout the winter of 1623-4 morale in the United Provinces was at its lowest since the muder of William the Silent in 1584. Maurice had achieved none of the victories he had dreamed of throughout the truce, and the initiative had been seized by Spinola. In January and February there was a period of exceptional frost which brought Spanish troops across the frozen waterways into the Veluwe to threaten Utrecht. Maurice sent Madame de 'Tserclaes on her travels again to seek a six-months truce, but there was no response from Isabella. With the thaw came devastating floods, and the garrison at Breda, a key city, mutinied for lack of pay. In the spring, however, the English at last took action. Mansfeld was summoned to London and James I agreed to send him to the aid of the Dutch.

Help too was on its way from France. The government was annoyed by its failure to settle the Valtelline according to the Treaty of Paris, and with the appointment of Cardinal Richelieu to the royal council in April 1624 Louis XIII found a minister determined to renew the efforts of Henry IV to break through the chain of Habsburg bases which encircled France. At this stage Richelieu was not strong enough in the council to challenge the *dévots* outright, nor was France strong enough to challenge Spain, but the basic purposes of Richelieu's policy in foreign affairs was quite clear: as he later set them down in 1629, these were 'to arrest the course of Spain's progress' and that France 'might enter the states of all her neighbours to protect them from Spain's oppression'. To these ends, accordingly, a marriage alliance was sought with England, the Treaty of Compiègne in June 1624 assured the Dutch of a subsidy of 400,000 écus, and the marquis of Coeuvres was ordered to prepare an assault on Spain's vital line of communication through the Valtelline.

Isabella was alarmed beyond measure by the extension of the area of hostilities and the growing number of Spain's enemies. 'This is a war which will last for ever', she wrote to Philip IV in September 1624, and, without much heed to the poor showing of the Dutch forces, she continued, 'If you do not see that the wants of our army are supplied to the minute we shall risk a disaster which will ruin all your states. I think it my duty then to spell this out plainly for you in good time, else if war breaks out next year in Germany, and France joins in with England, Your Majesty will find yourself face to face with the most awful difficulties one can imagine, and utterly unable to wage war in so many quarters at such a fearful cost. In such a case you would not have a hope, I will not say of victory, but of escaping utter defeat and ruin.'

The prophetic quality of Isabella's anxiety could for the moment be ignored. If French intervention was one day to deal the death blow to Spain's European policies, that day was still many years ahead. In the meantime, though Spinola had failed at Bergen and though English

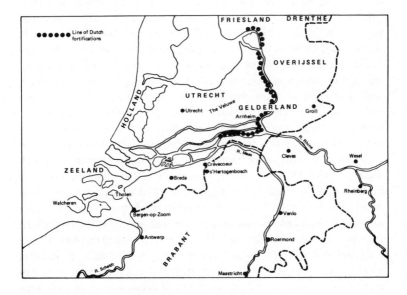

13. The war in the Netherlands 1621–48

hostility was expected to be troublesome, yet Frederick had been virtually abandoned by the German princes and the Palatinate had been cleared of Spain's enemies. Hungary and Moravia, moreover, had been defended, the Valtelline remained open, Dutch morale was at low ebb and, as the summer of 1624 reached its peak, Spinola was about to undertake a campaign against Breda.

Autumn 1624 to autumn 1625

At the end of August 1624 Spinola marched against Breda, a frontier fortress of great importance guarding the routes north to Utrecht and Amsterdam; it was also the favourite residence of Maurice of Nassau, which he himself had liberated in 1589 and which had been in his family for two centuries. It was well fortified, the surrounding countryside was little better than a quagmire, and Justinus of Nassau, Maurice's natural brother, garrisoned it with 7000 men. Not surprisingly, Isabella and the council of war opposed the operation, but Spinola had elected to restore his reputation in this way and would not be dissuaded from his purpose.

Because he set out so late in the season, the burghers of Breda, not anticipating an attack, had laid in only the usual stocks of winter supplies. Subsequently, as the Spanish army approached, they mistakenly admitted the hundreds of refugees fleeing before it, and Spinola wasted no time in confining the augmented population within his siege works. Despite the difficulty of working in waterlogged ground, his troops succeeded within seventeen days in digging ditches six feet deep, with protective walls five feet high, not only to encircle the town at a radius of half a mile from the walls but also to protect the besieging army itself from a relieving force. Breda was therefore doomed provided the army was supplied and paid, defended against attack and not called away to deal with other matters. It was the last condition which alarmed Philip IV, who warned Spinola 'to look to it that no fortress of our own is jeopardised for the sake of taking Breda', and it was precisely because Spinola refused to be diverted from his quarry that Maurice justified Philip's anxieties by taking Cleves at the end of September. In October he launched a daring raid on Antwerp with troops disguised as a Spanish convoy, which was identified and repelled only just in time, and in November the city was again attacked. But, despite the chorus of recrimination and alarm from Madrid and Brussels alike, Spinola kept the siege going with unwavering determination all through the winter.

In the Valtelline, meanwhile, the French expedition which had set out under the marquis of Coeuvres in November 1624 fulfilled its task admirably. Despite heavy snowfalls which blocked the passes, the troops occupied the entire valley by February 1625 and treated the papal garrisons with meticulous courtesy. Their success prompted Charles Emmanuel of Savoy to launch a swift attack on Genoa, in alliance with Lesdiguières, the independent-minded Huguenot governor of Dauphiné. The importance of the operation was appreciated by Wake, the English ambassador. 'It is very certain that the Spaniards are in very great labyrinth, and their weakness doth now evidently appear unto all men. They must defend Genoa or else their honour and all that they have in Italy will be buried in the ruin of that city, and when that source of their money shall be dried up [a reference to the Genoese banks which financed the government in Madrid] and the passage cut off for their transporting of Spaniards, Neapolitans and Sicilians, their armies in Germany will not be able to subsist long.' In the event, though Wake had hoped for English and Venetian ships to be sent in support, the only ships to be seen by Charles Emmanuel were those of the marquis of Santa Cruz bringing Spanish reinforcements into the port, and it did not take long for the duke of Feria to send the invaders packing.

In England after Charles's return from Spain, the government raised 12,000 men with whom Mansfeld was to recover the Palatinate, but the expedition was doomed from the start. James I could not bring himself to declare war on Spain, and when Mansfeld inquired how then he was to pass through the Spanish lines he was told 'to demand passage according to the amity between England and Spain'. In February 1625, nonetheless, Mansfeld set out for Calais, intending to disembark his men and march them overland to the Rhineland, but Richelieu refused to let him do so. Although French troops had already intervened indirectly against Spain in the Valtelline, Richelieu dared not yet risk anything which might result in open war, and Mansfeld's reputation made him in any case an unwanted guest.

Mansfeld therefore had no option but to sail up-Channel to Walcheren, but again he was denied permission to land. Maurice was ready to employ him for the relief of Breda but would not risk having him pass through the Netherlands without being free to watch his every step. While negotiations dragged on between Walcheren, London and The Hague, the unhappy troops, cooped up with foul water and contaminated food, died in their thousands. The remainder were at last put ashore. Without orders and, even more to the point, without pay, many of them deserted to the Army of Flanders.

Isabella's perennial anxiety that the conflict was being extended too widely was given substance in northern Germany, where concern at Maximilian's investiture and alarm at Tilly's presence in the Lower Saxon Circle led to talk of a new alliance against the emperor. 'It seems there is fuel enough if we bring coals and bellows', wrote Anstruther, the English ambassador, but it was Gustav Adolf not James who first proposed to set the fire ablaze. He offered to lead 50,000 men across Silesia into Bohemia and Austria, provided that two-thirds of the cost was met by the German princes along with England and the United Provinces; in addition he wanted free access to Bremen and Wismar, and the support of a Dutch fleet to patrol the north German coast in case of interference by Denmark or Poland.

The offer was refused. The States-General suspected that Gustav was more interested in Poland than in Bohemia and preferred to employ Christian of Denmark in his place. Christian's ambitions in the Lower Saxon Circle would compel him to engage the army of the Catholic League which appeared to threaten the Dutch frontier, and, were he successful, the way would lie open to restore Frederick to the Palatinate. James I agreed. His wife Anne was Christian's sister and it would cost less to support him than to underwrite Gustav's ambitious proposals. Gustav therefore withdrew to renew his war with Poland in the spring of 1625 and captured the rich Polish ports of Memel, Pillau and Elbing (see map 4), the value of whose customs dues exceeded that of the Swedish government's internal revenues. Without his leadership Brandenburg and Saxony refused to make a move, and it was only under Dutch pressure that the princes of the Lower Saxon Circle reluctantly elected Christian their director in May 1625.

With the spring of 1625 the siege of Breda ran into difficulties. Across a flooded landscape Spinola's engineers constructed sluice and counter-sluice to protect their earthworks and to prevent reinforcements' sailing into the city in barges over the fields from Sevenbergen, while the lack of forage became serious. Within the city too there were problems, though the plague, which caused great distress, served a grim purpose in reducing the number of mouths to feed, so that the supplies were not exhausted by the end of the winter. Maurice, fighting the last desperate campaign of his life, succumbed to illness in April. Before his death he secured the appointment of his brother Frederick Henry as commander-in-chief, but this could not prevent the surrender of Breda on 5 June. It was Spinola's great triumph, achieved against the opposition not only of the enemy and of the elements but also of his own government. His achievement, commemorated in Velasquez's *Las Lanzas* and Lope de Vega's *Triumphal Ode*, established his military reputation as he had intended, and the army of Flanders once again believed in its destiny to defeat the Dutch rebels.

Christian meanwhile advanced cautiously up the Weser until meeting with a serious accident at Hameln in the summer of 1625. He was thrown from his horse down an eighty-foot drop and was so badly stunned that for some days he was paralysed and taken for dead. Eventually he recovered his limbs and his zest for war, but Tilly had advanced north to block his progress and at the same time to keep a wary eye open for Mansfeld, who, following the loss of Breda, was raising men to join Christian.

Another soldier about to take the field was Wallenstein. Ferdinand, who had given him the Smiricky lands in pledge for a loan of 85,000 florins, had subsequently declared the domain of Friedland and Reichenburg an hereditary fief and had sold it to him outright as a bargain for an additional 65,000 florins. With the acquisition of more estates in 1624, the prince of Friedland enjoyed virtual autonomy over 2000 square miles between the Elbe and the Sudeten mountains. Here he created a self-sufficient military supply base. His manager, Gerhard von Taxis, controlled the activity of the peasants, directing their choice of seeds and methods of farming in order to produce a surplus of cereals; and armourers, smiths and weavers were imported from Flanders so that the warehouses were stacked with weapons and uniforms. Wallenstein's plan was to raise an army for the emperor's service and to make warfare a profitable business, not by the indiscriminate looting which characterised Mansfeld's armies, but by compelling the towns wherever he operated to pay heavily for protection from his troops. With the money thus raised he would then supply his army from his base in Friedland, and his troops, well paid and well supplied, would therefore be better disciplined and more effective than others'. Once victorious, Wallenstein then hoped to claim further rewards of land and titles from the emperor.

In February 1625 he had offered to raise 50,000 men but Ferdinand was uneasy about his intentions: in May he settled for 15,000 infantry and 6000 cavalry but with provision for the number to be increased as the occasion demanded. The Instructions of June 1625 laid down stringent conditions about the protection of property and the treatment of civilians but added, 'nonetheless we sanction the levy in conquered places and territories of sufferable contributions and loans'. No one in the Imperial chancellery presumed to define 'sufferable', while the clerks in the exchequer later pretended 'that without any remuneration on the part of His Imperial Majesty it was the duke of Friedland's intention to provide his armada with all its needs until such time as a state of peace might again be attained'. Wallenstein, on the other hand, regarded the army as his own private investment, heavily financed by de Witte, but expected the emperor to meet his expenses. But he had no illusions. In the last resort, as he put it, 'we must needs go *a la desparata* and take what we can get'.

In August 1625 Wallenstein set out for northern Germany. *En route* he reinforced the bridge at Dessau (see map 14) to oppose any enemy force trying to push eastwards into Silesia, and then persuaded Tilly to winter in the Weser valley while he himself occupied Halberstadt and Magdeburg. He did this in part because the emperor planned to assign these two secularised dioceses to his younger son, rather than to relatives of Maximilian, and also because Wallenstein wanted his own troops stationed by the Elbe so that von Taxis could send down supplies by barge from Friedland. Once established, he set about demonstrating his method of treating conquered territory. With little apparent fuss and after careful negotiations with each town, he secured the contributions he desired, and the Imperial secretary reports, 'the land was not wasted or burned, nor the people driven from hut and house, but all was cultivated and harvested'. Wallenstein had learned not to kill the geese which could lay golden eggs.

While the siege of Breda was brought to its successful conclusion and the armies of Tilly and Wallenstein were mobilised to meet those of Mansfeld and Christian, the emperor consolidated his position within the 'hereditary lands'. Bohemia was in no condition to make trouble, and Hungary proved to be surprisingly accommodating. This was partly because the elected leader of the diet, a Protestant and formerly an agent for Bethlen Gabor, had become a Roman Catholic and agreed to serve the needs of the emperor; matters were also improved in May 1623 by the renewal at Gyarmat of the Treaty of Sitva-Torok, which removed the immediate threat of Osmanli invasion and permitted the emperor to be less dependent upon purchasing Magyar co-operation. He even secured the election of his son Ferdinand as king of Hungary in October 1625.

In Upper Austria, since he had not yet settled all his debts to

Maximilian, he governed through Bavarian officials, who expelled Protestant clergy and required all but the nobles to attend mass. Ferdinand demanded of the Estates a fine of 1 million florins for their act of confederation with the Bohemian rebels, and when they protested that Maximilian had already taxed them for that offence insisted nonetheless on having at least 600,000 florins. The revolt of a desperate and disillusioned peasantry was quickly suppressed by Bavarian troops.

Outside Europe the general pattern of Habsburg success had been disconcertingly shattered so far as Madrid was concerned by a daring raid by the Dutch West India Company on Bahia in May 1624. Bahia was the capital of Brazil, which had come under Spanish rule with the rest of the Portuguese empire in the reign of Philip II, and had grown rich from the production of sugar. The Dutch fleet of over fifty ships swept into the port, making a rich haul of shipping, and disembarked a force sufficient to seize control of the town and subsequently to establish its authority in the province. When news of the action reached Madrid it provoked an angry and determined response: 'All the grandees, dignitaries, magistrates and government servants here, even those of the lowest class', reported Tarantaise, the Savoyard ambassador, 'have determined to make a voluntary offer to His Majesty which they think will amount to 2 million ducats in all', and within months an armada was despatched to South America. It arrived to discover that the population had risen against its new masters, and a hard-pressed garrison of 2500 Dutch in Bahia was forced to surrender in April 1625. By midsummer Brazil was once again under Spanish rule.

'Blessed be God who is thus defending His cause', exclaimed Olivares, and by the autumn of 1625 there was much to give satisfaction to the Habsburgs. The coalition of England, the United Provinces and Denmark was potentially dangerous, and the French were in possession of the Valtelline, but Tilly and Wallenstein were well positioned to contain the first and the French government was already running into criticism at home for its action in the second. In addition Genoa had been defended and Brazil recovered, the Turks had been brought to make peace, the 'hereditary lands' were well under control, and the great fortress of Breda had fallen to Spinola. 'Your Highness should reflect', wrote Tarantaise to Charles Emmanuel, 'how great are the vicissitudes of this world, for six months ago all the elements seemed to be uniting to bring this monarchy to ruin. Now they seem inclined to favour everything they do, and all the winds are wafting them on their way.'

Autumn 1625 to autumn 1627

The very success of the Habsburg governments in advancing towards their goals only increased the number of their enemies.

England and France, whose neutrality had been invaluable to Spain for more than a decade, had now to be reckoned as belligerents. In sending an invasion force against Cadiz in the autumn of 1625, Charles I clearly intended to revive the lost glories of the Elizabethan Age, but these were too hallowed in the national memory to provide reliable models for emulation: the Cadiz raid of 1596 had in fact been a disaster, and Cadiz itself had been strongly fortified since then. With high hopes, nonetheless, the States-General welcomed the first fruits of the English government's rediscovered enmity to Spain, released Viscount Wimbledon and other English officers in Dutch service to take command of the expedition, and supplied twenty of the eighty ships which, with 15,000 men, occupied the outer harbour of Cadiz in October. In the inner harbour, however, fourteen Brazil galleons and seven galleys were lined up in crescent formation so that any ship trying to get past the sunken hulks which blocked the entrance would be exposed to their combined fire-power, and troops streamed across Andalusia to reinforce the garrison. Wimbledon withdrew to open water in the hope of intercepting the bullion fleet or the East Indies fleet, bound for Cadiz and Lisbon respectively. In this too he failed and the expedition returned home disconsolate. For Spain, however, there remained the problem that Spanish shipping could no longer shelter from the Dutch in English waters before slipping across the Channel to Dunkirk.

Louis XIII's hostility, less open than Charles I's, was nonetheless evident in the Valtelline, where French garrisons had taken over the forts entrusted to papal troops. Despite the diplomatic treatment accorded his servants, the pope sent a legate to protest to Louis XIII, and the *dévots* published an *Admonitio ad regem* which declared it sinful to encourage heresy in the Valtelline out of envy of Spain. Richelieu's ministers produced counterblasts to justify the alliance with the Grisons, and the *Déclaration* of the bishop of Chartres went so far as to proclaim a doctrine of royal infallibility: 'the king made the alliance because he willed it; he undertook war because it is just and reasonable, or better, such a war is just because he undertook it'. It was unfortunate for Richelieu that the policy he defended against the Catholics should then be sabotaged by Huguenots. Rohan rebelled in Languedoc, Soubise raised a squadron which destroyed what remained of the royal fleet off the Normandy coast, and between them they made it impossible for France to sustain a war beyond her frontiers.

Coeuvres in the Valtelline appealed for clarification of his orders. The Grisons demanded that he implement the Treaty of Madrid (see p. 89) but Richelieu had advised him not to act too openly against the Roman Catholic population of the valley. His army, moreover, was needed in Languedoc. The Dutch government too was in a quandary. It was pledged to assist France against Spain in the Valtelline, but its own sailors refused to make this possible by attacking Soubise and the rebel Huguenot fleet. Olivares welcomed the pretence that France and Spain were not at war, since such a war would distract Spain totally from her objectives in the Netherlands; but, because Spanish shipping was being taken off the French Mediterranean coast, he had to retaliate by seizing French shipping in Iberian ports. From that it was but a short step to sealing the frontiers and both countries found themselves on the brink of a war which neither could afford to undertake.

An unexpected solution was proposed by de Fargis, the French ambassador, who was closely associated with the *dévots* and might possibly have received unofficial orders from Louis himself. He suggested to Olivares that the sovereignty of the Grisons be recognised and an annual tribute paid by the inhabitants of the valley, but that the latter be protected in their Catholicism and allowed to appoint their own magistrates. The forts were to be demolished and the matter of Spain's line of communication through the valley deliberately obscured. Although the assertion of the Grisons' sovereignty implied that Spain had no right of access yet, as the only troops capable of checking Spain's were now to be withdrawn to France, Olivares could be reasonably satisfied that the route was not closed. The terms were settled in March 1626 at Monzon, to the indignation of the Grisons, Savoy and Venice, who claimed they had been betrayed by France. Richelieu gave vent to his anger at de Fargis's unauthorised behaviour, but could not fail to recognise that it rescued him from an impossible situation. Beneath the barrage of abuse which was heaped upon de Fargis, it was another diplomat, Bassompierre, who remarked that in the government's relief at avoiding open war 'everyone was more concerned to blame the workman than to demolish the work'.

As one enemy withdrew, others re-formed. At The Hague in December 1625, the Dutch brought together England and Denmark in a new alliance with Mansfeld and Christian of Brunswick. Unlike the international combinations dreamed up in the fertile imagination of a Christian of Anhalt, this was soundly based in reality, since the Dutch agreed to furnish 50,000 florins a month to maintain 30,000 infantry and 8000 cavalry in northern Germany. The strategy agreed upon for 1626 was simple enough but potentially effective. Christian of Denmark was to engage Tilly along the Weser, giving Christian of Brunswick the opportunity to slip across Hesse into the Rhineland dioceses held by the Bavarian princes. Mansfeld meanwhile was to by-pass Wallenstein's army in the Elbe valley, raise the persecuted Protestants of Silesia and Bohemia, and attack Vienna. Bethlen Gabor, as of old, agreed to join in, but no one put much faith in his promises – nor in those of Charles I, who, in an excess of enthusiasm which took no account of his impoverished condition, committed England to provide £30,000 a month.

If the enemies of the Habsburgs had at last begun to organise themselves realistically upon a continental scale, Olivares was no less

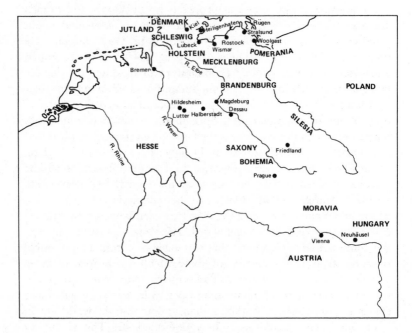

14. The campaigns in central Europe 1626–8

wide-ranging in his plans. His proposals, discussed at a conference in Brussels in May 1626, were to involve the Habsburgs, Bavaria, the Catholic League, Poland and the Hanse towns. The plan itself was not novel: it had matured in St Clemente's mind at the turn of the century and envisaged the destruction of the Dutch economy by denying Dutch merchants access to the Baltic trade upon which their country's livelihood largely depended. It had also been agreed in 1625 how to achieve this, by offering the Hanse towns the monopoly of Iberian trade with Europe provided that they denied Dutch merchants access to their ports; but, since the North Sea routes were controlled by England and the Dutch, the Hanse were not likely to derive much profit from the deal. What was novel was the wide range of measures proposed by Olivares to the Brussels conference, measures derived in part from Spain's new-found confidence in her ability to launch an effective naval force in northern waters. With the German coastline occupied by Imperial troops and Christian of Denmark contained by the League, it was hoped that the Hanse towns would be emboldened to defy the Dutch and accept the monopoly of Iberian trade, in the knowledge that Spanish shipping would be available to give them protection.

The first thing to establish was the support of the Flanders government – an easy matter, since the plan owed much to Spinola's reports on the value of the Flanders cruisers: 'we are continuing to disquiet the enemy and are keeping as many ships as we can at sea to do so'. Even Isabella, revealed in her correspondence with Madrid as a professional pessimist, agreed that 'it would be much in Your Majesty's service if you kept up war vessels in the Baltic Sea, as they would so hamper the trade which the Dutch carry on there that they would soon be brought to reasonable terms'.

Maximilian of Bavaria was uninterested, because his eyes were fixed on the Rhineland alone and he had shown no interest in the defeat of the Dutch, which was the whole object of the operation. He could not, however, ignore the armies of Denmark and Brunswick which threatened the Rhineland, and the participation of the Catholic League was thereby assured. The emperor agreed, determined to establish his authority more firmly in northern Germany, and to settle the religious issue once and for all in favour of the Catholic Church by the wholesale enforcement of the Peace of Augsburg. Wallenstein, though sceptical about Olivares's proposals and the emperor's intentions, was prepared to serve them if it allowed him to acquire a Baltic duchy and make him more wealthy, and more independent of Vienna, than he could be in

Friedland. The Hanse towns were cautious. They did not want the forces of the Counter-Reformation at their gates, but they saw merit in eliminating Dutch competition, provided that the Habsburgs effectively demonstrated that they could protect them by land and by sea. Poland too was interested. Sigismund longed to have his own fleet in the Baltic to challenge Sweden's, and to this end he pledged what support he could to the Habsburg plan.

The wide-ranging and ambitious schemes debated by the Dutch and their allies at The Hague, and by Spain and her allies at Brussels, affected an area stretching from the Atlantic to the Balkans, from the Baltic to the Danube, and involved every major power in Europe save France, which had retired from foreign affairs to undertake the siege of the Huguenot stronghold of La Rochelle.

Tilly wintered in Hildesheim and fell back on Hesse in the summer of 1626 to prevent Christian of Brunswick from entering the Rhineland. Christian's death in June put an end to the threat. Mansfeld meanwhile challenged Wallenstein at Dessau, where he looked for a brilliant crossing of the Elbe to restore his withered reputation, but he had not taken account of Wallenstein's careful defence works. He attacked them with 12,000 men and withdrew defeated into neutral Brandenburg with fewer than 8000. At the end of July, however, he was reinforced by Danish infantry, and in August he set off on a line curving east and south to reach Moravia. Wallenstein followed, carefully holding the inside of the curve to prevent any sudden break by Mansfeld into Bohemia, but he had not gone far when he learned that Christian of Denmark had moved forward into the ever-widening gap between himself and Tilly. Without hesitation he detached 8000 men to turn Christian's advance, and, when the Danes retreated, Tilly caught them and defeated them utterly at Lutter. Christian lost half his troops, and was thenceforth abandoned by all his German allies save the dukes of Mecklenburg.

Wallenstein with the rest of his men continued to shadow Mansfeld for nearly 500 miles across Europe in a well conducted if undramatic campaign. Mansfeld, finding himself continually barred from his objectives of Prague and Vienna, pressed on into Hungary to seek out Bethlen Gabor, who was once again late in the field. Throughout the late autumn they engaged Wallenstein near Neuhäusel without success. Bethlen made his peace, on the least favourable terms yet granted him, and Mansfeld, setting out for Venice, died in Bosnia during November. Despite prohibitions from Vienna, Wallenstein wintered his men in Moravia and Silesia; his threat of resignation served its purpose, since it was feared that should he disband Bethlen might return. Accordingly, the Bohemian revenues were assigned entirely for the upkeep of his army on Habsburg soil.

While Wallenstein defended the 'hereditary lands', the pacification and humiliation of Bohemia was completed by the publication of a new constitution which made no reference to the *Letter of Majesty* and which confirmed Bohemia's dependence upon the administrative hierarchy in Vienna.

In Upper Austria, however, the revolt which had been stifled in 1625 exploded with much greater force in the following year, the greatest popular uprising to occur in central Europe since the Peasants' Revolt of 1525. Throughout the winter, millennarian expectations of the fall of Antichrist had spread among the people, inflaming alike the victims of famine and persecution. When the entire population was required to attend the Easter Mass, Scultetus, the Calvinist preacher at Frederick's coronation (see p. 70), was smuggled into the country by Christian of Denmark's agents to encourage Protestant resistance. The immediate cause of revolt was the confiscation of Protestant books by house-to-house search, and between May and July 16,000 rebels took the field. Though religious persecution was the principal grievance, there were many other issues which brought Catholic peasants to fight alongside Lutherans, and in verses composed to maintain morale during the following winter the rebels set out the reasons for their behaviour: 'The duplicity of the Jesuits, the tyranny of the regent, thieving by the governor and swindling by officials, severe oppression of conscience and the excessive weight of taxation: it is these that have brought about in this country the uprising of the peasants.'

Inspired by their leader, Stefan Fadinger, whose magnetic personality made him a folk hero for many generations, and assisted by many nobles, whose expertise was indispensable for military success, the peasants held their own against the emperor's troops. They seized several towns, and were laying siege to Linz, the capital, until Fadinger's death led to a crisis of confidence. When Ferdinand offered to pardon all who submitted to his laws, the majority went home peacefully, but such apparent leniency displeased Maximilian, who arrived with reinforcements to provoke a new uprising in September. By the following spring it was over. 12,000 peasants are believed to have been killed, and, by a decree in May 1627, the Protestants were compelled to choose between conformity and exile.

In January 1627 Philip IV outlined to Isabella the extent of his plans for the year ahead. The Palatinate was to be held for Spain and Bavaria; an armed watch would be kept on French activity, especially in northern Italy; the Hanse towns were to be recruited as allies and bound by commercial treaties to Spain; the war with England and the United Provinces would be prosecuted with vigour; and Poland was to be encouraged to greater efforts against Sweden. By the end of the month, however, these projects were temporarily paralysed by the government's bankruptcy.

Once again the policy of mortgaging the future had failed, but it was Olivares alone who recognised that it was not simply a matter of renegotiating the debt. With his restless energy for identifying problems and inventing solutions, he had already proposed that Castile alone could not afford major undertakings of the kind outlined by Philip IV. Sensitive to the grievances of non-Castilians who neither saw their king nor enjoyed his patronage, he suggested the creation of a more widely based Spanish administration to replace the one dominated by Castile. In return the other kingdoms should bear some of Castile's financial burden, and he proposed a Union of Arms by which each kingdom would raise its own reserve of troops for service in the defence of all. It was a vain hope. The other kingdoms refused to be dragged down, as they saw it, into the bottomless pit of Castile's mismanaged finances. Even when the Cadiz raid engendered a short-lived mood of national unity in the face of danger, the Cortes of Aragon, Catalonia and Valencia each refused their aid, and in January 1627 there was nothing for it but to settle the bankruptcy by borrowing more money. This Olivares did by playing off a new group of Portuguese financiers against the Genoese, who for nearly a century had monopolised the business of lending to the crown, and, with a new set of loans to tide Castile over, interest payments could again be resumed.

France in the meantime, after seeking the alliance of England against Spain by the marriage of Charles I and Henrietta Maria, had drifted into war over the rights of Roman Catholics in England and English aid to the Huguenots of La Rochelle. Richelieu arranged several meetings with the Spanish ambassador to suggest joint naval action in the Channel, and, though their plans for an invasion of England never materialised, Spain was relieved of French hostility in a year when money was scarce. In the Netherlands it was so scarce, indeed, that Spinola dared make no move at all, and for the first time since the truce had expired the initiative passed to the Dutch. Frederick Henry in his first major campaign revealed his skill as a cautious but remorseless

director of siege operations by investing Groll, a powerfully defended
fortress in Overijssel which the Spaniards had occupied since 1606 (see
p. 34). It fell before the end of the summer.

In the Empire, however, the Habsburg cause prospered in 1627.
Wallenstein sent troops both to strengthen the defences of Hungary and
to reinforce Sigismund,because the Swedes, 'in whom we shall find a
worse enemy than the Turk', had advanced through Polish Prussia to
the estuary of the Vistula. With the rest of his army he cleared the
survivors of Mansfeld's operation out of Silesia and marched north to
join Tilly in Lower Saxony. Christian was in no position to resist their
joint attack. The Dutch had abandoned him as a poor investment,
Charles I had defaulted on his promise to provide £30,000 a month, and
the English fleet, which might have rendered him invaluable assistance
by entering the Elbe at Stade, had gone off to La Rochelle. In
September, therefore, Tilly and Wallenstein defeated Christian at
Heiligenhafen, and opened a way north through Holstein and
Schleswig to Jutland (see map 14).

Despite the bankruptcy and the loss of Groll, the Habsburgs
continued to prosper. The emperor was stronger than ever before
within the 'hereditary lands'; Denmark was about to be invaded; and
high hopes were still entertained for the successful execution of
Olivares's Baltic policy.

Autumn 1627 to midsummer 1628

In October 1627 an electoral diet met at Mülhausen. The electors of
Saxony and Brandenburg were outspoken about the contributions
levied on their own territories by Wallenstein's troops. The members of
the Catholic League had a similar complaint, and, though Maximilian
and the archbishop-electors were anxious for Tilly to invade Denmark,
they made it clear to Ferdinand that his requests for aid and his known
desire to have his son Ferdinand elected as king of the Romans – and
thereby guaranteed the succession to the imperial title – would be
rejected unless Wallenstein's powers were swiftly curbed.

When Tilly was wounded in October, however, it was Wallenstein
who assumed command of the Catholic League army as well as his own,
and there was nothing to check his triumphal progress through the
Jutland peninsula, where by Christmas he had 60,000 men in winter
quarters. In addition he sent another army into Mecklenburg, whose
hundred miles of coastline from Lübeck to the mouth of the Recknitz

included the ports of Wismar and Rostock. The dukes of Mecklenburg–Schwerin and Mecklenburg–Gustrow were Christian's last remaining allies, and by appropriating their territories as a base from which to execute Olivares's Baltic plan, Wallenstein privately intended it to replace Friedland as the nucleus of his personal empire. He also recognised that, since Christian was still powerful at sea, it was advisable to fortify the Mecklenburg ports and establish a fleet in the Baltic. He pretended support for the Spanish plan to destroy Dutch trade, intending that the first priority should be the defeat of the Danes, and wrote urgently to Isabella to secure the despatch of the Dunkirk fleet. He even suggested the cutting of a canal at Kiel to facilitate Spanish access to the Baltic and endeavoured manfully to be diplomatic to Gabriel de Roy, the Spanish agent sent to Wismar to superintend operations with the Hanse towns.

The Genoese envoy reported at the end of 1627 that the Hanse towns, 'though they may sympathise with their Protestant brethren, are trembling at the emperor's good fortune and so will probably bow before his commands'. Duke Frederick of Gottorp offered support if his own ships were given access to the Indies, and Count Schwarzenberg, the Imperial ambassador, appeared before a conference of the Hanseatic League at Lübeck in February 1628. It was a moment of great importance for the Habsburg cause, but nothing came of it. Schwarzenberg was too aggressive in manner and there were too many Protestants at the conference, too many exiles from Roman Catholic states and too many with grievances against the emperor's servants; above all, until Wallenstein could build his own ships, or secure those of Poland and Spain, the Hanse towns refused to expose themselves to attack by Sweden, Denmark and the United Provinces. Meanwhile the Dutch reinforced the Danish garrisons at Elsinore and Helsingborg, and effectively closed the Sound.

Wallenstein nonetheless consolidated his own position. In January he was made duke of Mecklenburg; in April, admiral of the Ocean and the Baltic. His new titles attracted widespread criticism. Maximilian's appointment to Frederick's title with the support of four electoral votes had been generally disapproved, but the elevation of a mere duke of Friedland to the titles and territories of two Imperial princes was held to be an unwarranted, over-hasty and provocative exercise of Imperial authority. The Flemish envoy advised Isabella that, unless she and Philip IV secured Wallenstein's dismissal, 'they would only confirm the very general belief that His Majesty has a secret understanding with the emperor to set up a universal monarchy and to make the Empire hereditary'.

Heedless of public opinion, Wallenstein increased the size of his army and planned to attack Stralsund (see map 14), an important port lying close to the eastern frontier of Mecklenburg and controlling communications between the Pomeranian coast and the island of Rügen. Rostock and other towns had paid him contributions to avoid having troops billeted within their walls, but Stralsund refused. Its wealthier citizens thought it cheaper in the long run to pay up, but the majority refused to give way, encouraged by the belief that Gustav Adolf would come to their aid. Wallenstein saw the danger. 'It must be stopped at once', he ordered Arnim, his commander in the field, 'and you must conclude with them by force so that they may not avail themselves of the assistance of the enemy.'

The enemy, however, was already at work. 'All the wars which are going on in Europe', wrote Gustav Adolf, 'are linked together and are directed to one end', which as he interpreted it was the defeat of the Reformation and the triumph of the Habsburgs. In 1621 he had written with rare prescience to the duke of Mecklenburg, when the latter had appeared to be indifferent to the elector Palatine's fate, 'Hodie illi, cras tibi' – 'Today him, tomorrow you'; and with Mecklenburg gone he anticipated the threat to Stralsund by sending in five tons of gunpowder. He then wrote to Christian of Denmark, one of his most persistent enemies, to invite him to join in an alliance to save Stralsund: 'I now see with little difficulty that the projects of the House of Habsburg are directed against the Baltic; and that by a mixture of force and favour the United Provinces, my own power and finally yours are to be driven from it.'

Christian agreed. After his defeats on the mainland he had no other course to adopt, and, since Stralsund stood on a triangular promontory connected by a causeway with the mainland, virtually surrounded by sea, the assistance of the Swedish and Danish fleets could be critical to its survival. As the enemies of the Habsburgs commented gleefully, 'the Eagle cannot swim'; Wallenstein needed at least a year to construct his own fleet, the Hanse refused to be committed at this stage, and Sigismund declined to transfer his squadron to Wismar until the Spanish fleet had entered the Baltic. Arnim nonetheless pressed on the attack, and when Wallenstein appeared at the gates the council capitulated. The citizens, however, took the law into their own hands, their fighting spirit aroused by the heady combination of physical danger, religious conviction and the assurance that support was on its way. As a result the siege had to be renewed.

While the fate of their Baltic policy hung on the siege of Straslund, Habsburg fortunes were vested in another siege, conducted many miles from the Baltic. Ever since 1612, Charles Emmanuel had nursed his ambition to acquire Montferrat, which controlled the route from Genoa to Milan and which belonged to the duke of Mantua (see map 8). When the duke died, in 1627, he left his territories to the duke of Nevers, whose son had married his niece. Charles Emmanuel, hoping to profit from a conflict, advised Olivares that there was an alternative candidate, the duke of Guastalla, who might be more amenable than the French prince to Spanish control, and offered to take the field in alliance with Spain. Since Mantua was an Imperial fief, Ferdinand ordered its sequestration pending a decision, but it was known that his second wife, who came from the ducal family of Mantua, favoured the French candidate. Not wishing to antagonise the emperor, nor Louis XIII, Olivares advised caution to Philip IV, and, since Charles Emmanuel had proved so unreliable in the past, wrote that 'though my greatest wish in the world is to see Your Majesty the master of Montferrat, I cannot find any way to justify you in dividing it with Savoy'.

Olivares's prudence was not reflected in the action of Córdoba, now promoted commander in Milan. Unaware of all the diplomatic ramifications of the Mantuan succession, but convinced this was a golden opportunity to safeguard by a swift *coup de main* the route from Milan to Genoa, Córdoba on his own initiative marched off to besiege Casale, the most powerful fortress in Montferrat.

For seven years the governments of Spain and Austria had increased in strength. Bohemia and Austria had been brutally but effectively brought to order, the Catholic cause in northern Germany triumphed at the heels of Wallenstein's army, and the Palatinate was occupied by the troops of Spain and the league. So far-reaching was the range of Habsburg policy across the whole of Europe, so all-embracing its scope, so successful its achievement, that the allies of the Habsburgs were becoming as alarmed as their enemies.

The United Provinces, on the other hand, had achieved little. Frederick Henry's capture of Groll was small compensation for Spinola's victory at Breda, the merchants were threatened with the loss of their Baltic trade, and the coalition of Protestant powers had as yet proved to be singularly ineffective.

If the Habsburgs' plans for the Baltic and for the security of their lines of communication were to depend in the summer of 1628 upon the outcome of the sieges of Stralsund and Casale, few could have doubted that they would be successful.

4

The Seven Lean Years of the Habsburgs 1628–35

July 1628 to December 1629

One important factor in explaining the almost uninterrupted course of Habsburg success up to 1628 was the absence of effective opposition from France. Though Richelieu's intervention in the Valtelline had been troublesome, the Treaty of Monzon had left Spain free to use the pass. Since then the persistence of Huguenot rebellion had ensured French neutrality in the activities of the Habsburgs. It was therefore ominous that in October 1628, after a long and arduous siege which had absorbed the personal attention of both Louis XIII and Richelieu, the Huguenots of La Rochelle surrendered to the king.

The victory put new life into the French government and Richelieu triumphantly introduced his memorandum on the international situation with the words 'Now that La Rochelle has fallen'. His proposal was simple. 'Outside our realm it must be our constant purpose to arrest the course of Spain's progress', though he recognised that France could not yet risk open war. Instead he laid down limited objectives for the immediate future. 'France should seek only to fortify herself, and to build and open gateways for the purpose of entering into the states of her neighbours so as to be able to protect them from Spanish oppression whenever the opportunities for this may present themselves.'

The most immediate opportunity for intervention existed in Montferrat, where Córdoba was hoping for a quick victory at Casale. Brushing aside the resistance of Charles Emmanuel of Savoy, Richelieu forced the pass of Susa in December 1628 and received the surrender of Turin. From there he sent reinforcements down the Po to Casale, which put new heart into the garrison. The intended coup was thus thwarted and a major campaign set in train.

At Stralsund too the Habsburgs had been denied victory. Wallenstein had blustered that 'the town shall yield though it were bound by chains to heaven', but while Danish and Swedish ships patrolled the coast and supplied the city there was nothing he could do, especially as he did not want to take the place by storm and damage it. The siege was abandoned in August, but Christian unwisely failed to leave well alone. Landing south-east of Stralsund, he seized Woolgast (see map 14), but when he tried to march on Mecklenburg he was intercepted on 2 September and defeated. Thereupon he fled to the coast, took ship for Denmark and sued for peace.

Spinola meanwhile left Brussels for Madrid in the autumn of 1628 to persuade Philip IV that unless Spain could afford to finance a series of major offensives it would be better to abandon the war altogether. In particular he explained that a full-scale attack in the Netherlands could mean nothing but a series of major sieges, occupying many years and costing millions of ducats. Olivares was scornful. The Romans, he claimed, had conquered the world with 100,000 men, while Spinola was unable to contain the Dutch with 90,000, and, when Philip IV refused to set aside more money for the Army of Flanders, Spinola refused to return to Brussels.

There was yet more bad news for Spain in 1628, when a third of the ships engaged in the West Indian trade were destroyed off Cuba in the battle of Matanzas Bay by a Dutch fleet led by Piet Heyn. Heyn was a national hero in the United Provinces for his privateering exploits, and his success on this occasion secured booty valued in Holland at 11 million florins. The directors of the West India Company celebrated by declaring a dividend of 50 per cent and the government was stimulated to launch a new offensive against the southern provinces in the spring of 1629.

The target was s'Hertogenbosch (Bois-le-duc; see map 13), one of the most important cities of Brabant, lying between two rivers and surrounded by swamp. Just as Spinola had done at Breda, Frederick Henry employed thousands of men to construct dykes and trenches; in addition he supplied them all by boat from his secure base on the Maas at Crèvecoeur. In Spinola's absence the Army of Flanders was commanded by Henry van der Bergh, the nephew of William of Orange and first cousin to Frederick Henry. After observing the skilful development of the siege, he decided to distract the Dutch from their quarry by attacking in a totally different quarter. Wallenstein released 20,000 men to join him, and in July he crossed the riverline at Arnheim, took Amersfoort and overran the Veluwe. Despite the very real danger, the States-General held to its plan, and while Frederick Henry continued the siege a second army was raised to attack Wesel, the indispensable link in the chain connecting the invading army with its base. In a brilliantly executed manoeuvre, Wesel was taken by surprise in August 1629, van der Bergh evacuated Dutch territory, and the fall of s'Hertogenbosch followed in September.

In Flanders and Brabant there was serious unrest. The failure to save s'Hertogenbosch, coupled with the ever-increasing burden of taxation, was blamed on Cueva; great nobles such as van der Bergh were as discontented with Spanish rule as their grandfathers had been seventy years earlier. 'Never have these provinces been more bitter in their enmity towards Spain', reported one Spanish observer. 'If the prince of Orange and the rebels were not kept by their fanatical intolerance from granting liberty of worship and from guaranteeing their possession of churches and church property to the clergy, then a union of the Obedient Provinces with those of the north could not be prevented.' Frederick Henry in fact wanted to allow liberty of worship in s'Hertogenbosch in order to reassure the southern provinces, but the successors of Gomarus demonstrated their power in the States-General to ensure that no concessions were made to Roman Catholics. Faced with such intransigence by the Calvinists, the Obedient Provinces had no option but to remain in their obedient condition, and the dismissal of Cueva temporarily restored a measure of support for Isabella's government.

In Italy the siege of Casale dragged on. The Spanish government vented its anger on Córdoba by bringing him to court martial for his unauthorised action; then, concluding that it was too late to back down without loss of honour, it allowed Spinola to take command of the siege. Ferdinand, too, decided to intervene. Anxious to repay something of his debt to Spain, he had also been provoked by the duke of Nevers, the French claimant to Mantua, who seized the duchy for himself and challenged the emperor's authority to determine the succession. Wallenstein urged him not to imperil the achievement of his ambitions north of the Alps, adding perceptively, 'let there be peace in Italy and there will be peace with France', but Ferdinand was determined to enforce his imperial perogative. The troops serving with van der Bergh in Flanders were recalled and sent south through the Valtelline to besiege Mantua in September 1629.

Pope Urban VIII was so enraged by this massive demonstration of Habsburg power in northern Italy that the *dévots* could no longer oppose Richelieu's plan to intervene on behalf of Nevers. Nor could the

Huguenots. Since the fall of La Rochelle they had made a desperate stand under the duke of Rohan in Languedoc, even appealing to Philip IV for assistance, but the royal army in a resolute show of strength had swept down the Rhône valley, seizing one Huguenot stronghold after another. Rohan could not halt its advance, and the surrender of his last fortress, Montauban, in 1629 compelled him to sign one of the more momentous of the many treaties ending civil war in France. The Grace of Alais, as it was termed, allowed the Huguenots complete freedom of worship wherever their churches were already established and protected them from discrimination in their careers. Their political and military privileges, however, were destroyed by the abolition of their separate law courts, assemblies and fortresses, and in this manner Richelieu ensured that the Huguenots should not again challenge the authority of the state. By the end of the autumn, therefore, Richelieu was in a stronger position than ever before to influence affairs in northern Italy.

Christian of Denmark, on the other hand, was more than ready to make peace. A meeting with Gustav Adolf in February had failed to rouse him to further action, and, since, for the immediate future, Denmark was unbeatable at sea, Wallenstein advised the emperor to offer generous terms. By the Peace of Lübeck, therefore, in June 1629 Christian renounced his family's claims to bishoprics in Westphalia and Lower Saxony and recognised the emperor's sovereignty in Holstein; in return he retained the throne of Denmark.

To strengthen his position against the Swedish invasion he feared, Wallenstein reinforced Sigismund of Poland, who was at war with Gustav, and recruited as extensively as he could throughout northern Germany. So great was his army, and so jealous was he of detaching any section of it for the Mantuan or the Dutch wars, that the emperor began to suspect his intentions. Moreover, the court was beset with the complaints of those who were compelled to sustain this vast army by their contributions. Maximilian objected that the army of the League had passed entirely into Wallenstein's hands, the elector of Brandenburg feared for his independence, and the emperor's brother echoed the thoughts of all when he wrote, 'we shall repent in the end of the excessive power given to Friedland'.

The Dutch of course seized the occasion to cultivate Gustav's friendship and hoped that he might prove to be a more dependable ally than Christian. The two countries were already bound by strong economic ties. Älvsborg, by virtue of its position north of the Sound, supplied timber and hemp to the Dutch dockyards without paying dues to the Danes, and was almost a Dutch colony; Sweden's metallurgical industries depended upon Dutch engineers and Dutch capital; Dutch agents advised Gustav Adolf how to organise and collect export dues in the ports he had captured along the Polish and Lithuanian coast, and Amsterdam was the market for most of Sweden's exports. Gustav's war with Sigismund displeased the Dutch, since it disrupted their vital trade in Polish corn, and they decided to help Sweden gain the victory as soon as possible so that the war might be brought to an end. Then, they hoped, Gustav might invade northern Germany.

The French, too, intervened on Sweden's behalf. Ferdinand's action in northern Italy had, as Wallenstein had forseen, prompted Richelieu to give encouragement to the emperor's enemies throughout Europe. Since Richelieu could scarcely deny Sigismund's right as a Roman Catholic to the throne of Sweden, his agents tried to make out that Poland was being used as an imperial catspaw. It was not too difficult an assignment. Sigismund was disgruntled that the policies of Olivares had failed to establish Poland as a naval power in the Baltic, and, when the Prussian ports of Memel, Pillau and Elbing fell to Gustav, he welcomed French proposals for a truce. At Altmark in September 1629 Sweden was granted for a period of six years Livonia and the right to collect the customs duties in the Prussian ports.

The tide had turned against the Habsburgs at Stralsund and Casale, in the Caribbean as in Brabant, and the king of Sweden, with Dutch and French support, was now free to invade the Holy Roman Empire. Nonetheless, in the midst of these disasters the emperor had achieved one spectacular success.

Roman Catholics had always complained that, despite the terms of the Peace of Augsburg, Calvinism had been afforded tacit recognition and that nothing had been done to stop the Protestants' extending their control over ecclesiastical territory. When Ferdinand proposed to outlaw Calvinism and restore to the Roman Church the lands which had been secularised since 1555, Maximilian and John George demanded that the matter be laid before the Diet, but Ferdinand, knowing only too well what would happen if that were done, decided to act on his own authority. In March 1629, by the Edict of Restitution, Calvinism was proscribed; two archdioceses, twelve dioceses and over fifty large convents and abbeys were restored to the Catholic Church; several free cities, such as Augsburg and Dortmund, were once again required to accept the authority of a bishop; and, because of the principle *cuius regio, eius religio*, wherever the Catholic Church was reinstated as the territorial authority Lutherans had to conform or emigrate.

The transfer of land and jurisdiction on so vast a scale was a triumph not only for the Counter-Reformation but also for the emperor, since it was he who issued the edict, without reference to any other authority; declared that its interpretation was a matter reserved exclusively for his own judgement; and empowered his commissioners to enforce their decisions with the aid of the imperial army. Though Wallenstein was an unenthusiastic champion of the Counter-Reformation, he was ready to demonstrate the power of the ruler from whom his own authority was derived. Throughout Swabia and Franconia his troops carried out the edict, and he was pleased to note that Ferdinand reserved for his own family not only Halberstadt and Bremen but also Magdeburg, which enjoyed a position of strategic importance on the Elbe between Brandenburg and Anhalt. Anxious to win over the Hanse against Sweden, Wallenstein tried to reassure them that the edict would not be applied to them, but elsewhere he was happy to reaffirm that 'he would teach the electors manners: they must be dependent on the emperor, not the emperor on them'.

January 1630 to December 1630

When Spinola died outside Casale in the spring of 1630 the Spanish army withdrew to Milan, while the French, who had invaded Savoy during the winter, seized control of Pinerolo (see map 8). On the other hand, the Imperial troops succeeded in taking Mantua from the duke of Nevers. The issue remained unresolved. Were the siege of Casale to be renewed, French reinforcements would have further to march than the Spanish troops from Milan, and the fact that Louis XIII had fallen ill with dysentery restricted Richelieu's freedom of action. He therefore persuaded the Habsburgs to accept a truce in northern Italy pending the outcome of an electoral diet in session at Regensburg.

Because of their opposition to the Edict of Restitution, the electors of Saxony and Brandenburg had refused to attend in person, and the emperor hoped that his Roman Catholic colleagues would allow him to pledge German support for Spain in the Netherlands and elect his son Ferdinand as king of the Romans, thereby guaranteeing his succession to the imperial throne. Richelieu therefore sent Father Joseph along with several of his best agents to Regensburg to undermine the emperor's position by rallying the Roman Catholics to the defence of 'German liberties'. Marcheville told the elector of Trier that it was Louis XIII's wish 'to deliver Italy and Germany from the oppression to which they had been reduced by the manifest violence and ambition of the house of Austria', and Brûlart reported so good a response to Richelieu's diplomacy that the electors, he claimed, could all be accounted good Frenchmen.

But French influence at Regensburg was a legend created by the French. Since the meeting at Mülhausen the Catholic electors had been resolved upon their policy. While Wallenstein marched and counter-marched across northern Germany, they needed no prompting in the matter of 'German liberties', and the Edict of Restitution, welcome though it was in many respects, was too obvious a demonstration of that Imperial authority which generations of German princes had tried to diminish. There was therefore no election of a king of the Romans and no support for Spain in the Netherlands. Furthermore, the electors insisted that the Imperial army be reduced in size and Wallenstein dismissed. The emperor had no option but to agree, and in August he ordered Wallenstein to resign his command to Tilly. Unlike de Witte, his financier, who took his life at the news, Wallenstein accepted the decision without public protest: with Friedland and Mecklenburg under his control, he could afford to wait upon events. The emperor too appeared unmoved. The removal of his over-powerful servant was not altogether unwelcome, and it permitted him to re-establish closer links with the Roman Catholic electors, thereby preserving the Edict of Restitution and forestalling French hopes of creating an independent Roman Catholic bloc hostile to the emperor.

Ferdinand in fact went one stage further, by adroitly turning the tables on Richelieu. Though Nevers had fled after the assault on Mantua, the emperor offered to confirm his succession to the duchy provided that Spain was guaranteed possession of Casale and Pinerolo and that Louis XIII withheld assistance from the emperor's enemies within the Holy Roman Empire. From the Habsburg point of view, this would have safeguarded Spain's major interests in northern Italy and bound France to assist neither the Dutch nor the Swedes. Father Joseph, the French negotiator, was put in a quandary. The *dévots* and many other Frenchmen would be outraged if Nevers were abandoned in order to leave France free to fight alongside Dutch and Swedish heretics, yet to accept the offer involved Louis in repudiating an alliance only recently (in June) concluded with the United Provinces.

The matter was referred to Louis, but the king was still seriously ill; and, when instruction failed to arrive, Father Joseph signed the Treaty of Regensburg on the emperor's terms. To what extent the treaty would be honoured would depend upon the outcome of a power struggle at the French court and of the Swedish invasion of northern Germany.

Because, in the summer of 1630, the Swedish invasion was expected daily, the emperor was advised to abandon not only Wallenstein but also the Edict of Restitution, so that the electors of Brandenburg and Saxony might be persuaded to ally with him in defending northern Germany. Ferdinand refused. The dynastic and religious advantages to be derived from the edict were in his eyes too important to be compromised, and at this stage he was not yet aware of the true strength of Sweden. Gustav's victories in the Baltic Provinces were discounted for having been won only against Poles; nor did his country seem to pose as great a threat as the more highly organised, more heavily populated kingdom of Denmark, which had been so easily defeated by Tilly and Wallenstein.

Gustav II Adolf, however, could dispose of resources far more valuable than those available to Christian. Sweden had become the principal European supplier of copper, producing 3000 tons a year, and could thus procure on the Amsterdam Exchange a constant supply of foreign currency to pay her armies wherever they served in Europe. In addition, whereas 5000 tons of iron had been produced in 1620, 20,000 tons a year were produced after 1630, and with Dutch help a flourishing armaments industry had been established. More valuable still were the customs duties to be collected in the Baltic Provinces, and, since the Truce of Altmark, the lucrative revenues of the Prussian ports.

Gustav, moreover, had shown himself to be an exceptionally gifted soldier. His greatest achievement was to revive the role of the infantry, who had become accustomed to scrumming together in massive formations, whether in defence or attack. By regrouping them in smaller units he enabled them to change front and to move their ground with remarkable speed and efficiency. Since smaller units were more exposed to attack, he positioned groups of cavalry among them and trained the musketeers to fire and reload three times as fast as those of other armies. Gustav also pioneered the use of light artillery, easily portable and relatively quick firing. His famous 'leathern gun', a three-pounder with a very thin bronze barrel, bound with rope and mastic enclosed in a sheath of hard leather, was developed before 1627, but its successor in 1629, an all-metal four-pounder, proved rather more effective. Three men were enough to transport and operate one on the battlefield and it was the possession of forty-two of these at Breitenfeld (see p. 131), against Tilly's ponderous twenty-four pounders, which helped to give the Swedes their victory.

Early in July 1630 the matter was put to the test when Gustav landed on the island of Usedom (see map 15). Subsequently he occupied Stettin, sent troops into Magdeburg to reclaim it for its Protestant administrator, and settled his troops in winter quarters across Pomerania and the Mark of Brandenburg.

Gustav's motives have been variously interpreted as defensive, offensive, imperialist or Protestant. Certainly he recognised the dangers to Sweden posed by the siege of Stralsund. 'The papists are on the Baltic. They have Rostock, Wismar, Stettin, Woolgast, Griefswald and nearly all the other ports in their hands. Rügen is theirs, and from Rügen they continue to threaten Stralsund; their whole aim is to destroy Swedish commerce and soon to plant a foot on the southern shore of our fatherland.' Oxenstierna agreed; many years later, when it would have been only too easy to disassociate himself from it all, he affirmed, 'it is certain that, had his late Majesty not betaken himself to Germany with his army, the emperor would today have a fleet upon these seas. And if the emperor had once got hold of Stralsund the whole coast would have fallen to him, and here in Sweden we should never have enjoyed a minute's security.'

Nonetheless, when Gustav told the *rad* that he proposed to occupy Pomerania, 'to guarantee Sweden's position for a few years to come', he had more than defence in mind. Pomerania was not only, after Livonia and Polish Prussia, the next target to offer itself as he conducted his successful campaign along the Baltic littoral, but also a base from which he could threaten both Denmark and Poland. At the same time Gustav believed his own propaganda, which cast him in the role of Protestant champion against the fell hand of the Habsburgs, so that for him the cause of Sweden and that of the Reformation were inseparable. His purposes were summarised, therefore, in two key words: *assecuratio*, the need for a secure base in northern Germany, and *satisfactio*, the indemnity he required from the north German Protestants to recompense him for saving them from the Edict of Restitution and the Counter-Reformation.

Strategist, imperialist, crusader, Gustav was essentially none of these. Like many of the participants who prolonged the European war, he was at heart a military adventurer, fighting for the sake of fighting and ready to chase the horizon on whatever pretext would best serve.

If the Swedish invasion of Pomerania was to prove calamitous for the Habsburgs, so too would be the outcome in November 1630 of a crisis at the French court. Since his appointment in 1624, Richelieu had been constantly threatened by the intrigues of the queen mother, of Anne, the king's wife, and of Gaston his brother. Louis respected Richelieu's ability, his loyalty and his indefatigable service, but he was a weak, indecisive man. His lonely and neglected childhood had made him particularly dependent upon the affection and support of others and left him vulnerable to the violent clash of temperaments generated at court and within his family. During the summer and autumn of 1630 the king's prolonged sickness kept him apart from his minister and exposed him to a determined attempt by Marie de Medici to reassert her maternal authority.

The struggle for power took the form of a conflict of principles over the direction of French foreign policy. While Marie advocated peace and the need to reduce the concessions granted to Huguenots by the Grace of Alais, Richelieu sought to establish France's international reputation as the acknowledged enemy of Spain. Were Louis to accept, for example, the Treaty of Regensburg, Richelieu argued, 'all foreign nations would regard an alliance with us as useless because of our unreliability, and would think that they could no longer find security except with Spain'. The issue was to be decided, the struggle for power resolved, by Louis's choice of a new commander for the army in northern Italy.

On 10 November 1630, after a violent and emotional scene such as the king had always dreaded, in which Richelieu and Marie confronted each other in his presence, it seemed that the cardinal was defeated. Louis appointed Marillac, Marie's nominee, to command the army in Italy and retired to his hunting lodge at Versailles, leaving the queen mother and her delighted followers to celebrate their triumph. But they deceived themselves. Louis had fled only to escape his mother's hysteria and, safe at Versailles, he ordered Marillac's arrest.

The Day of Dupes, as it was called, not only emancipated the king from the emotional tyranny of his mother but also confirmed once and for all his resolution to employ Richelieu as his minister and to endorse his policies. The humiliation was too great to be endured by the royal conspirators, and within a few months Gaston had fled to Lorraine and Marie to the Spanish court in Brussels. Marillac was executed, his more powerful brother, the chancellor, imprisoned, and French foreign policy was henceforth set firmly on a collision course with the Habsburgs. The Dutch had been provided with an ally more powerful than themselves.

It was ironic, if not indeed significant of the changing pattern of events, that amid all the activity generated by France and Sweden 1630 should have been a relatively peaceful year in the Netherlands. The administration in Brussels was unable to launch an offensive without more subsidies from Spain, and the Dutch had temporarily over-strained their resources at the siege of s'Hertogenbosch. Off the coast the initiative lay with the Dunkirk raiders. Though there were seldom more than thirty in operation at any one time in the years between 1626 and 1634, they captured 1499 craft and sank 336 for the loss of 120 of their own. Had such privateers been able to operate in the Baltic from the protection of the Hanseatic ports, as Olivares had planned, the damage done to Dutch trade would have been considerable.

Several Dutchmen, therefore, began to think it time to settle for peace, but not the Calvinist exiles from the south who now controlled the West India Company. In their determination to wage their crusade on the widest possible front, they used what was left of the company's profits to launch a remarkable invasion force across the Atlantic. Its objective was Pernambuco, and in 1630 8000 men transported in sixty-five ships were landed successfully in the centre of the richest sugar-producing region of South America.

January 1631 to February 1632

Spain's control of the Rhenish Palatinate made it possible, for the first time since 1543, to ship reinforcements down the Rhine to Flanders, and a new offensive was launched in the late summer of 1631. Instead of committing troops to the time-consuming and expensive business of siege warfare along the water line, the government sent 6000 men in a flotilla of thirty-five ships with several small craft to outflank the Dutch by attacking the islands of Zeeland. The first attempt at a landing was, however, foiled, and when a Dutch fleet caught up with the invaders in the Slaak near Tholen island (see map 13) it sank the ships and took most of the troops prisoner.

The failure of the Zeeland raid was a disaster by any standards, but so rapidly was the pattern of European conflict being altered by 1631 that events in the Netherlands were becoming less important for the rest of Europe. The irruption of France and Sweden into the conflict meant that issues were no longer polarised so directly as in the past between Madrid and The Hague, and in January 1631, as if to underline this trend, Sweden and France agreed at Barwalde to act together against the Habsburgs. Richelieu agreed to provide 200,000 reichstalers every May and November for a period of five years, and to acknowledge publicly that France was in alliance with Sweden. For his part Gustav had simply to refuse all offers of a separate peace before the treaty expired and to guarantee freedom of worship in Roman Catholic areas. Subsequently and separately he agreed to respect the neutrality of Bavaria and of the Catholic League.

'The king of Sweden', wrote Richelieu, 'is a sun which has just risen: he is young but of vast renown. The ill-treated or banished princes of Germany have turned towards him in their misfortune as the mariner turns to the Pole Star.'

John George of Saxony had other views. He commissioned Arnim, formerly in Wallenstein's service, to recruit whatever troops were available in northern Germany in order to deny their use to Sweden. He then summoned a convention of Protestant princes at Leipzig, where it was agreed to ally with the emperor provided that he revoke the Edict of Restitution. It was an offer of historic importance and it went ignored. Where Richelieu overestimated Gustav's attraction for the Protestant princes, Ferdinand underrated his military strength (see p. 125) and saw no need to purchase help by compromising over the matter of church property.

Maximilian, too, misread the situation. Anxious above all to safeguard his electoral title and his acquisition of the Palatinate, he was persuaded by Richelieu that the Habsburgs were not to be trusted in this matter while Spanish troops still occupied the Rhineland, and that Louis XIII alone could guarantee his position in the future. In May 1631 therefore, by the Treaty of Fontainebleau, France promised to defend the elector's new title and territories if he agreed not to assist the enemies of Louis and Gustav. It apparently went unnoticed that Gustav had already declared his intent of restoring the son of the former elector Palatine.

While Maximilian deceived himself into believing there was no threat from Sweden, Tilly, his commander tried desperately to hold the Catholic army together to meet this very threat. He was in great difficulties: 'no cannon in a condition to be used, no ammunition, no picks and shovels, no money and no food'; and without payment in advance Wallenstein refused to provision him from his warehouses in

Friedland and Mecklenburg. In April, therefore, he marched on Magdeburg in the belief that the city was well stocked with supplies. Gustav, meanwhile, surprised George William of Brandenburg by marching directly on him at Spandau, and terrified him into signing a treaty of alliance which was to cost the elector 30,000 reichstalers a month. Magdeburg fell in May, but, in what proved to be one of the worst episodes of the German war, the assailants got out of hand, the city was sacked and the supplies which Tilly needed so desperately were destroyed along with the city.

The events in northern Germany had an important consequence in northern Italy, where French troops were once again on the move to reinforce Casale. Ferdinand unexpectedly lost his nerve and, in order to meet the threat from Sweden, which so far he had tended to underestimate, decided to withdraw his army from Italy. He made a separate peace with Richelieu at Cherasco in June, by which Nevers was granted not only Mantua but also the fortresses of Montferrat and Casale. Subsequently, in a secret deal with Victor Amadeus, the successor to Charles Emmanuel, Richelieu purchased Pinerolo from Savoy.

Meanwhile the sack of Magdeburg had left Tilly with serious problems on his hands. His army was desperate for supplies, but Maximilian allowed him no freedom of action. Because of the entente between Bavaria and France, Tilly was forbidden to challenge Gustav Adolf in the field, and Saxony was closed to him lest any offensive move should drive John George into the Swedish camp. In the event Tilly had either to disobey orders or witness the desertion of his men. He invaded Saxony on 3 September, occupied Leipzig in good order on the 15th and in consequence was able to provision his army for the first time in months. John George immediately threw in his lot with Gustav, allowing him access to Saxony and the disposal of Arnim's troops, 'while the emergency continues' – a cautious proviso which warned Gustav that he had secured a reluctant ally.

With the Saxon army and his own, Gustav moved south, deliberately seeking a battle in order to enhance his reputation and to commit John George more firmly to his cause. Tilly, however, sat tight in Leipzig. His troops were loth to abandon the comforts they had so recently acquired within the city, and, since they were outnumbered, it was sensible to avoid an engagement in the open. Good sense, however, was not the principal attribute of Pappenheim, the second-in-command, who transformed a simple reconnaissance operation four miles north of

Leipzig into an assault on Gustav's camp and then expected the rest of the army to advance to his aid. 'This fellow', complained Tilly, 'will rob me of my honour and reputation, and the emperor of his lands and people', yet he felt in honour bound to join him. As a result the two armies met on 18 September near the village of Breitenfeld.

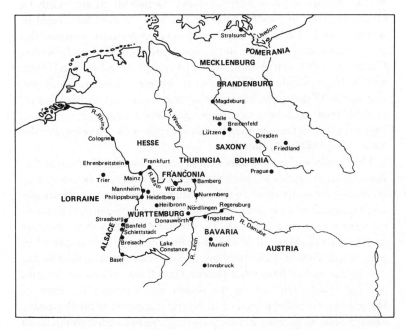

15. The campaigns in central Europe 1629–34

In the first encounter Tilly broke the Saxon line. Arnim tried to regroup but John George fled, taking with him two regiments of Saxons, who preserved sufficient composure to raid the Swedish baggage train before resuming their headlong flight. The day was saved for Sweden by the professional skills developed by Gustav Adolf. His small groups of infantry survived repeated attacks by the Imperial cavalry, the mobility and fire-power of the leather guns played havoc among Tilly's massed squares of infantry, and the cavalry, when Pappenheim's had turned their flank, displayed a remarkable degree of discipline simply by facing about and trapping him between themselves and their reserves. To add to his difficulties Tilly was wounded, and the wind, rising in an unexpected quarter, blew up a dust storm in the eyes of his men. 7000 Imperialists were killed, and a similar number of survivors was recruited that evening into the Swedish army: the remainder followed Pappenheim into Leipzig and then deserted.

Unaware that he was the cause of the disaster, Pappenheim complained bitterly that he had been let down, and went off to hold the Weser in case Gustav were to move westwards across northern Germany. Tilly meanwhile recovered sufficiently from his wound to withdraw to the Danube at Ingolstadt, where he prepared to defend the northern borders of Bavaria. But no one guarded the route to Bohemia. Gustav therefore sent Arnim, in company with Matthias von Thurn and a large number of émigrés, to liberate Bohemia from the Habsburgs. Wallenstein, having no authority to act on anyone's behalf save his own, withdrew circumspectly, leaving Arnim free to enter Prague in November, restoring the exiles to power eleven years after the Battle of the White Mountain.

The Habsburgs' powers were in disarray. Defeated in Zeeland and at Breitenfeld, outmanoeuvred in northern Italy and with Bohemia lost, there was yet much worse to come as Gustav advanced across Thuringia and Franconia to the hitherto unspoiled lands of the wealthy ecclesiastical territories of the Rhineland. The Roman Catholic princes meeting in Frankfurt-on-Main to debate the Edict of Restitution dispersed in panic when the bishop of Würzburg arrived as a fugitive in their midst, and by the end of November Gustav himself was master of the city. Though it was too late in the season to undertake the siege of Heidelberg, Mannheim fell and, as the crowning glory of the Protestant cause, a Spanish garrison in Mainz surrendered to Swedish troops on 20 December.

Gustav's occupation of the Rhineland was a disaster for Spain which the Dutch were quick to recognise by offering subsidies to Sweden. Richelieu was in two minds about the situation. Gustav was acting wholly independently of French interests – to have met these he would have had to have accompanied the Saxons into Bohemia – and French troops had to be rushed into Alsace to save it from the Swedes. This, on the other hand, was an advantage, since it established French power in an area hitherto dominated by Spain. The archbishop–electors of Trier and Cologne, moreover, turned in despair to Louis XIII rather than to Philip IV for protection, denied the Spaniards right of passage through their territories and offered France the use of the fortresses of Ehrenbreitstein and Philippsburg once they had been cleared of Swedish and Spanish troops.

Simultaneously, though not as a consequence of Gustav's action, Richelieu strengthened French power in the Rhineland by the successful invasion of Lorraine. Gaston of Orleans, Louis's brother, had fled there after the significance of the Day of Dupes had become clear, and Duke Charles had given him not only too warm a welcome but also his sister in marriage. On 31 December the French captured the fortress of Vic, and the presence of the Swedish army in the Rhineland made it impossible for a Spanish force to go to the duke's assistance. In January 1632 Gaston fled to Brussels and the French were empowered by the Treaty of Vic to garrison the duchy's Rhineland frontier and to have free access to Alsace.

Gustav sat out the winter in Frankfurt taking stock of his position. He had 80,000 troops garrisoned in Mecklenburg, Hesse, Magdeburg, Franconia, across the Lower Saxon Circle and in the Rhineland. The cost of maintaining them was met by the contributions he levied wherever they were garrisoned, and he planned to recruit 120,000 more. For all the many attractive qualities which won him the loyalty of Oxenstierna and his subjects, and the shrewdness with which he interpreted the actions of others, Gustav fought for fighting's sake. Objectives were little more than excuses. 'He had begun the work with God, and with God he would finish it' was his recorded intention to safeguard Protestantism, and he spoke equally vaguely of the need to reconstruct the Holy Roman Empire. Certainly his ambitions had grown apace, and the *assecuratio*, the safe base he had sought for Sweden in northern Germany, was forgotten as he talked of forming a *corpus evangelicorum* within the Empire, or even of becoming emperor himself. If the Elbe were no safe boundary for Sweden, could he then contain himself within the Danube and the Rhine?

Gustav's success made him arrogant with allies. None of Richelieu's envoys to Frankfurt could secure guarantees for any members of the Catholic League, save Trier, and the future of Bavaria looked to be uncertain. Bernard of Saxe-Weimar, a soldier of fortune in Gustav's employ, was rewarded with the bishoprics of Bamberg and Würzburg, to be the nucleus of a Franconian duchy, but established princes such as Gustav's brother-in-law, George William of Brandenburg, were treated with contempt. Frederick, the former elector Palatine, for whose sake Gustav was ostensibly engaged in the war, arrived at Frankfurt in February 1632 to be welcomed warmly as king of Bohemia, but so clearly was it demonstrated that Gustav proposed to treat him as a mere vassal that Frederick declined to accept his help. John George of

Saxony was repeatedly denounced as a traitor, and his son-in-law, George of Hesse-Darmstadt, was accused frequently and variously as a Saxon agent and as an Imperial spy. His wife, in describing their plight as reluctant and subordinate allies of Sweden, spoke also for others in the same predicament: 'It is hard to hand over the best and most valuable places in our land to a foreign king on so new a friendship, . . . to bring down the emperor's heavy hand and displeasure upon us . . . and to make enemies of the neighbours with whom we have lived at peace for countless years.'

March 1632 to December 1632

All the strategic considerations which had dominated Spain's policies for decades were rendered irrelevant by the destruction of her lines of communication to the Netherlands. In this moment of crisis Isabella coldly observed the one crumb of comfort to be had. The Swedish occupation of the Rhineland, she commented, would drive Maximilian of Bavaria more closely into alliance with the emperor; and both, she might have added, into the hands of Wallenstein. Throughout the winter of 1631-2 Wallenstein had mobilised his forces in Friedland, but he was in no hurry to take the field before the emperor had agreed to his terms. So desperate was Ferdinand's plight that Wallenstein was finally given a free hand to raise his own troops and to negotiate as he chose with allies and enemies. At the end of April he advanced on Prague in such strength that Arnim, recognising that he was no longer a match for Wallenstein, evacuated the city and withdrew in good order from Bohemia into Saxony.

Gustav meanwhile had invaded Bavaria. Having solicited the recall of Wallenstein, Maximilian could no longer assert his neutrality and he made his stand with Tilly along the line of the Lech near Ingolstadt. It was a strong position, made stronger by the arrival from Bohemia of 5000 reinforcements sent by Wallenstein, but Gustav was dangerously impetuous. Under cover of a smoke-screen and an artillery barrage, his troops constructed a bridge of boats, forced the river and stormed the cliffs. Tilly was mortally wounded and Maximilian was left to make a difficult decision. With his surviving forces he could hold either Munich, his capital, or Regensburg, a city not his own but without which there could be no communication with Wallenstein in Bohemia. In the event he sent his men to Regensburg while he himself rescued from Munich his treasury and state papers. Gustav entered the city in

May, to be indemnified with 200,000 reichstalers, but this, though humiliating to Maximilian, did not advance the Swedish cause, since Gustav could not move down the Danube to Vienna while Wallenstein held Bohemia. In June, therefore, he withdrew to Nuremberg and published his terms for the Empire. The Protestant princes, grouped in four Imperial circles, were to form a *corpus evangelicorum*; Protestants were to be tolerated throughout the Empire; Sweden was to acquire northern Germany from the Vistula to the Elbe, and Brandenburg, by way of compensation, was to have Silesia.

The proposals did not have to be taken seriously. Maximilian's brave decision to defend Regensburg rather than his own capital allowed Wallenstein to join him with an army in July, and they took up their position on a long ridge overlooking the Swedish camp at Nuremberg. Reluctant to risk an attack, Gustav chose to sit things out, but, whereas Wallenstein, with Bohemia at his back, could supply his men for months on end, the Swedish army began to run short of provisions. In September Gustav moved against the ridge only to be driven back, and, for the first time since his landing at Stralsund, he tried to buy time by offering to negotiate. Wallenstein, sensing his advantage, refused. Gustav therefore broke camp intending to march on Upper Austria, where some of the Lutherans exiled in 1627 had returned to lead a new uprising. This would have made things very difficult for the emperor, but Wallenstein behaved coolly. Instead of following the Swedes at a disadvantage, he struck north-east for Saxony. Gustav correctly interpreted this as a threat to his northern base and, since he had no faith in John George's reliability, had no option but to retrace his own steps to Nuremberg and set out in pursuit of Wallenstein.

Wallenstein deliberately avoided an engagement, content to prolong the chase indefinitely, and it was not until 12 November that he was brought to battle, at Lützen. Having sent 12,000 of his men under Pappenheim to Halle, he was in fact taken by surprise, and he was fortunate that the Swedish attack was so long delayed by heavy mist that Pappenheim was able to return for the final stage of the battle. Nonetheless, Wallenstein had to withdraw to the south, leaving the field clear for the Swedes to reassert control in Saxony and renew communication with the Baltic ports. For Sweden, however, the victory at Lützen was won at too great a price, for it was there that Gustav Adolf was killed. He had always boasted that 'a general who keeps himself out of danger can gain neither victories nor laurels', ignoring the fact that a general with these ideas rarely stays a general for long.

So wide-ranging was the conflict in Europe, so complex the interaction of alliances, that the immediate effect of Gustav's death was to ease the pressure not on the Catholic rulers of Germany but on those of Poland. Wladislau IV, like his father Sigismund, was an ally of the Habsburgs. He had thus encountered the enmity not only of Sweden but also of France and the United Provinces, whose agents went as far afield as Constantinople and Moscow to urge the Turks and Russians to combine in the destruction of Poland. Though the Osmanli sultan declined the invitation, the patriarch Filaret had good cause to accept. Wladislau had formerly been a contender for the tsarist throne, but, apart from settling that old score, Filaret also hoped to recover Smolensk and the land east of Dneiper, which Poland had occupied during the civil wars in Russia (see pp. 54–5). When he attacked Smolensk in 1632, Sweden, despite the Truce of Altmark, sent Wrangel with an army from Prussia to assist him. Had Gustav survived Lützen, he would have followed Wrangel, with consequences difficult to imagine, but in the confusion caused by his death Swedish troops in Poland were withdrawn, and Wladislau was well able to cope with the Russians alone.

In Flanders, meanwhile, a serious crisis had arisen. Opposition to Spanish domination of the Brussels administration had been allayed only temporarily by the dismissal of Cueva (see p. 120), and, when in 1631 van der Bergh was replaced as commander-in-chief by the Spaniard Santa Cruz, he and several of the nobles decided to join the Dutch. In the spring of 1632 the count of Warfusée, president of the council of finance in Brussels, went to The Hague to offer their services: for themselves they wanted pensions and titles, for the Roman Catholic Church a guarantee of toleration and for the French-speaking provinces the opportunity, should they so wish, to be assimilated with France. The States-General welcomed their defection and a tactfully worded proclamation of May 1632 invited all the inhabitants of the Obedient Provinces to follow the praiseworthy example of their forefathers in liberating themselves from the heavy and intolerable yoke of the Spaniards and their adherents. It added that Frederick Henry would at once march south to help them and, for the first time in the Eighty Years War between Spain and the Dutch, gave solemn assurances that the southern provinces would be maintained 'in their privileges, rights and liberties, as well as in the public exercise of the Roman Catholic religion, desiring for ourselves to live, deal and converse with the same as good friends, neighbours and allies'.

The Dutch proclamation was effective propaganda among those who no longer believed in the power of Spain to protect them or their faith. In June, when Frederick Henry advanced into the region of the Maas, accompanied by van der Bergh, who had formerly been stadtholder there, there was little resistance and the towns of Venloo and Roermond (see map 13) surrendered without a shot. Maastricht, however, refused to open its gates, and, since it was protected on both sides by the Maas, Frederick Henry had to undertake a difficult siege. The operation required the total circumvallation of the town, with bridges constructed over the river above and below the city, but a massive undertaking of this kind was Frederick Henry's forte and he prosecuted it with patient vigour. Isabella recalled the troops sent to cover Gustav's movements in the Rhineland and Wallenstein released Pappenheim for a period in the summer, so that the besieging force was under attack by as many as 30,000 infantry and 10,000 cavalry. Frederick Henry's lines of supply, however, were safe by water, and he advanced his siege works without delay until the city, to avoid certain sack, surrendered in August.

After the fall of Maastricht, van der Bergh called in vain for a general rising. The townsmen were too cautious, and the nobles who had not already joined the Dutch awaited a lead from France. It was indeed a remarkable opportunity for Richelieu to extend the northern frontier of France and destroy Spanish power in Flanders, but he dared not take it. Abroad Gustav Adolf had jettisoned the French alliance and Wallenstein had been recalled to take action against him; at home Montmorency, with the support of the king's brothers, Gaston, and of Charles of Lorraine, was leading a rebellion in Languedoc over its privileges as a *pays d'état*. All Richelieu's efforts therefore were directed to defeat the rebels and to invade Lorraine, whose duke was compelled to accept a greater measure of French control.

Without direct intervention by Richelieu, only the baron of Noyelles tried, and failed, to raise the garrison at Boucham before fleeing to France. The rest of the nobles, restive though they were, accepted Isabella's reminder that the Habsburgs had more titles and appointments in their gift than the republican oligarchs of The Hague, 'where a loutish and ill-mannered burgomaster can often lay down the law'. Her final concession was to summon the States-General for the first time since 1600. Some members called for separate independence, but the majority approved a resolution that peace negotiations be opened with the Dutch. Isabella agreed. With Albert and Spinola dead, and her own life coming to its end, she was anxious to establish a settlement. So too

was Olivares. The failure of the Zeeland raid and the loss of Maastricht
had convinced him that the war could not be won. Moreover, the fleet
was lost in a storm and attempts to augment Castilian revenues by
raising money in Catalonia had failed.

Public opinion in the United Provinces was less hostile to the idea of
negotiations than in the past. During the year the Dunkirk raiders had
taken or sunk as many as 200 Dutch vessels for the loss of fifteen of their
own, and so great had become the cost of the war in Pernambuco that
many merchants were willing to welcome any settlement which put
paid to the now unprofitable West India Company. But the company
was still powerfully influential, and the Calvinist ministers, strangely
silent when the States-General had issued its proclamation to the
southern provinces in May, once again preached the necessity of
liberating Flanders not only from Madrid but also from Rome.
Negotiations foundered therefore over Roman Catholic rights and
a demand that Philip IV assist the Dutch in Pernambuco, regardless
of the fact that this would provoke rebellion against him in Portugal.

In the event, as Frederick Henry withdrew for the winter, Olivares
began to change his mind about the war. The young cardinal–infante
Ferdinand, an able prince who chafed under the clerical role imposed
upon him, persuaded him that he, Ferdinand, was the very man to
succeed Isabella and put new life into the defence of Flanders. Again the
Spanish government was deluded by the attraction of yet one more
effort against the Dutch, and, with the news of Gustav Adolf's death
and the consequent possibility of reopening the Rhineland route, began
to make plans for sending Ferdinand to the Netherlands. With this in
prospect, and aware that Wallenstein was competent to maintain the
security of the Empire, Olivares could be excused for hoping that the
tide might again be turning in Spain's favour.

January 1633 to May 1635

Determined though the Spanish government was to send the cardinal–
infante to Brussels, it was unable to do so while Isabella lived, and still
less while she and her States-General sought to reach a settlement with
the north. Frederick Henry was under no such restraint and in 1633
took Rheinberg, the last of the Spanish strongholds on the lower Rhine.
This opened the way for the invasion of Brabant, but Frederick Henry
knew his limitations. His speciality was siege warfare, in which he

excelled, and he chose not to hazard his reputation by campaigning in the open. The year ended in the Netherlands, therefore, without further loss to Spain. Isabella died in December and, under the provisions of Philip II's decree of May 1598, direct rule was formally re-established. As a result the States-General was dissolved and its peace negotiations abruptly terminated.

Elsewhere the year was one of considerable activity following upon Gustav's death. His chancellor, Axel Oxenstierna, in Frankfurt-on-Main when the news broke, moved swiftly to Dresden to keep a watchful eye on John George. From there too he arranged matters in Sweden, where Gustav had been succeeded by his young daughter Christina. The *riksdag*, summoned at Oxenstierna's orders to receive the news of Gustav's death, entrusted the conduct of the regency to the nobility of the *rad*. This in effect gave Oxenstierna all the power he needed. Not only was he an able and loyal public servant, but in addition his leadership was acknowledged by the other noble families. Moreover, he held the most important office in the administration and of the other four great offices of the kingdom one was held by his brother, another by a cousin.

The situation in Germany was less easy to control. John George wanted to unite the Protestants under his own leadership and negotiate a separate peace with Ferdinand. 'Should the war last longer the Empire will be utterly destroyed', wrote his commander, Arnim. 'Our beloved Germany will fall a prey to foreigners and be a pitiable example to all the world.' In the belief that John George would be the key figure in any new negotiation, Richelieu sent the marquis of Feuquières to Dresden. Oxenstierna meanwhile summoned to Heilbronn in March 1633 representatives of the Franconian, Swabian, Upper Rhenish and Electoral Rhenish Circles, which Gustav had designated to be the nucleus in the Empire of a *corpus evangelicorum*. He also invited George William of Brandenburg, in order to keep him out of John George's clutches, and persuaded the whole assembly to remain in alliance with Sweden. Feuquières realised just in time what was happening and rode in haste to Heilbronn to secure the acceptance of Louis XIII as joint protector with Sweden of the new (Heilbronn) league, and John George had no option but to become its reluctant ally. Feuquières also ensured that French subsidies would be paid no longer to Sweden, as under the Treaty of Barwalde, but directly to the League itself. However, Oxenstierna forestalled his attempt to secure general recognition of Bavarian neutrality.

Bavaria in fact was already under Swedish occuption. Bernard of Saxe-Weimar, who had taken command of the army after Lützen, joined forces with Horn, the Swedish commander in Alsace, and ravaged the duchy throughout 1633. At Maximilian's request Wallenstein sent one of his lieutenants, Aldringer, to Bavaria, but with orders to keep the Swedes under surveillance and under no circumstances to hazard an engagement. Wallenstein, moreover, did nothing to prevent Bernard from taking Regensburg, the vital link between Bavaria and Bohemia – strange inactivity which dismayed not only Maximilian but also Oñate, Spain's ambassador to the Empire, who was desperately trying to establish a safe route for the cardinal–infante and his army. More strangely still, when Oñate ordered the duke of Feria to bring the advance guard down from Innsbruck into Bavaria, Wallenstein refused to let Aldringer go to his aid. Baffled by his orders, and resenting the ignominy of inactivity, Aldringer finally took matters into his own hands and in September joined forces with Feria north of Lake Constance. Together they then relieved Breisach, which was under attack by Swedish troops, and thus ensured the Spaniards access to Alsace and the Rhineland.

The peasants of Upper Bavaria rebelled: impoverished by the devastation of their land, bewildered by the collapse of authority, and influenced by refugees from Upper Austria who had fought in the peasants' rising of 1626, nearly 10,000 took up arms – against whom it was not entirely clear. The Swedish, Spanish and Imperial commanders, however, had no difficulty in discerning the danger to themselves, and made common cause to defeat them.

Peasants were easily forgotten and it was Wallenstein who now monopolised everyone's attention. Ferdinand was mystified by his orders to Aldringer, suspicious of his correspondence with Arnim, John George and Richelieu, and outraged by the panoply of sovereignty he maintained in Friedland. Oñate believed that he was dangerously out of control and the young Ferdinand of Hungary urged his father to appoint him commander-in-chief in Wallenstein's place. At the same time the enemy princes with whom Wallenstein corresponded could neither trust him nor be trusted by him. It would in fact be wrong to impute a coherent strategy or even low cunning to his actions. He was undeniably in a situation of tortuous and perilous complexity; he was also ageing rapidly, gouty and subject to fits of depression in which only his brother-in-law Trčka and his general Holk could approach him. The firm signature of 1623 had become a crippled scrawl, and it is probable that he had no longer any clear idea of what he wanted, let alone the means to achieve it. His army was still a powerful force, but Wallenstein increasingly relied on his commanders to hold it together, and of these Pappenheim, the most influential with the troops, was gone and Holk died of plague during a brief summer campaign in Saxony. In August Ferdinand sent Count Schlick ostensibly to urge an assault on the Swedes but in secret to sound out the other commanders, Piccolomini and Gallas in particular, as to whether they would obey Wallenstein 'in the event of any change in his position which might arise for reasons of health or any other reason'. Aldringer's defection in Bavaria was an ominous coincidence.

In October 1633, during a campaign in Silesia, Wallenstein captured Thurn and, instead of sending him to Vienna for execution, released him in exchange for the Silesian fortresses held by Bohemian exiles. It was a profitable exchange but it angered Ferdinand and gave rise to a suspicion that he was plotting with the émigré nobles. It is probable that he was. Wallenstein had a romantic vision of a united, independent Bohemia, standing proudly as a bulwark against the Osmanli Turks, and this last point had become an obsession. Even in 1629, in the midst of enforcing the Edict of Restitution and sending troops to s'Hertogenbosch and Mantua, he had written, 'it would be better to turn our arms against the Turks. With God's help our emperor would be able to place the crown of Constantinople on his head within three years.' Trčka, at any rate, wrote to Kinsky, leader of the Bohemian exiles in Dresden, that Wallenstein was ready 'to throw off the mask'; and Feuquières, through Kinsky, promised French support if Wallenstein would seize the Bohemian crown.

During the winter Wallenstein realised that he could no longer trust his officers. The exaction of an oath of loyalty at Pilsen in January 1634 was a pointless measure exhibiting his desperation, and when news came that the emperor had dismissed him he fled, carried in a litter, to his fortress at Eger. There he was murdered by his own men. Piccolomini was rewarded with most of the Trčka estates, and Gallas, the new lord of Friedland, became second-in-command to a new commander-in-chief, the emperor's son Ferdinand.

The lines were now drawn more clearly in Germany than for many years. On the one hand there was the Heilbronn League of the German Protestants in alliance with Sweden and France; on the other two major Habsburg armies, led by Ferdinand of Hungary and the cardinal–infante Ferdinand, about to join forces in southern Germany. The advantage lay with the Habsburgs. Oxenstierna and Richelieu were uneasy allies, as revealed by their correspondence over Philippsburg and other Rhineland fortresses captured by Swedish troops and claimed by the French. It was also difficult to control Bernard of Saxe-Weimar, whom Oxenstierna had reluctantly appointed commander-in-chief instead of his own son-in-law Horn. Bernard demanded the fulfilment of a promise made by Gustav Adolf to create him duke of Franconia, and this being done caused difficulties with the other German princes of the League.

In Germany, the Spanish Ferdinand marched through the Valtelline into the Tyrol, while his cousin, the Austrian Ferdinand, advanced up the Danube to meet him. Bernard of Saxe-Weimar therefore attempted to disrupt their purposes by seeking to lure the Austrians into following him into Bohemia, where Arnim had successfully advanced from Saxony to the gates of Prague. Though Bohemia was in great peril, Ferdinand of Hungary, by luck or good judgement, left it to its fate. He took Regensburg and pressed on up the Danube. Bernard, whose lines of communication lay up the Danube, therefore had no option but to turn about and follow in his train. Arnim, without support, failed to take Prague and withdrew.

In the middle of August Ferdinand crossed the Danube at Donauwörth and, finding a Swedish garrison in Nördlingen, decided to protect his flank by destroying it. Horn and Bernard arrived soon after to reinforce the town, but their troops were demoralised and tired from their fruitless campaign and the region was short of supplies. On 2 September the cardinal–infante arrived, so that the combined Habsburg army of 33,000 now had the advantage over the 25,000 of the Heilbronn League. Though they had little chance of success, the League commanders recognised that after the wasted summer it was vital to preserve the League by some show of action, and the battle began. Both sides made serious errors in the preliminary skirmishes, but in the event the battle became a test of endurance between the Spanish and Swedish infantry. After seven hours of fighting, in which the Spaniards claimed to have withstood fifteen charges, the Swedes finally fell back, and then, becoming entangled with Bernard's horse, their retreat turned into a rout. 'The enemy', reported Ferdinand of Hungary, 'scattered in such a way that ten horses are not found together. Horn is taken, and no one knows whether Weimar be dead or alive.'

Spain and Austria had never been closer. The two young cousins in the excitement of their victory behaved like blood brothers, and their elders followed suit in October 1634 by drawing up the Compact of Ebersdorf. This pledged the emperor and the Roman Catholic German princes in his retinue to give full assistance to Philip IV, as duke of Burgundy, in suppressing the Dutch revolt. The agreement did not carry the signature of Maximilian of Bavaria nor did it consider what might happen should France come to the defence of the United Provinces, but it was nonetheless a long-awaited diplomatic triumph for Spain. Meanwhile Ferdinand of Hungary carried all before him in Württemberg, and the cardinal–infante, accompanied by Piccolomini, marched swiftly through the Rhineland to bring his army to Brussels in November.

Despite the great victory achieved at Nördlingen, the emperor now accepted the fact that the Edict of Restitution remained the one major obstacle to peace within the Empire. Until it was rescinded the German Protestants could not be divorced from their alliance with Sweden. He was also influenced by his son Ferdinand, whose interests were dynastic rather than imperial. Devoted almost exclusively to Austria, Bohemia and Hungary, where Roman Catholicism had been immeasurably strengthened since 1609, Ferdinand of Hungary did not believe the edict was worth a farthing if it condemned the 'hereditary lands' to perpetual war with northern Germany. As a result of this decision, John George agreed to discuss terms, and in November 1634 signed the Preliminaries of Pirna, the all-important prelude to a truce in the following February and subsequently to a peace treaty which was to serve as the model for other settlements between the emperor and the German Protestant princes.

In the preliminaries it was declared that the emperor was willing to offer an amnesty to all save the family of the former elector Palatine, the Bohemian exiles and those who remained obdurate in future. In particular the reservation was intended to reassure Maximilian of Bavaria that his acquisition of the Palatinate was not to be questioned and thus to secure his eventual agreement to a final settlement. With an eye to other princes who might be interested, it was agreed in the preliminaries that Calvinism was not to be given official recognition but that Lutherans might retain all ecclesiastical territory in their possession in November 1627. This was to abandon the Edict of Restitution – suspended in theory for period of forty years – but it did allow the Roman Catholics to enjoy the benefit of the substantial recoveries they had made between 1618 and 1627. John George agreed that the emperor's younger son Leopold might retain Bremen and Halberstadt, but a Saxon administrator was restored to Magdeburg. In addition, the Saxon conquest of Lusatia was confirmed. Finally, as a major concession to the emperor, John George promised to break off his alliances with foreign powers. He took this to be merely a negative undertaking, but, as Arnim warned him in vain, its effect was to make him the ally of the emperor against Sweden and thus to exchange one enemy for another.

The members of the Heilbronn League were frightened and disorganised. They met Oxenstierna in Frankfurt to discuss their plight, but had to disperse in haste as the cardinal–infante approached *en route* for Brussels. Their anxieties were exploited by Richelieu, who offered them the Treaty of Paris in the same month that John George signed the Preliminaries of Pirna. He agreed to provide 12,000 troops and generous subsidies to all who continued the struggle against the emperor. In return he demand guarantees for the security of Roman Catholics in the Empire, a promise that no prince would follow Saxony's lead by negotiating a separate peace, and that not only Schlettstadt and Benfeld in Alsace but also the bridgehead of Strassburg, all in Swedish possession, be ceded to France, giving her virtual control of Alsace. Oxenstierna was unable to prevent the German princes from signing the treaty but withheld his own agreement, and in the event Bernard of Saxe-Weimar did little to earn his subsidy. He failed in his assignment to hold the Rhineland between Mannheim and Mainz, and the Spaniards recovered Philippsburg in January 1635.

The pressure of events was driving the governments of France and the United Provinces into a course of action which each in earlier years would have repudiated. Frederick Henry had never supported the intolerance of the counter-remonstrants and in 1632 he had given full support to the peace negotiations which followed his capture of Maastricht. Now he joined with the Calvinist ministers and the directors of the West India Company to prosecute the war at all costs. His change of heart was attributed by some to Hercule de Charnacé, the experienced French negotiator of the treaties of Altmark and Barwalde, who may have offered French support to make the House of Orange supreme within the United Provinces. More influential, however, was the simple logic of events. The peace negotiations of 1632 had foundered long before the Habsburg victory at Nördlingen. There was therefore, in his opinion, no option but to renew the war with greater determination than before, and to secure at any price a French declaration of war against Spain.

To this end the Dutch government offered to partition with France the Spanish Netherlands, and the instructions to the states' ambassadors laid down that 'the provinces in which the French tongue is generally spoken should be assigned to the crown of France; those remaining should and ought to be left to the United Provinces'. In the event, however, because the projected frontier was to run in the west from Blankenberge on the coast, north of Bruges to Rupelmonde, the ambassadors had to assign to France a considerable part of Dutch-speaking Flanders. Moreover, so desperate was the need to secure the French alliance that the States-General agreed to guarantee the rights of Roman Catholics throughout the Spanish Netherlands.

The proposals were strongly opposed not only by the Calvinist clergy but also by moderate men such as Pauw, who sought the liberation not the conquest of the southern provinces and feared the consequence of having France as a neighbour. Richelieu too disliked the offer, and for a similiar reason: 'It could happen soon afterwards that, lacking any barrier between ourselves and the Dutch, we should find ourselves entering upon the same war with them as they are presently engaged in with the Spaniards.' Moreover, he was still reluctant to challenge Spain outright. Neither he nor Louis XIII was fit, the government was in debt and there was no reserve of trained soldiers upon which Richelieu dared trust the defence of France, let alone the invasion of Spain. But the collapse of the Heilbronn League, the negotiations at Pirna, which threatened to neutralise the Empire, and the arrival of the cardinal–infante in Brussels demanded desperate measures, and in February 1635 France and the United Provinces published their formal alliance. France was to supply 30,000 men for the Dutch army, thus technically maintaining the pretence of not being engaged in war with Spain, while the Spanish Netherlands were given the choice of rising as an independent state against Spanish rule or of submitting to conquest and partition.

Oxenstierna felt threatened on all sides. The council of regency was becoming critical of his conduct of the war, the Truce of Altmark with Poland was about to expire, Denmark threatened war and the German princes were looking either to the emperor or to France. Confident nonetheless that, no matter how dangerous the situation for Sweden, France could not manage without her, Oxenstierna went to Paris in April 1635 to demand a French declaration of war against both Spain and the emperor. He secured the Treaty of Compiègne, which tactfully ignored the disputed matter of Alsace and guaranteed the rights of Roman Catholics in the Empire without contesting the Swedish occupation of the bishoprics of Mainz and Worms. Richelieu, however, would not declare war. The Dutch in February had forced him as far as he thought it prudent to go, and Louis XIII refused to undertake the support of Protestant princes across the Rhine. Consequently the treaty was never ratified.

In the rationalised account of his policies which he subsequently composed for his *Testament politique* Richelieu wrote; 'If it is a sign of singular prudence to have held down the forces opposed to your state for a period of ten years with the forces of your allies, by putting your hand in your pocket and not on your sword, then, when your allies can no longer exist wihout you, to engage in open warfare is a sign of courage and great wisdom.' Courage perhaps, but not necessarily wisdom. It is true that in 1632 Richelieu had written to an agent in Madrid that 'nowhere is Spain in a position to resist a concentrated power such as France over a long period, and in the final analysis the outcome of a general war must necessarily be calamitous to our Iberian neighbours'. In the months following Nördlingen, however, the dangers in the short term seemed insuperable, and, though Louis's own memoranda were confidently bellicose, those of his ministers were filled with uncertainty.

In the event the main issue was not the need to satisfy allies but the French government's own fears for the security of the Rhineland. Lorraine had come increasingly under French rule since 1630, and Duke Charles was now an exiled soldier of fortune, hoping to return to Nancy in triumph at the head of a Spanish army. Alsace was a more complex area, a congeries of rival jurisdictions, but the French, who had followed fast upon the heels of the invading Swedes, had profited by their withdrawal after Nördlingen to make themselves masters of the diocese of Basel in Upper Alsace; the county of Montbéliard, from which to command the Burgundian Gate between the Vosges and the Jura; and the strongpoints of Haguenau, Bouxwiller, Bischwiller and Saverne. The most important areas still outside their control were Breisach, where an Imperial garrison had held on despite Swedish victories elsewhere, and Strassburg, whose citizens might still allow the Habsburgs access to the Rhine bridge. As a result, the renewed power of Spain and Austria in the Rhineland, which by the compact of Ebersdorf was to be directed to the defeat of the Dutch, was interpreted by Louis XIII and Richelieu as an immediate threat to Alsace and Lorraine.

Paradoxically, it was one simple consequence of the Habsburg presence in the Rhineland which crystallised everything not in terms of strategy or political necessity but of honour. Spanish troops entered Trier in March 1635 and carried off the archbishop–elector to Germany as a prisoner. Since 1631 he had placed himself under the protection of Louis XIII, and at an emergency meeting of the royal council it was unanimously agreed that his arrest was an insult to France that could be avenged only by war. On 19 May 1635 a herald was therefore sent to Brussels to proclaim Louis XIII's declaration of war against Philip IV of Spain.

At the very moment when, as by a miracle, the government of Spain was poised to strike a final blow against the Dutch rebels, whose intransigent opposition had dominated Spanish foreign policy since 1599, she was compelled to deal with an enemy not of her own choosing; an enemy, moreover, superbly placed to disrupt her lines of communication and supply, and whose national resources of wealth and population, no matter how badly they might be organised in 1635, made her capable, as Richelieu had foreseen in 1632, of outlasting Spain in any war of attrition. The French declaration of war, whatever Richelieu's fears might have been for the consequences to France, proved to be for Spain an unmitigated disaster and assured the triumph of the United Provinces.

5
The European War 1635–45

In the long run the French declaration of war transformed the entire pattern of conflict in Europe by making the Spanish–Dutch war peripheral to the struggle for power between Bourbon and Habsburg. In the short run it nearly proved disastrous for France.

Richelieu had been able in the past to employ as many as 50,000 troops on occasion to intervene as and when he chose in the conflicts of other states. He now needed three times that number merely to defend the long line of the French frontier, which at every point, from the Pyrenees, the Rhineland and the Netherlands, was vulnerable to invasion by Spain. It was an undertaking for which France had only her famous Guards and the four great regiments of Picardy, Piedmont, Champagne and Navarre. These were the apple of Louis XIII's eye, carefully supervised by him even in such matters as the appointment of individual officers, but their numbers were inadequate for the task in hand. As a measure of the government's desperation the feudal levies were summoned to the kingdom's defence, even though the military obligations of the *noblesse de l'épée* had long ceased to have any value. After commanding them in Lorraine, Louis XIII condemned them out of hand. 'I regret to have to tell you that our nobles are unreliable. As soon as they are asked to exert themselves . . . all they are fit for is to help their king to lose his honour. If one sends them no more than three hours' distance from here in the direction of Metz or Nancy, they begin to grumble and claim that they are being sent to their perdition and threaten to decamp.'

The expedient was never repeated and it was necessary to contract out the recruitment of troops to colonels, whose terms of employment made them very nearly autonomous. This in turn presented another problem. It was a matter not only of scraping together sufficient troops but also of finding reliable commanders to lead them. France had very few, and the success of a campaign was endangered alike by the courageous stupidity of some as by the craven unreliability of others. Two nobles, for example, Du Bec and St Leger, exposed their inadequacies at their first engagement and, too proud to face criticism at home, chose exile among their country's enemies. The only two men of any military talent available to Richelieu were Bernard of Saxe-Weimar, the German commander defeated at Nördlingen, and the duke of Rohan, a Huguenot and a former rebel. Rohan was desperately anxious to be of use. Since the Grace of Alais he had been at a loose end, writing to his mother, 'I have the feeling that since the capture of La Rochelle and the waning of the religious wars in France all theatres of war no longer concern me.' To his credit he had kept the Huguenots out of the Languedoc rebellion and Richelieu was prepared to run the risk of employing him.

The payment of troops was yet another problem which the government was ill prepared to meet. Its finances were already in disorder and the royal council simply noted, with classic understatement, that 'by increasing His Majesty's forces, which are already very large, it will become difficult for him to pay them all on time'. It resolved accordingly that the troops would have to live off the land, with the unrealistic proviso that 'they must not become completely undisciplined and disobedient'. The government in fact had no idea of the cost of the war to which it was now committed. Campaigns, as the Spaniards had learned, were determined by sieges, siege warfare was primarily a matter of organisation and finance, and the only way to win a war was to outlast the enemy's finances.

In the circumstances, therefore, Richelieu's plans for making war in 1635 seem to have been prepared with bland indifference to his inadequate reserves of men, commanders and money, since he undertook to harass Spain in northern Italy, to strengthen the defence of Alsace and to assist the Dutch against the cardinal–infante. Rohan served him well in Valtelline. He was welcomed by the Grisons, who appreciated the tact displayed in sending them a fellow Protestant, and with their support Pastor Jurg Jenatsch was able in September to lead a rebellion against Spanish control in the valley. When the Habsburgs rushed in troops from both Milan and the Tyrol, Rohan's army helped to disperse them and by the end of the year the Valtelline was closed to Spain.

Elsewhere Richelieu's plans were unsuccessful. The north Italian

states of Savoy, Venice and Tuscany pledged themselves to take Milan,
but their campaign was short and fruitless. Bernard of Saxe-Weimar,
whose hopes of creating an independent duchy of Franconia had been
destroyed at Nördlingen, was promised territory in Alsace and given 4
million livres to maintain 12,000 men and 6000 horse in the Rhineland.
Nonetheless, the Spaniards consolidated their hold in the Lower
Palatinate, and Gallas, after a brief incursion into Lorraine, settled
down for the winter at Zabern with his army in control of the Vosges
Gap.

In the Netherlands a French army forced its way across Luxemburg
to join Frederick Henry near Maastricht. The allied army, numbering
32,000 infantry and 9000 cavalry, sacked Tirlemont and invested
Louvain. It was then that sickness struck the French camp, that many
began to desert for lack of pay, and that Piccolomini, leading a relief
force sent by the emperor, crossed the Rhine at Mainz and cut the

16. The campaigns in France, the Rhineland and the Netherlands 1635–43

French lines of communication with their bases in France. In these circumstances Frederick Henry declined to pursue the campaign. As an expert in siege warfare he preferred not to commit his forces unless he was adequately covered, and when the French complained of his lack of initiative they were bluntly told to go elsewhere and leave the Dutch to fight their own war.

Since there was no returning through Luxemburg, the remnant of the French army had to be shipped home in great humiliation by the Dutch. Their departure was celebrated in Brussels, where morale had been raised not only by the triumphant arrival in the previous year of the cardinal–infante Ferdinand, but also by his tactful demeanour as Philip IV's representative. In addition, the citizens of the Obedient Provinces derived much satisfaction from the presence of Piccolomini's force, incontrovertible evidence of Imperial support for their cause. With Piccolomini Ferdinand relieved Louvain and then seized Schenkenschans at the junction of the Waal and the Rhine. This was a particularly bold and imaginative achievement, because Schenkenschans was a key point of the lines of defence created by Maurice in 1605, and Maastricht was all but cut off from the United Provinces.

Elsewhere the Habsburgs had had other victories to celebrate. Ferdinand of Hungary occupied almost the whole of the right bank of the Rhine, and, with his troops securely quartered in Württemburg, Swabia and Franconia, the Habsburg kingdoms welcomed the rare luxury of having neither friend nor foe billeted upon them. The emperor therefore enjoyed a most advantageous position of strength within the Empire. The negotiations initiated at Pirna with John George of Saxony were finally completed in May 1635 by the Treaty of Prague, and other German princes were invited to subscribe to its terms.

Maximilian of Bavaria was reluctant to do so, but, since both France and Sweden had declared their support for the former elector Palatine, whose family was excluded from the amnesty granted by the Peace of Prague, he had no option but to sign. The emperor made things easier for him by securing the dioceses of Hildesheim, Minden and Verden for members of his family and by offering his own daughter, forty years younger than Maximilian, in marriage to the elderly widower. Once Maximilian had signed, the archbishop–electors of Mainz, Trier and Cologne followed suit. So too did George William of Brandenburg. Boguslav of Pomerania had promised him the reversion to his duchy, but since Swedish troops were currently in occupation the elector needed the emperor's help to expel them. Thereafter all the remaining German Protestants, except for a handful of Calvinists, gave their assent to the Peace of Prague.

As a result, by the very clause to which Arnim had taken exception at Pirna (see p. 144), the signatories of the peace were now obliged as allies of the emperor to assist him against Sweden, so that in theory Catholics and Protestants were at least combined in one army under the command of the emperor's son.

Sweden in 1635 was in no position to withstand any Imperial assaults. Her allies in Germany made their peace with Ferdinand. Richelieu withheld French subsidies because the Treaty of Compiègne (see p. 145) had not been ratified, and the expiry of the Truce of Altmark (see p. 122) left Sweden exposed to Polish hostility at the very moment when her resources were dangerously overstrained. In Stockholm the conduct of the war, indeed the war itself, came under censure, and Oxenstierna, more or less the prisoner of a mutinous garrison in Magdeburg, could not return home to take charge of affairs. In his absence the council of regency so bungled its negotiations with the Poles that its minimum terms were made public before a settlement had been reached. Since the Poles were angry with Sweden for her intervention in the Smolensk war, they were in no mood to make things easy, and it needed the full force of French intervention to patch matters up. Eventually, by the Truce of Stuhmsdorf, Sweden had to accept the loss of the Prussian ports, whose port dues produced an income of over 550,000 reichstalers a year. In return she was recognised in possession of Livonia and, with the signing of the truce, was spared the responsibility of maintaining troops in the south-east corner of the Baltic.

Without French subsidies and the income from the Prussian ports, this was the worst possible moment for Swedish troops to have to live off the land, since the area available from which to exact contributions had been substantially reduced by the Imperial victories and by the loss of allies as a result of the Peace of Prague. Everything therefore depended upon Baner, whose army represented Sweden's one remaining asset in northern Germany. With it he had to safeguard the line of communication from Stockholm to Frankfurt, and above all to defend Pomerania. Baner, like many other commanders, hoped to create for himself an independent duchy in Germany, but in 1635 his only concern was to survive. His entire army of 23,000 was in a state of mutiny, and agents of John George and of Christian of Denmark made matters worse by offering to recruit the mutinous colonels and their regiments.

By August he and Oxenstierna had quietened things down by making concessions to the officers, but it was clear from Baner's despatches in October that so many men were deserting to the Saxon army that he doubted his ability to hold the line of the Elbe. At the end of the year, however, 10,000 reinforcements were released from the Polish frontier, the first fruits of the Truce of Stuhmsdorf, and with their arrival the soldiers began to believe that with Baner lay their best opportunity for profit. Morale was improved by a successful series of skirmishes with the Saxons in the valley of the Elbe, culminating in 1636 with a major victory at Wittstock (see map 18). This left Oxenstierna free to return to Stockholm, where he rescued Christina from her mother, who sought to marry her off to a Dane, and reasserted his authority over the regency administration.

While Oxenstierna took stock of the situation in 1636, Richelieu faced the worst crisis of his career as Spain, Austria and Bavaria, in a rare combination of military might, planned the defeat of France. The cardinal–infante and Piccolomini, reinforced by the Bavarian cavalry under Werth, invaded Picardy, while Gallas and the exiled Charles of Lorraine attacked through the Vosges Gap into eastern France. Coincidentally there were widespread urban riots and peasant revolts against the cost of the war (see p. 162).

By July the allies had made good progress, except for what seemed to be a minor check to Gallas at the village of Saint-Jean-de-Losne, between Champlitte and Langres. Ferdinand overran the region between the Somme and the Oise, by-passed Amiens and by mid August had taken Corbie, barely fifty miles north of Paris. The danger was dramatically brought home to the French by Werth's cavalry, which pressed on to Roye and Montdidier and whose outriders swept through Pontoise into the suburbs of Paris itself. Richelieu, on the brink of a breakdown, managed to organise defences and the supply of reinforcements, while Louis XIII set a splendid example of royal leadership, calming the frightened, rallying the dispirited and riding out at the head of his troops to meet the enemy halfway at Senlis.

It was a brave gesture, but what really saved France was the village of Saint-Jean-de-Losne, which, against the odds, resisted Gallas so successfully that it was renamed Saint-Jean-Belle-Défense. Since Gallas could not take the village, his advance lost momentum, some of his men began to desert and he himself became uneasy about Bernard of Saxe-

Weimar, who was manoeuvring on his left flank in the Rhineland. The news of Wittstock gave him the excuse he needed to withdraw from a situation which increasingly exposed his inadequacies as a commander. As a result Ferdinand and Piccolomini were left stranded to the north of Paris. Werth advised a spirited dash into the capital, but Ferdinand was running short of supplies and men and, no doubt correctly, believed that he could not go further without the support of Gallas. He therefore withdrew and France was saved.

In the autumn of 1636 a diet of electors at Regensburg elected Ferdinand of Hungary king of the Romans. It was in many respects the high-water mark of the emperor's reign. He had seemed to be stronger when the Edict of Restitution was being enforced, but had then been too dependent upon the unreliable strength of Wallenstein. In 1636 his achievement was more solidly based. Throughout Bohemia and Austria, though not in Hungary, where the Osmanli threat compelled caution in dealing with the nobility, the administration had been centralised at the expense of local franchises and privileges, and the power of the Protestants reduced. Within the Empire he exercised an authority greater than any emperor for three centuries. No longer was there a Catholic League or an Evangelical Union to resist his policies or restrict his freedom of action: instead he was leader of a coalition of princes of both faiths, bound to him by treaty to serve him against Sweden and France. But the work had taken its toll of his health, and at fifty-nine he was a very tired old man. 'The Roman Empire needs me no more', he said thankfully, and died in February 1636, leaving his son Ferdinand to succeed him unchallenged.

Rohan meanwhile had run into serious difficulties in the Valtelline. The inhabitants of the valley demanded automony, the Grisons insisted on their sovereignty, and, when Rohan agreed to the latter provided that the rights of Roman Catholics were protected, the Grisons turned against him. Richelieu in 1636 could spare no troops for Rohan, and in March 1636 Jenatsch led a successful revolt against the French occupation. Rohan dared not face Richelieu's anger and joined Bernard of Saxe-Weimar, in whose service he died in the following year, while the Spanish viceroy in Milan negotiated rights of transit through the valley by recognising the absolute sovereignty of the Grisons.

The events of 1636 demonstrated very clearly the risk taken by France in declaring war on Spain in 1635. Far from harassing the Spanish lines of communication, she herself was subjected to an assault which all but carried the day. There was nothing, moreover, to encourage the view that things would be easier in the future. What was evident was the advantage derived by the United Provinces from French involvement in the war. If Ferdinand and Piccolomini, reinforced by Werth and Gallas, had been free to advance north from Schenkenschans, the fate of the republic would have been in doubt. On the other hand, because Ferdinand had to concentrate all his reserves in preparation for the invasion of France, the Dutch recovered Schenkenschans in the spring of 1636.

In the following year the States-General ordered a seaborne attack on Dunkirk. Frederick Henry disliked the plan, but, as Dutch shipping suffered so heavily from the Dunkirk raiders, he had no option but to assemble the army for embarkation at Rammekens. When several weeks of contrary winds prevented the fleet from putting out into the Channel, however, he transferred the army inland and took everyone by surprise by marching on Breda. Once again he demonstrated his genius as a military engineer. His operation, brilliantly planned, defended and executed, like those of s'Hertogenbosch and Maastricht in the past, was the talk of Europe, and in October the city surrendered.

Within the Empire, Baner invaded Saxony, which seemed to be but poorly defended. Gallas, with uncharacteristic daring, abandoned his brief to cover Bernard of Saxe-Weimar in the south-west, took the Swedes by surprise at Torgau (see map 18) and drove them back to Pomerania. The setback convinced Oxenstierna that Sweden could not fight on unaided, and he resolved to solicit a new alliance with France.

Richelieu for his part no longer had reservations about declaring war on the emperor. By the Treaty of Hamburg in March 1638 he guaranteed an annual subsidy of 1 million livres (400,000 reichstalers). In return Oxenstierna abandoned Sweden's claims to territory in the Rhineland. Both sides agreed not to negotiate separately with their enemies, and they incorporated in the treaty their first thoughts about a possible settlement to the war. They laid down that there should be a general amnesty within the Holy Roman Empire, and the restoration of the political, constitutional and religious conditions pertaining 1618. They also demanded 'satisfaction' for their own efforts, but by tacit agreement no specific references were made to their respective claims to Pomerania and Lorraine.

April 1638 to May 1643: I. The eclipse of Spain

Encouraged by Gallas's absence in Saxony, Bernard of Saxe-Weimar at last made his move. In February 1638 he took Rheinfelden, east of Basel, and from there advanced on Breisach, the most important link in the chain of Habsburg communications. With French support he began the siege in August, and in December the city surrendered. Richelieu's delight at the news was modified only by anxieties about Bernard's intentions, but fortuitously, in July 1639, Bernard succumbed to smallpox, leaving the army to Erlach, his second-in-command.

This produced a swift reaction from an unexpected quarter. The young Charles Louis, son of the former elector Palatine and living in exile in Holland, resolved to buy out Erlach and with his troops restore his family's fortunes in the Rhineland. The scheme was both imaginative and bold; his mistake was to travel across France, where he was arrested and detained until Richelieu himself had succeeded in securing Erlach's services. The new contract, drawn up in October 1639, established that the troops were to be paid directly by the French government and were therefore to obey orders from the French commander-in-chief.

The French army was becoming a more useful weapon of war. Its administration was being radically overhauled by two able civilians, Servien and Sublet de Noyers, the young commander Turenne was beginning to show his paces, and in 1638 a small force had invaded Spain to lay siege to the Basque port of Fuenterrabia. In 1639 the siege was abandoned, despite the success of a naval squadron in defeating the attempts of Spanish ships to relieve the town, but, by way of compensation, other troops invaded Roussillon, a Pyrenean province lost to Spain in 1494. In addition, French influence was extended in Savoy, where Victor Amadeus died in 1637 leaving infant children. His widow Christine, a sister of Louis XIII, attempted to govern in the French interest; her brothers-in-law favoured the Habsburgs (one of them, Prince Thomas, was already serving in the Army of Flanders) and since the duchy was an imperial fief they called upon the emperor to appoint them as regents. In 1639, to settle the matter, Richelieu sent troops to establish Christine's authority beyond question.

Despite the misfortunes suffered by Spain, Olivares had not lost his resilience, and in 1639 he prepared an armada of over seventy ships, commanded by Oquenda, to sail to Flanders. He recognised that the fall of Breisach and the French occupation of Savoy, Alsace and Lorraine had made it impossible to reinforce the Army of Flanders except by sea, but this alone would not have called for the armada of 1639, since, with the connivance of Charles I, Spanish troop-ships had for several years been able to make for the safety of English territorial waters, thence to be smuggled across the Channel with the help of the Dunkirk squadron. Olivares's intentions were breathtaking – if not foolhardy. Oquenda's task, apart from transporting reinforcements, was to seek out and destroy the Dutch fleet. Then, in a fascinating revival of the Baltic schemes of 1627, he was to join the Danish fleet in an attack on Älvsborg, Sweden's outlet on the North Sea, and deny the Dutch access through the Sound to the Baltic trade upon which their wealth depended.

Though the odds were heavy against the venture's succeeding, it was nonetheless fortunate for the Dutch that in this crisis they had a seaman of exceptional ability in charge of their fleet. Frederick Henry as admiral-general exercised very little co-ordination between the individual states' colleges of admiralty, and followed the general custom of appointing as his representatives men of noble rank but little naval experience. In 1636, however, he had selected Maarten Harpeertszoon Tromp, who was first and foremost a sailor, and one to rejoice in the opportunity of a naval battle with Spain. When Oquenda arrived in the Channel in September 1639, Tromp, though heavily outnumbered at that moment, immediately launched his attack. His seamanship was demonstrably superior to Oquenda's and, for fear of losing their ships on the Flemish sandbanks, the Spaniards ran for the protection of English waters, and of the English shore batteries covering the Downs roadstead between Dover and the North Foreland. Charles I was content to play host to the Spanish fleet for as long as they paid him, but the Dutch, who were once again in dispute with England over the North Sea fisheries, were in aggressive mood. The States-General ordered Tromp to ignore English neutrality and attack when he was ready.

Tromp had barely twenty ships with which to challenge the shore batteries and the Spanish fleet of seventy, but in the dockyards of the United Provinces a tremendous effort was made to reinforce him by converting merchantmen into men-of-war. Within three weeks Tromp's numbers had been trebled. He exploited the inexperience of the Spanish captains by sending in fire-ships, which caused some to panic and run aground while the rest put to sea in disarray. Although Oquenda survived the Battle of the Downs which followed, and arrived safely in Dunkirk, most of his fleet was destroyed, and with it Spain's last chance to defeat the Dutch.

The problem for Spain was not simply that she could no longer maintain her lines of communication with Flanders by land or by sea, since this was as much a symptom of her condition as its cause. The root of her ills lay in her inability to finance the armies and fleets upon which in the past her security and power had depended. The conflict with the Dutch had been extended, both in its geographical range and in its duration, beyond the resources of the Spanish empire, and the intervention of France as a belligerent had exacerbated the problem. Worse still, the very foundations of the homeland itself were in danger.

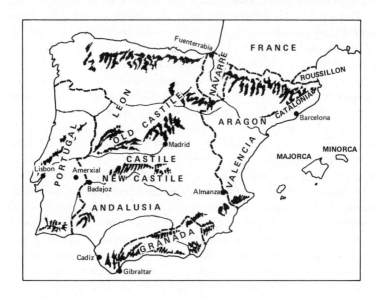

17. Spain and Portugal

The Spanish monarchy, monolithic though it appeared to its enemies, was in reality a federal union of five kingdoms – Castile, Aragon, Navarre, Granada and Portugal – which shared a common loyalty to one royal family but preserved their separate constitutions, customs and liberties. None was more independent than Catalonia, itself one of the three separate kingdoms of Aragon. It regarded Castile as an allied but foreign power with whom it had neither economic links nor historical associations. As a Mediterranean state it had taken no part in Castilian enterprises in America, nor for that matter in the Netherlands; it resented being dragged into Castilian wars and refused to become more closely associated with a kingdom burdened beyond belief with overseas commitments and domestic debt. It had therefore rejected Olivares's proposals to establish a union of arms (see p. 112) and also his appeal in 1632 for financial aid. Olivares recognised that this was to some extent the fault of previous monarchs. Catalans had had no benefit from association with Castile, no sight of their common ruler and no honours, pensions or employment at his hands. Nonetheless, from the Castilian point of view the Catalans were inexcusably self-regarding, 'entirely separate from the rest of the monarchy', as Olivares himself put it, 'useless for service and in a state little befitting the dignity and power of His Majesty'.

In 1636, for example, Olivares had not dared to invade France from Catalan soil, so uncertain was he of the attitude of the inhabitants, and when the French besieged the Basque port of Fuenterrabia the Catalans refused to send help, as though Catalonia in some peculiar way was not at war with France. In 1639, with the French invasion of Roussillon, the pretence could no longer be maintained, and the viceroy was ordered to raise men and money by force. As the viceroy himself put it, 'The Catalans are naturally fickle. . . . Make them understand that the welfare of the nation and the army must go beyond all laws and privileges.'

With the winter of 1640 troops were billeted in Catalonia to bring home the fact that the country was in real danger from France and that it had some responsibility to contribute to its own defence. The Castilian troops, however, almost as foreign to the Catalans as the French they had driven back, went unpaid and therefore seized what they needed. By the spring their presence had provoked risings in many areas; by the summer the whole kingdom was in revolt. The Catalans appealed to France for aid, Louis XIII was proclaimed duke of Barcelona, and in January 1641 a Castilian army was defeated by French and rebel forces outside the walls of Barcelona.

Two months earlier rebellion had broken out in Portugal, led by the duke of Braganza, whose family had a claim to the throne. The kingdom had passed to Philip II in 1580 with the most stringent provision for the maintenance of its liberties and self-government. By the reign of Philip IV there was bitter complaint that the Castilians who enriched themselves at Portugal's expense had failed to protect her colonies in South America. The Castilians, on the other hand, could retort that the Portuguese had contributed nothing towards the relief of Pernambuco, and that Philip IV might well have succeeded in his negotiations for a truce in the Netherlands but for his scrupulous refusal to abandon Brazil to the Dutch. In 1636 Olivares ordered the collection of a 5 per cent tax on property, a tax hitherto confined to Castile but extended on this occasion to Portugal to help pay for a new expedition to South America. Whatever its justification, the levy was unconstitutional and led to rioting in 1637. Only when Braganza and other leading nobles hesitated to give a lead was order temporarily restored.

Subsequently it was rumoured that Olivares planned to abolish the Cortes and incorporate the kingdom into Castile. It was then that the influence of Braganza's wife became important. She came from one of the proudest families in Spain – her brother was duke of Medina Sidonia and captain-general of Andalusia – and apart from her particular ambition for her husband she shared the general hatred of her class for Olivares. In December 1640 she persuaded Braganza to proclaim himself John IV of Portugal; in the following autumn her brother resolved to make himself master of an independent Andalusia. Olivares learned of Sidonia's treason in time to save the province for the crown, but nothing could save Portugal, where the people rallied to their new king with a patriotic fervour all the more intense for having been denied an outlet for nearly three generations.

In the Netherlands, meanwhile, the cardinal–infante was losing heart. He had saved Antwerp in 1638 and survived two attacks on Hulst in 1639, but he could not fight successfully on two fronts at once and in 1640 lost Arras, the capital of Artois, to the French. Wearied, indeed prematurely aged, by the barrage of endless and impossible demands to send aid to Castile while struggling to hold both the French and the Dutch at bay, he reported in 1641 that 'if the war with France is to continue we have not the means to take the offensive. The Spanish and imperial armies are reduced to such a state that they can undertake nothing. The only solution is to establish supporters in France and use them to make the Paris government more amenable.' It was a vain hope. The dukes of Bouillon and and Guise, who were genuinely opposed to the war with Spain and who hated Richelieu's exercise of power, needed no prompting from Spain to promote a conspiracy in April 1641, but once again the attempt by factious nobles to unseat Richelieu failed.

The one source of consolation to Spain in 1641 was the first real evidence of dissension between Frederick Henry and the States-General. The prince had enjoyed no major triumph since the fall of Breda in 1637, and there was public speculation about his ability as a soldier. More germane to the dispute was the marriage of his son

William to Mary, the daughter of Charles I. The king had swallowed his pride over the Battle of the Downs in his anxiety to find allies against his Parliament, and when the Civil War broke out Mary and her mother, Henrietta Maria, set up court at The Hague. When Frederick Henry tried to mobilise military support for the royalist cause, the regent class, already suspicious of his purposes in seeking a royal marriage for his son, reasserted its uncompromising Calvinist and republican nature and maintained that if any help were to be given it should go to the English Parliament. The dispute was a bitter one, and an official declaration of neutrality by the State-General merely papered over the cracks.

The death of the cardinal–infante in November 1641 was closely followed in 1642 by that of Richelieu. No man had done more from 1623 to 1634 to disrupt the ambitions of the Habsburgs by sapping Spanish lines of communication, by exploiting the emperor's difficulties and by alliances with Bavaria, Sweden and the United Provinces. When all that had failed to prevent the triumph at Nördlingen, his decision to bring France openly into the conflict had almost brought her to the brink of destruction, but by the time of his death it was becoming evident that the war was going well. Roussillon and Perpignan, lost to Spain in 1494, had been recovered, Alsace and Lorraine were under French control, and French armies were carrying the war forward in Flanders and in Spain itself. Turenne had demonstrated his genius and in the young duke of Enghien another general of quality had been discovered. Violent, morose and wayward, at the age of twenty-two he had already proved himself a brilliant commander-in-chief on the Flanders frontier.

Success was so immoderately expensive that ultimately the victories proved to be of less consequence for France than the measures taken to pay for them. Initially the government tried to finance its alliances and its own minor engagements abroad by creating more offices for sale within the administration, but long before the full burden of warfare was experienced, in 1636, it had been found necessary to borrow on an overwhelming scale. In order to finance the loans by which France waged war between 1630 and 1648, taxation was increased threefold, the most remarkable rate of increase in the history of the *ancien régime*.

As taxes mounted so did the arrears of payment, and troops had to be used more widely than in the past to assist the collectors to confiscate goods and chattels. This led to a series of revolts in many regions of France, principally but not exclusively in the south and west, throughout most of the war years. The pattern was similar in most cases: disturbances in the spring, declarations of loyalty to the king and complaints against his ministers who burdened the poor with extra taxes, confrontation with royal troops, and dispersal when harvest time came round.

Even in 1636, the very year when Paris was threatened by Habsburg armies (see p. 153), the government had to contend with riots in Amiens and Rennes and widespread peasant revolt in the south-west. The *croquants*, as the rebels were termed, had no unified command, but a common concern to take vengeance on tax officials, of whom a great number were murdered. Some of the provincial nobility provided local leadership, and the authority of one, La Mothe la Forêt, was for a time widely recognised, but the movement was sporadic, breaking out and reappearing like a moorland blaze. Nearly one-quarter of France was affected, between the Loire and the Garonne, and assemblies of armed peasants could number 60,000 on occasion. The governor of Angoulême secured a brief respite in August, but the use of troops to collect taxes in the winter led to a violent renewal of rebellion in the spring. This time, however, Richelieu was able to dispose of the army, and the rebellion was ended with the slaughter of 14,000 peasants.

The revolts thus threatened but never actually destroyed the government, which in fact made itself even more powerful under the inexorable pressures of financing the war. The *élus*, the officers responsible for the principal tax, the *taille*, became disgruntled by the sale, and thus the reduplication, of their positions and by the greater difficulty of collecting the tax from an increasingly desperate and impoverished peasantry. As a result, many of them either failed to carry out their duties or appropriated more than their traditional share of the money they raised. To counter this, Richelieu began to employ intendants directly responsible to the royal council: first as itinerant commissioners; then, after 1635, on permanent location in the provinces. There, wielding the exceptional powers assigned them by the council, they raised their own *fusiliers* to suppress resistance, supervised the work of tax collection and, in 1642, took over from the *élus* the assessment of the *taille*.

In this unexpected administrative revolution, able and ambitious men were established in parallel with the existing bureaucracy, but with the authority to emasculate it. Their concern lay with the two most critical areas of local government – taxation and order – and in all things they answered directly to the king's ministers. The measures taken to finance the war thus paved the way for the absolutism of Versailles.

Richelieu's death was followed almost immediately by the dismissal and disgrace of his great adversary Olivares. In an unusual display of activity, Philip IV had himself marched against the Catalan rebels in the summer of 1642, but he was forced to abandon the campaign when French troops reinforced Barcelona and advanced into Aragon. Olivares was made the scapegoat for the humiliation endured by the king, and for all the failures of the past five years. He was dismissed in January 1643 and died shortly afterwards, almost insane with grief at the collapse of his ambitions for Spain. Like Richelieu he had done much, in a country less amenable than France to central direction, to improve the efficiency of the royal administration. Like Richelieu, too, he had displayed a sure grasp of strategy, sensitive to any event which might endanger the security of Spanish lines of communication. In addition, his recognition of the importance of the Baltic in the Dutch economy had led in 1626, and again in 1639, to diplomatic and military planning on a truly continental scale, even though he lacked the resources and the commanders to achieve his purposes.

It was apparent that Louis XIII was unlikely to survive Richelieu by more than a few months. His death would then expose France to the hazards of a regency – even perhaps to civil war – and provide Spain with opportunities for intervention. There was therefore a good case for Spanish commanders to bide their time in 1643, but Don Francisco de Melo in Flanders was anxious to make his mark as a worthy successor to the cardinal–infante. He invaded France, therefore, with an army reinforced by the emperor, hoping to break the line of fortresses guarding the head of the Oise valley by laying siege to Rocroy (see map 16). The campaign was bungled. Enghien, at the head of a relieving force greater than Melo's, was allowed to emerge unmolested from a narrow defile to fight on open ground, where his superior numbers gave him the advantage. The Habsburg front collapsed under the French attack until only a nucleus of 8000 Spanish *tercios* held firm. Such was their reputation that Enghien proposed a truce, but in the confusion of negotiating a cease-fire across the battlefield shots were exchanged and the battle renewed. The *tercios*, overwhelmed but not disgraced, fought to the last man, and with them died the legend of their invincibility.

Of the troops who fought at Rocroy, only Enghien and his most senior officers knew that Louis XIII was dead and that the whole direction of French foreign policy might be altered by his widow, who, with two sons under age, proclaimed herself regent. The situation resembled that of 1610 after the death of Henry IV. Anne of Austria, as sister of Philip IV, of the cardinal–infante and of the empress, had always maintained a secret, indeed treasonous, correspondence with Madrid and Brussels, and her first act, as Richelieu had always feared, was to recall from exile those, such as the duchess of Chevreuse, who had conspired against the cardinal and opposed the war with Spain.

Quite unexpectedly, however, Anne appointed as chief minister an Italian cardinal, Mazarin, who had attracted Richelieu's attention in the Mantuan war and had subsequently become his principal subordinate. It was rumoured that a special relationship pertained between the queen and Mazarin, interpreted by some as a secret marriage, by others as a condition of tactful adoration by the minister; it has also been suggested that, since she was too feckless and irresponsible to cope with government, she chose the most efficient agent available to do it for her. Neither explanation takes account of the maturing effect on Anne, late in life, of the birth of her two sons. As the mother of princes she was at last responsible for something which mattered to her, and, in her anxiety to preserve their kingdom and their throne from enemies at home and abroad, she recognised that Mazarin alone might do for them what Richelieu had achieved for their father.

His abilities were immediately put to the test. The nobles who had imagined themselves in positions of power were angry with Anne for frustrating their ambitions. Among the conspirators were Vendôme, Henry IV's illegitimate son, and the irrepressible duchess of Chevreuse, only just returned from sixteen years of exile. The *importants*, as they were called, were no match for Mazarin, who arrested and exiled them before their plans were complete. The war with Spain continued.

April 1638 to May 1643: II. The emperor, the Empire and Sweden

Baner, like Mansfeld, Wallenstein and Bernard of Saxe-Weimar, wanted to set himself up as an independent prince, and but for lack of funds would have raced to Alsace on news of Bernard's death to compete with Richelieu for control of his army. His one hope thereafter was to attract the emperor's notice and secure the appropriate reward to purchase his services. As a consequence of the Treaty of Hamburg (see p. 155) the receipt of French subsidies allowed him in 1639 to lead the Swedes in a major offensive to the walls of Prague. The emperor, as Baner had intended, began to negotiate the price of his treason until the devastated condition of Bohemia compelled the army to withdraw for lack of supplies. In the following year he joined forces with the Bernadines (the soldiers formerly led by Bernard of Saxe-Weimar and subsequently employed by France) at Erfurt. Together they numbered over 40,000 men, well placed to deliver a formidable attack anywhere within the Empire, but Baner, pursuing his fruitless negotiations with Ferdinand, forfeited a major opportunity and achieved nothing.

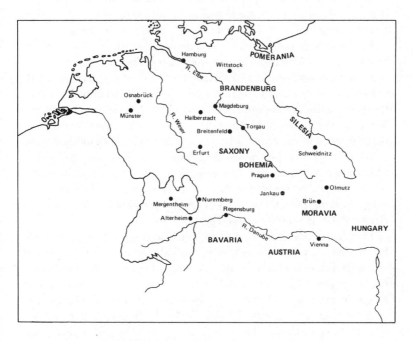

18. The campaigns in central Europe 1635–43

In September 1640 the first full session of the Diet to meet since 1603 was summoned to Regensburg. This was an assembly which had formerly been at the mercy of rival pressure groups, united only in its opposition to Imperial policies, but Ferdinand III was confident of his power to achieve his purposes. As an indication of the changed circumstances of Imperial politics, the delegates agreed that the Imperial army be stationed outside the city in case of attack by Baner, a defence measure which at any other diet would have been denounced as an act of intimidation. In the event, and unexpectedly, the precaution was justified. Baner realised that he had wasted his opportunity in the summer, marched on Erfurt in the late autumn and persuaded the Bernardines to join him in December. Together they advanced at speed on Regensburg, arriving on the north bank of the Danube with only the frozen river between them and the city. Ferdinand was in his element. As the only German prince with any recent military success to his name, he took pleasure in demonstrating his ability: the troops were called in and held the city until the river thawed in January 1641. Baner had to withdraw for lack of supplies to Saxony – and thence to Halberstadt, where he died in the spring.

The Diet, however, had not been summoned to observe the victor of Nördlingen put his troops through their paces. The emperor wanted to negotiate a general settlement. Sweden was becoming more powerful, as Baner's winter attack had illustrated, and Ferdinand hoped to secure the best possible terms from the German princes before matters got worse. Earlier in 1640 he had met the electors at Nuremberg and agreed that the terms of the Peace of Prague would have to be modified if the Calvinists were to lay down their arms. He had also persuaded Maximilian that to secure a permanent settlement it might be worth relinquishing a portion of the Palatinate. Safe conducts therefore were issued to bring the Calvinists and even a representative of the former elector Palatine's family to the Diet.

The discussions went well from Ferdinand's point of view, both before and after Baner's incursion, until the arrival of the representatives of the new elector of Brandenburg. Frederick William was a twenty-year-old Calvinist who had been educated for a time at The Hague in company with the elector Palatine's children. Contemptuous of his father and of his policies, he had chosen to live outside Brandenburg and had had to be ordered home in December 1640 when George William was on his death bed. Frederick William recognised the difficulties under which his father had laboured in attempting to govern and defend a scattered and vulnerable patrimony: the Mark of Brandenburg was a battleground for the emperor and the Swedes, Pomerania was under Swedish occupation, Cleves was dominated by the Dutch and East Prussia was a fief of the king of Poland. He intended nonetheless to make something of his inheritance. Determined and opportunist, he was able to interpret the run of events more skilfully than his father had done, and, if rewarded on occasion with some remarkable good fortune, had at least the wit to recognise it when it came his way.

The one thing clear to Frederick William was that the Peace of Prague was of no advantage to Brandenburg. It guaranteed no conquests, since George William had made none, and it imposed on his people the burden of maintaining troops to serve an emperor who was unable to protect them from Sweden. Those of his father's advisers who had supported the peace were dismissed, and representatives were sent to Regensburg to denounce the 1635 settlement before the Diet. At the same time Frederick William began immediately to negotiate with the one power he believed capable of destroying his inheritance, and succeeded in securing a truce with Sweden in July 1641. Two months later these countries were formally at peace.

The effect of this was to rally to his side several Protestant princes whose objections to the 1635 settlement had found no champion in the elector of Saxony, who had been only too well pleased with its terms. The mood of the Diet began to change and, encouraged by this example of unilateral negotiation with an enemy, the members dared to question the emperor's proposals. Simultaneously, and independently of the Diet's deliberations, representatives of France, Sweden and the emperor agreed at Hamburg in December 1641 to begin their own negotiations for peace, holding separate meetings at Münster and Osnabrück to discuss matters relating to France and Sweden respectively.

No matter what was being debated at Regensburg or Hamburg, the war still went on. After Baner's death Wrangel tried to hold the fort, but with neither an inspiring commander nor pay the Swedish army mutinied and threatened to sign on with the Bernadines. In November Torstensson arrived to put matters right. Elderly and rheumatic, he was also very tough, very experienced and with a reputation for successful audacity which to some extent reconciled his men to the savage discipline he imposed. He brought with him 7000 native Swedes to form the nucleus of his army, and enough money to settle the mutiny. French subsidies had been increased that year to 480,000 reichstalers, and in addition the Swedish government had adopted the dangerous expedient of selling off crown land to pay for the war.

With his army reinforced and restored to obedience, Torstensson defeated the Saxons in 1642 at Schweidnitz. He then advanced nearly 200 miles to the south-east in an astonishing campaign through Silesia into the heart of Moravia, and his outriders pressed on to within twenty-five miles of Vienna before Piccolomini and the archduke Leopold had even began to organise their defences. Yet it was all to no avail.

Torstensson had overstretched his own lines of communication and had to retreat into Saxony – leaving a garrison in Olmutz, which successfully held this remarkably isolated outpost of the Swedish empire until 1650.

Leopold pursued him to Breitenfeld, where, for the second time in the war, the Swedes won a major victory. One quarter of the Imperial army was killed, another quarter recruited into the Swedish army, and Sweden once again enjoyed the fruits of military ascendancy. Leipzig paid 150,000 reichstalers to purchase immunity from Torstensson's men, and Sweden was able to make war pay for itself while the army, growing in numbers because of the loot to be had, began to raid further afield into the lands of the Habsburgs and their allies.

Throughout Torstensson's campaign the negotiations at Münster and Osnabrück in Westphalia hung fire. Until the disaster of Breitenfeld in November 1642 the emperor was convinced that events were moving satisfactorily his way and was in no mood to rush things: given time he hoped to see evidence of a split between Sweden and Brandenburg, and also between Sweden and Denmark. The French too bided their time, confident that the emperor would soon be defeated by Torstensson and would then have to reduce his terms. Matters were brought to a head when the elector of Mainz invited all the German princes to a conference at Frankfurt-on-Main, where Ferdinand hoped to settle his disputes with the Germans independently of France and Sweden. The latter powers, however, published an invitation to all German princes and cities to join their conferences with the emperor in Westphalia. The emperor forbade acceptance of the invitation, but Frederick William, recognising the advantages he might enjoy over the emperor with the Swedes at Osnabrück, ignored the ban. So too did Maximilian of Bavaria. His army, led by Franz von Mercy and his cavalry commander Werth, was beginning to recover its reputation and the emperor's need of its services increased Maximilian's bargaining power. He had also been given assurances by Mazarin that his rights in the Palatinate would not be questioned. By the spring of 1643, therefore, Ferdinand was compelled to agree that the Westphalian conferences should be accorded the status of a diet, so that whatever was determined there should become a law of the Empire.

June 1643 to August 1645

Rocroy left Spain so defenceless in Flanders that Ferdinand was obliged to send Piccolomini to help. In the meantime he depended increasingly on Maximilian's revitalised Bavarian army to hold south-west Germany, where Mercy and Werth fought brilliantly against the Bernadines.

More important to the Habsburg cause was the news of fighting between Sweden and Denmark. Christian had recovered from his humiliation at the hands of Wallenstein, and, lured by the offer of Bremen and Hamburg, had taken a few tentative steps towards a possible alliance with the emperor. Like the emperor, his prime concern was to weaken the power of Sweden. To this end he had tried to exploit Baner's difficulties with his mutinous troops in 1635, received with honour Gustav Adolf's widow after the failure of her attempt to marry Christina to a Danish prince, and planned with Olivares in 1639 a joint attack on Älvsborg. Oxenstierna commented fairly when he said of Christian that he had 'repeatedly tucked us under the chin to see if our teeth were still firm in our heads'. The latest dispute arose over the Sound dues. Sweden's exemption from these was not in question, but Denmark refused to exempt ships plying from Baltic ports under Swedish occupation and no longer countenanced the deception by which many Dutch ships sailed under a Swedish flag.

Late in the autumn of 1643 Oxenstierna ordered Torstensson to abandon a campaign in Silesia and take Denmark by surprise. By January Torstensson was master of the Danish mainland, waiting impatiently for the Little and Great Belts to freeze to allow his troops access across the ice to Copenhagen. Louis de Geer, the Dutch entrepreneur with a fortune invested in Swedish metallurgical industries, had commissioned a private fleet in the United Provinces which gave Sweden temporary command of the Sound and made easy the capture of Gotland and Osel, two islands belonging to Denmark which commanded shipping lanes in the eastern Baltic. Meanwhile Horn attacked the Danes in Skåne, one of the provinces of Danish-occupied Sweden, in the hope of reaching the coast and of launching an invasion across the Sound.

In the event, the Little Belt failed to freeze and Horn was delayed by unexpected resistence at Malmo. Torstensson was therefore trapped in the Jutland peninsula and, if Gallas, who had had the wit to chase after him, had also had the sense to keep sober, the emperor might well have recovered his influence in northern Germany. Torstensson left Wrangel to hold the mainland and with almost contemptuous ease gave Gallas the slip at Kiel. When Gallas turned to follow he defeated him.

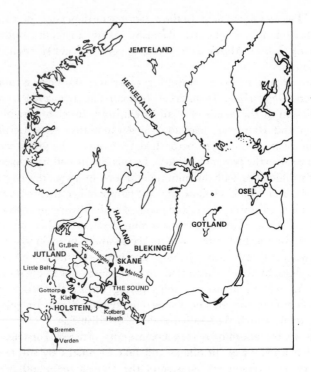

19. Denmark and Sweden

Denmark was therefore still in danger from Swedish armies in Jutland and Skåne, but Christian saved the day at sea. He drove off de Geer's fleet in May, and for several weeks engaged the Swedish navy in a running battle among the Danish islands. The battle reached its climax on 1 July off Kolberg Heath, between Kiel Fjord and the island of Fehmarn. The Danes were driven into the fjord, but the Swedish admiral was killed and Christian, though wounded, was able to conclude the action victoriously.

Sweden's attack on Denmark was unpopular in Paris. Mazarin objected that French subsidies designed to achieve the defeat of the emperor were being misappropriated to finance a private vendetta between the Baltic powers, but he dared not repudiate the alliance, because other events in Germany were causing him anxiety. Maximilian of Bavaria could not be won from his alliance with Ferdinand, and the best of the French army, exultant after its victories over Spain, was being defeated in the Black Forest by Mercy and Werth. Moreover, a Spanish embassy had arrived at Münster. Mazarin was content to discuss peace terms within the Empire, but it was vital to French interests elsewhere that Spain be excluded from the negotiations, since even the briefest of truces might allow Philip IV the opportunity to settle his finances and restore order to the Iberian peninsula before resuming the war with France. Consequently in March 1644 the duke of Longueville, who led the French delegation, refused to meet the Spanish ambassador, on the grounds that his credentials credited Philip IV with the titles of king of Navarre and duke of Barcelona, both of which the French claimed for Louis XIV.

The Spaniards vigorously opposed the manoeuvre to exclude them. Not only were they alive to the advantages of a truce, but in addition they were anxious to be present at all the negotiations, to ensure that the emperor did not abandon their interests in the Rhineland. This was the serious reality behind the superficial disputes about protocol which delayed the formal opening of the Westphalian conferences until December 1644, and which prevented any real business being achieved in 1645. Procedural disputes also reflected the ambivalent views of the countries represented at the conferences. Salvius and Johann Oxenstierna, for example, represented two opposed factions in the Swedish government, the one anxious to negotiate, the other seeking to prolong the war. Similarly, of the Dutch delegation, Knuyt of Zeeland and Pauw of Holland advocated war and peace respectively. On more trivial grounds, d'Avaux and Servien, the two assistants to the duke of Longueville, were so jealous of each other that they could not bring themselves to agree on anything and each insisted on reporting separately to Mazarin.

Although 1645 was a year in which little seemed to be achieved in Westphalia, it was a time of great danger for Austria. Torstensson invaded Silesia in February, and was advancing rapidly across Bohemia with Imperial and Bavarian troops on his flank when he challenged and defeated them at Jankau. In addition, as a result of Swedish and French diplomacy, George Racoczy of Transylvania followed the example of his predecessor Bethlen Gabor and invaded Habsburg Hungary, to be acclaimed by the Protestant nobility. Ferdinand rushed to Vienna to organise its defences and awaited with anxiety the junction of the two invading armies. The day was saved by the garrison at Brünn in Moravia, which held out for five months against Torstensson and made it impossible for him to join Racoczy and the Hungarians. Racoczy abandoned the struggle and the emperor purchased peace in Hungary by the Treaty of Linz, which guaranteed full freedom of worship to the Protestants.

Attracted by the news that the Bavarian cavalry was engaged in Bohemia, Turenne invaded the Upper Palatinate in the spring of 1645, only to be defeated at Mergentheim by Mercy, who had been reinforced at the last moment by Werth and the battered survivors of Jankau. Later in the summer the French tried again. Enghien, with Swedish reinforcements, forced his way through to the Danube and challenged the Bavarians at Allerheim, near Nördlingen. Both sides suffered heavy casualties. Mercy was killed and his troops withdrew, leaving Enghien to claim a victory which in fact gained him no advantage, since the Bavarians still held the line of the Danube at Donauwörth. Both Maximilian and Ferdinand could therefore congratulate themselves on surviving a year of danger and invasion.

Sweden and Denmark meanwhile had been negotiating a peace settlement at Brömsebro. Christina had come of age in the previous year, a determined and intelligent girl who recognised that Sweden was being impoverished by warfare, and especially by warfare in regions so widely scattered as Jutland, Bavaria and Moravia. She recognised too that until peace had been achieved she could not afford to dispense with Oxenstierna. As a first step therefore, and with the *riksdag*'s support, she opened negotiations with Christian of Denmark, though as a daughter of Gustav Adolf she wanted to retain every acre acquired since 1643. Christian had no bargaining power at his disposal save Christina's own determination to end the fighting, but she was brought to modify her terms to some slight extent by Dutch and French intervention – the French wanting Sweden to settle quickly with Denmark in order to renew the war in Germany, the Dutch afraid that Sweden was already too powerful in the Baltic and might endanger their vital commercial interests.

The Treaty of Brömsebro, concluded in August 1645, secured substantial gains, including the strategically valuable islands of Gotland and Osel, and the provinces of Jemteland and Herjedalen, whose acquisition provided Sweden with the great natural frontier of the Kiolen Range against Norway. Free trade between Sweden and Denmark was abolished, because Sweden was now expanding her own mercantile marine and saw no reason to allow the Danes advantages in Swedish-controlled ports. On the other hand, she insisted on exemption from the Sound dues for herself and for all the ports in her empire. In pledge of this Denmark had to concede for a period of thirty years the south-western province of Halland, which brought Sweden at last to the shores of the Sound. Finally, the dioceses of Bremen and Verden, administered by Christian's son, were to remain under Swedish occupation.

The Dutch were relieved that Sweden had not acquired sole control of the Sound and immediately offered diplomatic support to the Danes, at the price of a reduction in the dues on their shipping. Mazarin too felt the need to counterbalance Swedish power in the Baltic by making an alliance with Denmark, and promised Christian that France would endeavour to recover Bremen and Verden for his son. As for Sweden, the treaty was of the utmost importance, since, unlike the successes achieved in Germany, the acquisition of Halland, Herjedalan and Jemteland were to be of permanent value. Once the treaty had been concluded, Christina applied her energy to the deliberations in baulk at Osnabrück and to force the emperor's hand made a separate truce with John George of Saxony at Katschenbroda.

With Brandenburg and Saxony lost to him, and Bavaria restless under the pressure of French inducements, Ferdinand recognised that he had lost the substantial advantages he had enjoyed as emperor in the year of his accession. Spain as an ally was now a broken reed, making demands which Ferdinand could no longer meet, while his own kingdoms of Austria, Bohemia and Hungary were again subject to annual invasion. As the winter began, therefore, he determined to bring the war to an end and, by sending his chief adviser, Trautmannsdorf, as a plenipotentiary to Westphalia, gave other princes confidence in the sincerity of his intentions.

6

The Making of Settlements
1645–60

The conclusion of the Eighty Years War 1645–8

The federal assembly of the United Provinces, the States-General, was not a sovereign body. Its members were the spokesmen of their own individual and sovereign provinces, and their unanimity was necessary before action could be authorised. To avoid general paralysis of the administration, the tradition of unanimity, observed at all levels of government, had given rise to another tradition, by which the dissentient voices to a majority decision were won over by the chairman of each committee or assembly. Sir William Temple, during a tour of duty in the United Provinces, thought this to be an admirable practice: 'In these Assemblies, tho' all are equal in voices, and one hinders a result, yet it seldom happens but that united by a common bond of interest, and having all one common end of public good, they come after full debates to easy resolutions . . . so as the smaller part seldom contests hard and long what the greater agrees of.'

Temple exaggerated the reasonableness of Dutch politics. More typical perhaps was a case in 1639 when Amsterdam was in dispute with the States-General over the issue of naval licences. The States-General sent a deputation to state its case, but the Amsterdam council refused to meet it, on the grounds that its members 'were not competent to be received in the council, still less so with the object of making proposition to an individual member of the Assembly of Holland, without the knowledge of the Estates of that province, which was a sovereign assembly and was only in alliance with the States-General'.

The sovereignty of an individual province, invoked so readily in a minor dispute over naval licences, was of paramount importance in matters of war and peace, where each campaign had to be financed by the separate agreement of each province and treaties endorsed in the same manner. Since Holland provided over half of the republic's income, her voice was generally respected, but not always obeyed. She was vulnerable, for example, if the inland provinces failed to pay their contributions to the navy, which was supplied almost entirely from the dockyards of Holland, and could retaliate only by threatening to withhold her contribution to the army. The mediatory role of the House of Orange was, therefore, of considerable importance. As captain-general, as admiral-general and as stadtholder in five of the seven provinces, Frederick Henry was well placed to build up a party in federal committees to give central direction to the war with Spain. In particular he had won control of a small standing committee of the States-General for the direction of foreign policy; the members of this committee were bound by an oath of secrecy not to divulge information even to their own provinces – until 1643, when the Estates of Holland forbade their representatives to take the oath, thus demonstrating their suspicion of the House of Orange and affirming the principle of provincial sovereignty.

Frederick Henry lived in a manner wholly at odds with the sober republicanism of Holland's regents. He built palaces, made royal marriages for his children, maintained a lively court and was attended by the nobility of several countries. So effectively did his public appearance disguise his status as the servant of the Estates that it was feared he might resolve the anomaly by arrogating sovereignty to himself. The French, indeed, no longer addressed him as Excellency but as Highness, a term properly reserved only for *Hun Hoogmogenden*, Their High Mightinesses of the States-General, and it was rumoured that with French support he was planning to make Antwerp an independent principality for his own family. All manner of complaint was therefore made against him by the Estates of Holland. His capture of Sas van Gent in 1644 was compared unfavourably with the achievement of the French, who had followed up their victory at Rocroy (see p. 163) by storming across southern Flanders, taking Gravelines, Mardyck, Cassel, Ypres and Menin. At the same time he was condemned by the counter-remonstrants for advocating religious toleration in the south, and was unfairly blamed for the clauses in the treaty of 1635 which had abandoned the Walloon provinces to France.

The States-General had already had to intervene between Frederick Henry and the Estates of Holland to insist upon Dutch neutrality in the English Civil War, but the prince continued to seek ways of helping the House of Stuart. The outbreak of war between Sweden and Denmark in 1644 brought matters to a head (see p. 169). Since Christian had declared for Charles I, Frederick Henry resolved that the United Provinces should support him against Sweden. The regents of Holland took the opposite view. Of all the United Provinces, Holland relied the most on the Baltic trade and objected the most strongly to Danish control of the Sound, especially when Christian rescinded the convention by which Dutch ships sailing from Baltic ports under Swedish occupation were exempted from the Sound dues. Many of the regents, moreover, had invested heavily in Sweden and supported Louis de Geer, who raised a private fleet to clear the Sound. Holland therefore welcomed Sweden's request for an alliance against Denmark, and it was only by exerting his personal influence with the Zeeland delegates that Frederick Henry was able to prevent unanimity on the matter in the States-General. In 1645 Holland took her revenge, withholding her subsidies for the army until the prince agreed that a fleet of 300 merchantmen be convoyed through the Sound without paying dues to Denmark. When the war ended in the Treaty of Brömsebro, however, the Estates of Holland began to fear that too much power had passed to Sweden and, perversely, blamed this upon Frederick Henry.

At the same time the Dutch, out of jealousy and frustration, were becoming disenchanted with the French alliance. French troops had advanced only too successfully along the Flemish coast, while Frederick Henry made little headway in the north. In 1645 he prepared to march on Antwerp, but at the last moment he diverted his troops towards Ghent, having heard that several influential families were ready to have the gates opened at his arrival. Since Ghent lay in the region assigned to France under the treaty of 1635, he first sought French permission to exploit the opportunity and, if successful, to occupy the city until a final settlement was negotiated. Although the French agreed, a French detachment nonetheless appeared near the city as the Dutch approached, and Frederick Henry immediately withdrew, too indignant at the apparent duplicity of his allies to consider the possibility of a joint attack.

To crown it all, the French took Dunkirk. For many years this nest of privateers had hampered Dutch shipping, and it was aggravating beyond measure that, just when Spain was in decline, it should pass into the hands of a powerful and unreliable ally. The mood was exploited by the Spanish government, whose only thought was to end the Dutch war in order to defend itself against France. Its agents therefore spread rumours that France was negotiating a separate peace and that Louis

XIV planned to marry the infanta and exchange Catalonia for the Spanish Netherlands.

The peace party in the United Provinces was most strongly entrenched in Holland, and especially in Amsterdam, where Andreas Bicker and his colleagues maintained that there were greater profits to be made by legitimate trade than by war and piracy. This was patently true of the Baltic trade, which was the staple of Dutch commerce, but it was now claimed that the principle applied equally to the East and West Indies. As early as 1644 the directors of the Delft chamber of the East India Company had agreed, 'a merchant would do better honourably to increase his talent and send rich cargoes from Asia to the Netherlands instead of carrying out costly territorial conquests which are more suitable for crowned heads and mighty monarchs than for merchants greedy of gain'.

The privateers of Zeeland disputed the case, as did the directors of the West India Company, which had made itself master of the slave markets of Brazil and the colony of New Netherlands in north America. The company, however, was 18 million florins in debt, and its position had been complicated by the success of the Portuguese rebellion. Where the directors and the privateers wanted to pursue the conflict with Portugal in South America, Bicker and his colleagues – having sold their shares in the company most profitably after the exploits of Piet Heyn – preferred to trade legitimately with an independent Portugal and thereby have access both to Brazil and to the salt pans of Setubal.

Another issue which was hotly debated was the future of Antwerp. In Amsterdam the regents concluded that to restore the southern city to its former independence was only to create a formidable rival to their own. Frederick Henry's determination to liberate the city was therefore no longer applauded as a legitimate war aim but condemned as a self-seeking ploy to provide the House of Orange with the nucleus of an independent principality. Thereafter Frederick Henry was made the scapegoat for all the problems of the past few years, and a flood of pamphlets exaggerated the antithesis between princes who lived only by war and a merchant class which sought peace for everyone. The Delft directors had contrasted the military ambitions of crowned heads with the peaceful desires of 'merchants greedy for gain', and a contemporary dissertation on the state of France pointed the relevant moral. While the nobility ruled France, it claimed, 'nothing is to be hoped for the common man; the commons there would be happy indeed if they could live under a republic in which the common man does not suffer too much from wars and may live quietly in peace with his family in his own home'.

The propaganda was successful. Despite its treaty with France, the States-General ordered Pauw to negotiate peace with the Spanish representatives at Münster, and by the end of 1646 a treaty had been drafted which won the assent of all but the privateers of Zeeland and the strict Calvinists of Utrecht. The latter were hopelessly confused. Though they would not settle with Spain neither could they approve the alliance with Catholic France. The death of Frederick Henry in March 1647 removed the one man capable of waging war in the field and of mobilising support for it in the States-General. The new prince, William II, enjoyed nothing of his father's influence and the peace party carried the day.

At the eleventh hour there were alarming indications of a Spanish military revival in Flanders, where the new governor, the archduke Leopold, recovered Armentières, Commines and Lens in 1647; but Spain was so anxious to defend herself from France that she had no wish to delay a settlement with the Dutch. In the event she even accepted the States-General's demand that s'Hertogenbosch be ceded and that no guarantees for Roman Catholics be written into the treaty. As a result, Europe was taken aback in January 1648 to learn of the sudden conclusion of the Treaty of Münster to end the Eighty Years War between Spain and her former subjects of the Netherlands. By the treaty

(1) the United Provinces were recognised as independent;
(2) the Scheldt remained closed, so that Antwerp remained permanently blockaded;
(3) Dutch conquests in Flanders and Brabant, including Maastricht and s'Hertogenbosch, were confirmed, without any protection for their Roman Catholic populations; and
(4) Dutch conquests overseas were also confirmed, along with the right to trade freely in both the East and the West Indies.

The terms were more favourable to the Dutch than any offered or sought in 1609, but ratification by the States-General was delayed for several months until the delegates of Zeeland and Utrecht finally agreed to accept the verdict of the majority. So it was that the Portugese ambassador was able to record, in a moving despatch of June 1648, that 'the peace was proclaimed here . . . at ten o'clock on the morning of the fifth of this month, that day and hour being chosen because on that day and at that time eighty years ago the counts of Egmont and Hoorn had been executed by the duke of Alva in Brussels, and the States wished their freedom to begin at the same day and time as these two gentlemen had died in defence thereof'.

The making of the Peace of Westphalia 1645–54

Trautmannsdorf arrived in Westphalia in December 1643 with orders from the emperor to secure a settlement (see p. 173). His bargaining position had already been undermined by the unilateral action of Frederick William of Brandenburg and John George of Saxony (see p. 173). It was weakened further by Maximilian of Bavaria, whose suspicion of Spain's intentions in the Rhineland was so intense that he failed to discern the ambitions of France in that quarter. Consequently, with French and Swedish troops on the loose in his own duchy, he urged Trautmannsdorf to ignore the interests of Spain and surrender with all speed to the demands of France and Sweden. These two countries, moreover, had recognised the advantage to be gained by maintaining a united front against the emperor, and their refusal to sell each other short, despite many private disagreements, explains the magnitude of the concessions which Trautmannsdorf was compelled to make during the following years.

Mazarin did not oppose a general settlement of German affairs provided that it excluded Spain and left her isolated in her war with France and the United Provinces. He also intended to drive a hard bargain to extend French influence in the Rhineland. For more than two years Trautmannsdorf refused to yield in principle over Spain, but finally accepted in practice that Charles of Lorraine, as Spain's co-belligerent against France, should not be admitted to the negotiations. In the duke's absence it was agreed that France remain in occupation of Moyenvic, Baccarat and Rambervillers and retain the bishoprics of Metz, Toul and Verdun, ceded in 1559.

Further south, the French demands for the Breisgau and the forest cantons east of Basel were rejected. Instead the emperor ceded his rights and possessions in the Sundgau and Lower Alsace – the more readily perhaps because Lower Alsace did not belong to him. Those drafting the treaty therefore had a difficult time defining the nature of French sovereignty in the bishopric and city of Strassburg and in the six other free cities which retained their membership of the Diet. Mazarin, untroubled by the small print, which he was confident he could interpret to his own advantage at a later date, claimed a seat for France in the Diet; when this was refused he secured by way of compensation Breisach, Philippsburg and other important centres on the right bank of the Rhine.

The French demands seemed almost modest in comparison with Sweden's opening bid for an indemnity of 12 million reichstalers, Silesia, Pomerania and nearly every former bishopric in northern Germany. For domestic reasons Christina was anxious to conclude the war; she was also determined to honour her father's claims for *assecuratio* and *satisfactio* (see p. 126) and declared in addition that the religious and political situation pertaining in 1618 should be restored.

In these circumstances it took two years to settle the problem of Pomerania alone. Though no one could drive the Swedes from the duchy, Frederick William refused to abandon his claim to it and demonstrated once again his ability to play a weak hand consummately well. He married into the House of Orange to win Dutch support for his interests in Cleves, and persuaded Mazarin that Brandenburg should be made powerful enough to prevent any future expansion of Imperial power into northern Germany. He then offered to partition Pomerania, accepting the eastern section, despite its lack of ports, in return for compensation elsewhere. The Dutch, in order to deny Sweden at least one section of the German coastline, approved the plan; so too did Mazarin. As a result of their representations, Trautmannsdorf finally agreed to confirm the elector's rights in Cleves, Mark and Ravensburg (see p. 44) and awarded him the dioceses of Halberstadt and Minden, to strengthen Ravensburg; the diocese of Cammin with the port of Kolberg, adjacent to Pomerania; and the reversion to Magdeburg on the death of its existing administrator. In this way Frederick William acquired territory much greater in extent than that surrendered to Sweden and of greater strategic importance for the future, because it established a series of links in a chain binding the Rhineland duchies to Brandenburg.

Once Brandenburg had been settled, Sweden secured control of the mouths of the Oder, the Elbe and the Weser by the emperor's recognition of her occupation of the islands of Rügen, Usedom and Wollin, along with Stettin, Stralsund, Wismar, western Pomerania and the bishoprics of Bremen and Verden. As ruler of these last three she was allowed three seats in the Diet, but not the electoral title she had hoped for, and Bremen had an additional value as 'a bridle for the Jute', a base from which to threaten Denmark. The demand for Silesia, from which to check a hostile Poland, was refused, and in consequence Sweden demanded a larger indemnity. It was on this issue that negotiations ground to a halt in the winter of 1647–8.

While the principal bases for a final settlement were being laid in 1646 and 1647, the fighting went on remorselessly, the appetite for plunder unassuaged. There was political calculation too, since a victory conferred valuable advantages in the conference halls of Westphalia. In this respect it was France and Sweden who profited the most.

In 1646 a French army advanced across the Spanish Netherlands to take Courtrai and Dunkirk; a second occupied Elba and launched an attack on Naples; a third, in company with Swedish troops desperate for loot, invaded Bavaria to compel Maximilian to withdraw from the war. So widespread was the devastation that Maximilian lost heart and in March 1647, by the Armistice of Ulm, Bavaria, Cologne and the members of the Franconian and Swabian Circles declared their neutrality. It availed them nothing. Since the Bavarian troops led by Werth were taken into Imperial service, those of Sweden and France refused to withdraw, and when Maximilian learned that the Protestant princes and Sweden sought the restoration of the elector Palatine he hastily renewed his alliance with the emperor.

Charles Louis, son of the former Elector Palatine, presented the negotiators with one of their most difficult problems. The emperor was pledged to support Maximilian and to leave the Rhenish Palatinate available for the use of Spain. France and Sweden, on the other hand, had so frequently committed themselves to Charles Louis's restoration that they could scarcely back down in negotiating the final settlement. A compromise was mooted. Maximilian was to retain his electoral title and the Upper Palatinate; Charles Louis would have an electoral title created for him and recover the Lower Palatinate.

None of this gave satisfaction to Spain. Her exclusion from the negotiations, the extension of French influence in Alsace and Lorraine and the plan to reinstate a Calvinist in the Lower Palatinate were nothing less than disastrous, nor was the catalogue of bad news yet complete. In 1647, for the sixth time in less than a hundred years, the government declared itself bankrupt: in Naples, where the harvest of 1646 had failed disastrously, the efforts of the viceroy, Arcos, to finance an attack on Elba by imposing new food taxes on a famine-stricken population provoked rebellion. Masaniello, a young fisherman whose mother had been punished for smuggling corn, led the attack on the viceregal palace, emptied the prisons and compelled Arcos to rescind all taxes. When Masaniello, driven insane by the gratification of his lust for power, was assassinated by a former supporter, the rebellion lost momentum, but the countryside remained in turmoil throughout the summer. It was not until April 1648 that Arcos was able to restore his authority.

In January 1648, the treaty of Münster (see p. 178) took everyone by surprise but did not stop the war. French and Swedish troops defeated the Bavarians at Zusmarshausen and systematically devastated the duchy for the second year running, to punish Maximilian for failing to remain neutral. The French also won a great victory at Lens in the Spanish Netherlands and the Swedes invaded Bohemia. In Bohemia, however, the mood of the people had changed: the Swedish invasions since 1639 had aroused such horror that, in the popular mind, the emperor had come to represent security and the hope of peace. When the Swedes occupied the Kleinseite opposite the citadel of Prague, it was the citizens themselves, for the first time in the seventeenth century, who rallied against the enemy at their gates. Throughout the summer they held on grimly, praying for relief or news of a peace settlement. The German princes did the same, and the delegate from Brandenburg spoke for all in affirming that Germany's suffering should not have to be prolonged 'until Spain and France had finished their game'.

Mazarin in fact was only too ready to hasten the end, since his victories were achieved at the price of serious disaffection at home. He had raised loans between 1643 and 1645 on such a scale that government expenditure reached its peak for the entire war. Thereafter, since he could not increase the revenue from taxation to service these loans, further loans were denied him and he was forced to sell more offices, withhold the salaries of the *officiers* and invent new taxes – expedients which did little to ward off bankruptcy but a great deal to bring dissatisfaction to a head. When the Paris *parlement* was asked to approve his measures, its members, in a manner without precedent, united with those of the other sovereign courts (the *chambre des comptes*, the *cour des aides* and the *grand conseil*) in May 1648 to prepare a manifesto of their grievances. They referred to the suffering of the peasantry and, at greater length, to the non-payment of their own salaries and the sale and reduplication of offices: more significantly, they condemned not only the government's financial policies but also the employment of intendants to take over so much of their administrative duties (see p. 162).

Faced with the united opposition of his senior civil servants, judges and officials, and aware that their manifesto was acclaimed everywhere as the true voice of the people, Mazarin hastily withdrew the offending edicts and recalled his intendants. By the end of the summer the government was virtually bankrupt.

If France were to wage war successfully with Spain, and without the aid of the Dutch, who had made their own peace, she had to extricate herself without delay from the German war, on the terms already agreed with Trautmannsdorf. Once this was realised in Westphalia, the Swedish government, unwilling to be left on its own, became more accommodating about the indemnity, and with all the representatives under orders to complete the work the few outstanding matters were speedily resolved. Sweden settled for 5 million reichstalers, Calvinism was officially recognised in the Empire and 1624 was agreed upon as the date after which land taken from the Catholic Church would have to be restored – a solution favourable to the Protestants except, by special exclusion, in Bavaria and the Habsburg lands, where the rulers had already recovered every acre of secularised land. Though Sweden and France failed to secure a ban on the election of a Habsburg as emperor, there was general agreement that the election of a king of the Romans should not take place in the emperor's lifetime. The most serious concession wrung from Trautmannsdorf was that the members of the Empire, including the emperor, were to be neutral in the war between France and Spain, even if Franche Comté, itself a member of the Diet, were invaded by France.

All the agreements and compromises negotiated since Traut-mannsdorf's arrival in December 1645 were finally put together in the two treaties of Münster and Osnabrück (see p. 167) and agreed to in October 1648 for ratification by the governments concerned in February 1649. These two treaties, along with the Treaty of Münster between Spain and the United Provinces and the Treaty of Brömesbro (1645) provided or confirmed solutions to nearly every international crisis which had occurred in the first half of the seventeenth century. Indeed, around these terms and their elucidation could be written the history of European conflict since the death of Philip II.

The main points of what was collectively to be known as the Peace of Westphalia may be summarised as follows.

1. To all intents and purposes the separate states of the Holy Roman Empire were recognised as sovereign members of the Diet, free to

20. The making of the Peace of Westphalia

control their own affairs independently of each other and of the emperor.

2. The principle of *cuius regio, eius religio* was reaffirmed, but construed to relate only to public life, so that attendance at the established church was no longer compulsory and freedom of private worship was permitted. Moreover, any subsequent change of religion by the ruler was not to affect that of his subjects.

3. Calvinism was recognised within the Confession of Augsburg and was thus protected by the Augsburg settlement of 1555. The Edict of Restitution, shelved in 1635, was abandoned and, except within the Bavarian and Austrian lands, the retention of all land secularised before 1624 was allowed.

4. In matters of religion there were to be no majority decisions taken by the Diet. Instead both sides were to meet separately to prepare their cases and disputes were to be settled only by compromise.

5. Maximilian retained his electoral title and the Upper Palatinate. His family retained the bishoprics of Osnabrück and Paderborn.

6. A new electoral title was created for Charles Louis on his restoration to the Lower Palatinate.
7. John George of Saxony was confirmed in his acquisition of Lusatia.
8. The terms of the Treaty of Xanten (1614), assigning Cleves, Mark and Ravensburg to the elector of Brandenburg, were confirmed. In addition, Frederick William acquired eastern Pomerania and the bishoprics of Cammin, Minden and Halberstadt, along with the succession to Magdeburg.

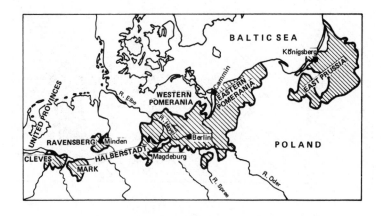

21. Brandenburg 1648–60

9. The emperor's claim to hereditary rights in Bohemia, Moravia and Silesia was established. The Sundgau was surrendered to France.
10. The duke of Nevers was confirmed in his inheritance of Mantua, Montferrat and Casale (Treaty of Cherasco, 1631).
11. Sweden had acquired her mainland provinces of Jemteland, Herjedalen and Halland, with the islands of Gotland and Osel by the Treaty of Brömsebro (1645). The Peace of Westphalia confirmed her control of the river-mouths of the Oder, the Elbe and Weser – virtually the entire German coastline – by the occupation of western Pomerania, Stettin, Stralsund, Wismar, the dioceses of Bremen and Verden and the islands of Rügen, Usedom and Wollin. She was paid an indemnity of 5 million reichstalers.
12. France acquired the Sundgau and, in effect, Lower Alsace, though the six free cities along with the city and bishopric of Strassburg retained their membership of the Diet. In Lorraine, her occupation

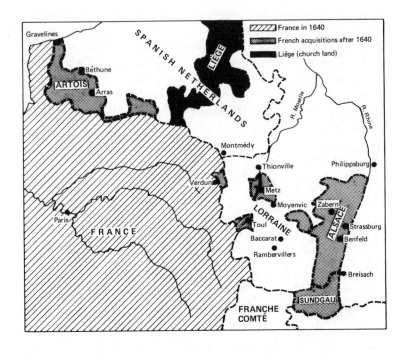

22. *French gains on the north-eastern frontier 1643–59*

of the bishoprics of Metz, Toul and Verdun (Treaty of Câteau-Cambrésis, 1559) was confirmed, along with her more recent gains of Moyenvic, Baccarat and Rambervillers. Other acquisitions included Pinerolo in Savoy, and Breisach, Philippsburg, Zabern and Benfeld on the right bank of the Rhine.

13. The United Provinces were declared independent of Spain and also of the Holy Roman Empire. The Dutch retained their conquests overseas and in the Spanish Netherlands, including Maastricht and the meiery of s'Hertogensbosch, without any guarantees of the rights of Roman Catholics. They were to trade freely in the East and West Indies but Antwerp remained under blockade.

14. Spain was excluded from the Westphalian settlement. Having been forced to give way on all points to the Dutch, her position in the Rhineland was substantially weakened by the French acquisitions and by the restoration of the elector Palatine. The apportioning of Lorraine was determined without reference to Spain or to her ally

the duke. Left alone in her war with France, no prince of the Empire, not even the emperor himself, might come to her aid, unless Imperial territory was involved – and for this purpose Franche Comté, despite its membership of the Diet, was specifically excluded.

It was easy to criticise the peace for its betrayal of the religious principles inherent in the conflict. Pope Innocent X uttered his formal condemnation of it as 'null, void, invalid, iniquitous, unjust, damnable, reprobate, inane, empty of meaning and effect for all time'. More poignantly, the Bohemian scholar Comenius gave vent to the cry of the Calvinist exile: 'They have sacrificed us at the treaties of Osnabrück. . . . I conjure you by the wounds of Christ that you do not forsake us who are persecuted for the sake of Christ.' But the truth of the matter was expressed by an anonymous writer: 'This war has lasted so long that they [the German princes] have left it more out of exhaustion than from a sense of right behaviour.'

What, then, had been achieved? The remarkable thing was that within the Empire so little had been changed. Alsace and western Pomerania were now in foreign hands; Saxony, Brandenburg and Bavaria had increased their territory, the elector Palatine had lost much of his, and Bohemia had been brought entirely under the control of Austria. Apart from this, the situation established in 1648 was fundamentally that of 1618. The Catholic powers had hoped to recover the land secularised since 1559, the emperor to revive Imperial authority, and Sweden to control the destinies of the German Protestants; but none of these ambitions was achieved. The Empire remained, as it had been since 1559, an untidy collection of autonomous states, some Catholic, some Protestant. If the fighting had stopped in 1621, in 1629, or even in 1635, there might have been many changes to record, but its wearisome prolongation had finally brought Germany full circle, to perpetuate for another hundred years the political fragmentation of the past hundred.

Yet there were some significant differences of emphasis and direction. The Palatinate was not again to be the hub of international Calvinist politics; and, if Saxony was a spent force, Brandenburg was a potent new one. The efforts of Ferdinand II to impose Imperial authority, of a kind which no emperor had exercised for centuries, came near to success in 1629 and 1635, but the oligarchic, federalist, centrifugal forces within the Empire, assisted by the armies of Sweden and France, had rendered vain his unifying, authoritarian and monarchic aspirations, and, in so doing, had ensured the survival of religious diversity within the Empire.

Ferdinand III accepted this because his ambitions lay in a different direction. As head of the House of Austria, his power had been strengthened by the years of war. Hungary was a problem that had yet to be solved, but the other 'hereditary lands' had been reduced to order. In Bohemia and, no less important, in Upper and Lower Austria, the Estates had been deprived of their powers, the administration was centralised on Vienna and religious uniformity was established. In addition, Ferdinand was recognised as the hereditary sovereign of Bohemia, Moravia and Silesia. The contrast between the overall position of Ferdinand III and that of Rudolf or Matthias indicates the full measure of the revolution which had taken place. The price, in territorial terms, had not been high – Lusatia, sold to Saxony for support against the Bohemian rebels, and the Sundgau; Trautmannsdorf had brilliantly contrived that the gains of Sweden and France were made at the expense of powers other than Austria. Consequently, the Austrian house of Habsburg was left free to fulfil its dynastic ambition outside the Empire, to make Austria once again the Eastern March against the Osmanli Turks, and, in pursuit of its mission to liberate Hungary, to create the Danubian monarchy.

Mazarin had secured the creation of a separate Estate for the Imperial Free Cities, in the belief that they would constitute a powerful force to restrain the emperor; 'it is principally they who have the money, the lands and the munitions of war'. Events proved him wrong. The great days of the Free Cities had long been over, and their political authority declined further as the virtual withdrawal of the emperor from the direction of Imperial affairs allowed the princes to assume the dominant rôle.

Economic trends and differences of emphasis are less easy to discern than shifts in political power and are the subject of considerable debate. That there was misery endured throughout the hideous progession of campaigns and sieges, with the slaughter, plague and famine which attended them, cannot be questioned. It was not, however, so widespread or devastating as was sometimes put about later by propagandists to heighten the achievement of their princes in creating prosperity out of adversity. Not only is it impossible to assume a uniform condition, whether of improvement or of decline, before or after the wars; but there is also disagreement about the nature of the evidence and how to interpret it (see *The Thirty Years War*, ed. T. K. Rabb).

Population figures for example, even when reliable, are not always interpreted in the same way. A fall in numbers, evidence of deaths or permanent migration to one historian, is taken by another to indicate merely a temporary evacuation or a failure to investigate correctly the compensatory number of births.

Much of the decline, where evidence of decline can be established, is often attributed to events preceding the outbreak of war; most regional studies, however, leave little doubt that in the areas selected for scrutiny the consequences of the war itself were disastrous. Though the warfare was destructive it was not universal. The areas worst affected were those of the greatest strategic importance – the Saxon plain, the Rhine crossings, the roads across the Black Forest and those leading to Vienna and Prague. Hamburg, Bremen, Lübeck and Danzig, on the other hand, grew rich from the war and were spared the presence of enemy troops within their gates.

Whatever the precise nature and extent of the economic consequences of the German wars, the conclusion of the conflict was the prerequisite of recovery, and recovery could be surprisingly rapid. A good harvest safely gathered in made all the difference: wooden houses were rebuilt, traders moved freely across the land and births began to outnumber deaths. The danger was that the Westphalian settlement might not hold as the means of implementing its details were worked out at Nuremberg between April 1649 and June 1651. Troops might refuse to disband because there was not enough money to pay them off or because they could envisage no way of life other than that of warfare and plunder. More dangerous to the peace of the Empire was the ambition of a commander or of a government which might start it all off again. Spain was angry at her exclusion from the settlement and might feel justified in renewing the war in the Rhineland, and Karl Gustav, Christina's heir-presumptive, had military ambitions which were thwarted by the peace.

In the event, the bankrupt condition of Spain and the desire of Mazarin, Christina and Ferdinand III to address themselves to domestic problems ensured the execution of the treaties. Negotiations went on at Nuremberg until June 1651, Frederick William made an abortive raid on Jülich in that year, Spain retained Frankenthal until 1653 – when the emperor offered to cede Besançon, an enclave within Franche Comté – and the last Swedish garrison outside northern Germany was not withdrawn until 1654; but for most Germans it was the harvest of 1650 which was celebrated as the first fruits of the peace.

On 22 August 1650, in the city of Ulm and throughout its neighbouring villages, thanksgiving feasts and services were held, when the memories of past sufferings and the hope of a peaceful future were alike commemorated in a prayer written specially to be said in every pulpit.

We thank you, Dear Lord, that you have given us peace after years of suffering turmoil and war, and that you have granted our pleas. We thank you for pulling us like a brand out of the fire, allowing us to rescue our life almost as if it were itself war booty. . . . Oh Lord, you have indeed treated us with mercy that our city and lands, which had previously been full of fear and horror, are now full of joy and happiness. We beseech you, who has saved us from the sword, mercifully to let our corn grow again, that we may multiply and prosper once more. . . . Oh God, the lover of peace, grant us henceforth permanent peace and leave our boundaries and houses in calm and peace that the voice of the war messenger shall not frighten us and the man of war touch us not.

Postscript I: *The United Provinces and the Treaty of Westminster 1654*

With the signing of the Treaty of Münster the Dutch entered upon their golden age. Their international authority was sustained by their primacy as a commercial nation, and both were reflected in a lively, self-confident culture, characterised especially by the works of Rembrandt, Hals and Vermeer and an astonishing number of genre painters. No people could have been more proud of the independence they had achieved and the wealth they had acquired; none could have taken more delight in their landscapes, their cities and themselves. Before the passion faded they employed artists in great number to hold a mirror to their achievement, to show them themselves and to immortalise the present. The great age of the United Provinces thus found eternal expression in the great age of Dutch art.

The peace satisfied nearly everyone but William II, who wanted to avenge the execution of his father-in-law, Charles I of England, renew the alliance with France against Spain and keep the House of Orange in the forefront of Dutch politics. The Estates of Holland, on the other hand, were burdened with their own debt of over 140 million florins and looked for economies to be made. At their insistence the States-General immediately reduced the army from 55,000 to 32,000, but William, by playing upon the prejudices and anxieties of the nobility and of the Calvinist clergy, prevented further cuts from being made in 1649. The regents of Holland therefore refused to pay the regiments maintained out of Holland's contribution to the federal government. Indeed, they went further, and appealed to the thrifty instincts of the Dutch taxpayer to persuade him that the cost of a standing army in peace-time imposed unnecessary strains upon the economy. 'There is no need to have a garrison in every town', wrote one of their propagandists, 'to pay salaries to military governors, colonels and innumerable other officers; it is unnecessary that the military should go about in clothes plastered with gold and silver while the common people have to eat dry bread.'

William retaliated by undertaking a tour of the chief cities of Holland, accompanied by 400 troops, in order to frighten the civic authorities into withdrawing their demands for demobilisation. His action was modelled on that of Maurice of Nassau in 1618 (see p. 51), but the public on this occasion was weary of war and there was no religious controversy to cloud the issue and inflame the passions. William was coldly received; a few of his more outspoken critics were removed from office as a result of his visitation, but their policies were not repudiated. The tour ended in humiliation outside the gates of Amsterdam, where the regents refused to let him enter.

In the following year he arrested six prominent members of the Holland Estates and ordered his nephew, the stadtholder of Friesland, to seize Amsterdam by a surprise attack. The affair was bungled but the threat of cvil war was serious enough to prompt both sides to agree to a compromise in August. Three months later, William died of smallpox. Though his widow was pregnant there was no immediate heir to succeed him, and the regents celebrated their good fortune by striking a medal inscribed, 'The last hour of the prince is the beginning of freedom.' The golden age was to be uncompromisingly republican.

By a curious irony the Dutch found themselves at war within a few months of William's death and with the very regicides of England whom he had sought to attack. The perennial conflict over the herring fisheries, the rivalry over trade in the East Indies and the hostile reaction to the execution of Charles I had led to strained relations between the two countries, but it was the Commonwealth's Navigation Act of 1651 which finally brought about the war. It forbade the import of foreign goods unless carried in British ships or in those of the country of origin, and so effectively threatened the Dutch carrying trade that the States-General sent Tromp to enforce Dutch freedom of navigation from Gibraltar to Denmark. When his fleet encountered an English force and refused to salute the flag, the war began.

It was the one type of war that the Dutch could not afford to fight. England was still primarily an agricultural country and could withstand the temporary dislocation of her foreign trade; not so the United Provinces, which had everything to lose from warfare with a rival who could deny them access to the herring shoals and obstruct the passage of their transports through the Channel. Moreover, while the Dutch had reduced their fleet between 1648 and 1651, the English had increased theirs, and had found in Monk and Blake two admirals as skilful as Tromp. The latter tried to save the day by a series of convoys, but the effort foundered on the ill discipline and obstinacy of the civilian captains. Whenever Monk or Blake attacked, they scattered in an attempt to save their own cargoes and thus delivered themselves into the enemy's hands.

The Dutch were humiliated, their trade suffered and the partisans of the House of Orange made capital out of the English victories. John de Witt, the new grand pensionary of Holland, desperately tried to end the war, but, when Cromwell demanded a military alliance of the two countries against the Catholic states of Europe, de Witt declined so dangerous an offer. Eventually he persuaded Cromwell that if the war continued the Orange party might seize power and provide the exiled Charles II with an excellent base and willing allies. Cromwell took the point and by the Treaty of Westminster (1654) simply required the Dutch to recognise English sovereignty in the Narrow Seas, to pay for the privilege of fishing in English waters and to deny assistance to Charles II.

These terms represented for the Dutch an unhappy footnote to the Treaty of Münster, but since they were avenged by victory in the Second Anglo-Dutch War, of 1656–7, they did little lasting harm. Nor did this unexpected demonstration of England's naval power significantly detract from the overall wealth and political influence enjoyed by the United Provinces for the next two decades of their golden age.

Nonetheless, the Anglo-Dutch war indicated that the problems of the next half-century would be different from those of the past. The Dutch had made themselves great by challenging the power of Spain in Europe and of both Spain and Portugal in the West and East Indies. By 1650 the situation was entirely changed. France had emerged as the most powerful state in Europe, dangerously close to Dutch territory, and England was beginning to challenge the Dutch for commercial supremacy not only in America and in the East but even where they plied for cargoes in the ports of Europe.

Postscript II: Sweden and the treaties of Copenhagen and Oliva 1660

The ending of the German war went almost unnoticed in Sweden as the country moved to the brink of a civil war.

In order to pay for the war after 1632, Oxenstierna had begun to convert the rents in kind from crown lands, and sometimes the lands themselves, for cash. What began as a cautious experiment was swiftly transformed into a rake's progress by the greed of his noble colleagues in the *rad* (royal council), who plundered the royal estates with the irresponsible selfishness of triumphant mercenaries. Oxenstierna was too old to control them, and twenty-two families obtained between them lands worth one-fifth of the ordinary revenues of the kingdom.

As a result the administration ran short of money, and the peasants of the royal estates, accustomed to enjoy considerable independence under an absentee and generally tolerant landlord, were abandoned to the mercies of nobles anxious only to exploit their investment. When the *rad*, in order to compensate for the fiscal consequences of its greed, invited the *riksdag* (the assembly of the four Estates of the realm: the nobles, the clergy, the townsmen and the free peasantry) to approve a series of indirect taxes, the Estate of the peasants withheld its consent. Together with the clergy and townsmen it demanded *reduktion*, the recovery of all crown land; and, when the *rad* refused to surrender its gains, the *riksdag* rejected the tax proposals.

For some years the impasse went unresolved, until the failure of the harvest in 1650 brought discontent to a head. The *riksdag* met for the unprecedented period of four months, and the speeches of the peasants' Estate, in conjunction with the demonstrations of starving villagers, caused consternation among the nobles. Oxenstierna confessed that he was afraid to visit his country estate, and another noble drew an unhappy parallel with events elsewhere: 'They all want to do as they have been doing in England and make us all as like as pig's trotters.'

The crisis played into the hands of Christina, a woman of intrepid self-assurance, self-willed and determined to abdicate rather than fulfil the expectations of her subjects by marrying to produce an heir. Since in addition she intended to become Roman Catholic, she kept her plans secret until she had negotiated the recognition of her cousin Karl Gustav, the commander-in-chief, as hereditary prince. The *rad* disliked the proposal and could see no reason for her haste. At the height of the crisis, therefore, Christina pretended to endorse the *riksdag's* demands, until the nobles took fright and gave way over Karl.

Four years later Christina abdicated and left Karl X to find a solution to his kingdom's problems. Bankruptcy was imminent. The revenues from the Baltic ports were insufficient to meet the government's needs, the Stora Kopperburg (see p. 54) was almost exhausted and there was nothing left but to recover the crown lands. As the nobles had accepted Karl only in order to avoid *reduktion*, its introduction would have caused rebellion and Karl therefore proposed a compromise. Royal estates deemed 'indispensable' to the running of the administration, along with a quarter of the remainder, were restored to the crown: in return, the nobles were guaranteed permanent possession of what they retained.

This limited *reduktion*, while pleasing no one, was grudgingly accepted by all, but the tensions in society were less easily resolved. Karl therefore proposed to reunite the nation by going to war. Moreover, his government was still too impoverished to maintain its army in northern Europe by any means other than war and plunder, and it was not difficult to find an enemy. John Casimir, who succeeded his brother Wladislau as king of Poland in 1648, reasserted his family's claim to the Swedish throne when Christina abdicated – despite the fact that he was already at war with Russia. In a series of lightning campaigns in 1655, Karl entered both Warsaw and Cracow, the joint capital cities, and drove John Casimir into exile. A tentative move by Frederick William of Brandenburg to sneak advantage from the Swedish invasion by gaining full independence for his duchy of Prussia, a Polish fief, was firmly checked by Karl, who compelled him to supply him with troops and to pledge him half the revenues of the duchy. The Russians, meanwhile, transferred their hostility from Poland to Sweden.

Karl's success was evident. It was equally clear that he had no notion what to do with it. He had not enough troops to control the population against its will, and, though he was initially received without much opposition, his confiscation of supplies and the desecration of Catholic churches roused the peasantry to revolt. Karl plunged blindly into the interior in a vain attempt to impose his authority, while behind his back John Casimir returned to Warsaw and the Russians seized their opportunity to invade the Baltic Provinces.

With 500 miles between himself and his base in Pomerania, Karl demonstrated his brilliance as a soldier by bringing his army safely to the coast. Unhappily, he then betrayed his political ineptitude by laying siege to Danzig, a move which immediately alarmed the Dutch and brought them to the aid of the Russians and the Poles. In these difficult circumstances for Sweden, Frederick William demanded and secured from Karl full sovereignty in Prussia, as the price of his continued support.

It was at this moment that Frederick II of Denmark joined in the war, hoping to recover the losses of 1645. Karl seized upon this as an excuse to abandon a position which was rapidly becoming untenable, only to adopt a new one even more fraught with danger. Within eight weeks he brought his army across Pomerania and Jutland to the shore of the Little Belt, over which, when the water froze in January 1658, he rushed across to the island of Funen, losing two squadrons of cavalry through the ice. The manoeuvre merely left him stranded on Funen, while in his absence Frederick William went over to John Casimir, who had regained control of Poland. By an unexpected stroke of luck the Great Belt too began to freeze, and for seven days, in a thrilling race against the thaw, Karl moved, with 5000 men and artillery, from one island to the next, until Zealand, with Copenhagen, was at his mercy. Frederick, betrayed by the elements, could only surrender.

The Treaty of Roskilde, concluded in February 1658, was the most important in Swedish history, since it established the boundaries of modern Sweden. Halland, pledged to Sweden for twenty years in 1645, was ceded in perpetuity, along with the coastal provinces of Skåne, Blekinge and Bohus. In addition the Danes surrendered Trondhiem in Norway and the island of Bornholm.

By losing Skåne, the Danes lost control of the Sound, which could thus be closed only by the two countries acting in co-operation. Karl immediately demanded that it be closed to Dutch warships, in revenge for Dutch intervention at Danzig, and, when Frederick refused to commit himself, began to think of appropriating to himself the triple crown of Scandinavia. Moreover, the reversion to peace merely revived the former problem of what to do with the army: Karl dared not dismiss it for fear of his Baltic enemies, nor could he afford to maintain it in idleness. Consequently, within five months of the treaty of Roskilde, he had it shipped over to land on Zealand.

This time the Danes in Copenhagen resisted him so strongly that, instead of the swift success he had hoped for, Karl was forced to undertake a siege which promised to be both long and bloody. Simultaneously the inhabitants of Trondhiem and Bornholm rebelled against their change of ruler, and Frederick William invaded Pomerania. Most serious of all was the blockade of the Sound by the

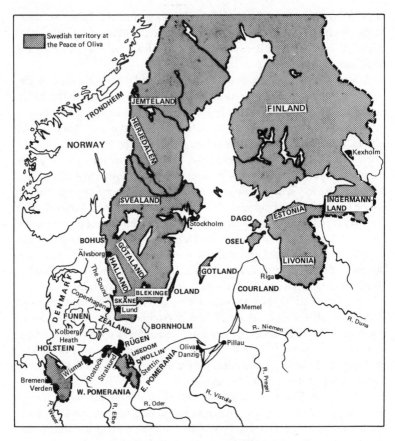

23. *The Swedish Empire in the Baltic 1610–60*

navies of France, England and the United Provinces, acting in rare concert because their trade with the Baltic was too valuable to be put at risk by Sweden. If Karl therefore could not win the war against Denmark, neither could he himself be defeated, and the impasse was resolved only by his death from camp fever in 1660.

A council of regency immediately came to terms with Frederick in the Treaty of Copenhagen. Sweden restored Bornholm and Trondhiem and abandoned the attempt to close the Sound. In every other respect, the Treaty of Roskilde was confirmed.

At the same time, through the intervention of France and Austria, a conference met at Oliva to resolve the disputes between Sweden and her other enemies and to bring peace to the Baltic for the first time in the seventeenth century. As a result,

(1) John Casimir acquired from Sweden the southern part of Livonia, but renounced his claim to the Swedish throne;
(2) Frederick William agreed to evacuate Swedish Pomerania rather than be left to fight on single-handed, but won general recognition of his sovereignty in Prussia; and
(3) the Russians formally confirmed Sweden's possession of the Baltic Provinces.

Within sixty years Sweden had established her Baltic empire and within another sixty years she was to lose most of it. It was too vast an empire to be maintained by so small a country with limited resources of manpower and wealth. It was, moreover, strategically impossible to defend for any length of time an empire whose provinces were scattered along the Baltic littoral, perpetually exciting the hostility and greed of the inland powers. Denmark and Poland were no longer as powerful as they had been in 1600, but Frederick William was forging the new state of Brandenburg–Prussia and the tide of Russian history was on the turn. In vain did Swedish commanders plunge into the hinterland – as Gustav Adolf did in Bavaria, Torstensson in Moravia or Karl X in Poland – in search of the security of natural barriers; none were to be found east of the Urals or north of the Danube. The empire was finally to collapse under the combined assault of the inland states, while another Swedish commander, Karl XII, lost his sanity and his empire in a headlong pursuit of enemies which took him far beyond Poland and Russia into the heart of Asia Minor.

Postscript III: France and the Treaty of the Pyrenees 1659

Although the settlement between Spain and the United Provinces in January 1648 deprived France of a powerful ally, Mazarin remained confident that Spain was on the brink of defeat: handicapped by revolts in Portugal, Catalonia and Naples, and deprived of allies and Rhineland bases by the negotiations being concluded in Westphalia, she would not long sustain a war against the concentrated power of France.

French expectations of an easy victory were shattered when the opposition of the four sovereign courts brought the administration to a halt in the summer of 1648 (see p. 182). More damaging was the violence which followed as the army officers and nobles took arms against the government and each other in a civil war without principle. It was nicknamed the Fronde by one of the participants who likened his supporters to 'schoolboys who sling mud (qui frondent) in the gutters of Paris'. The *officers*, appalled by the unexpected consequences of their opposition, made their peace with Anne of Austria at Reuil in March 1649; the nobles persisted in their Fronde for several years.

Condé, formerly the duke of Enghien, fought to assuage the slightest affront to his vanity, which had become intolerably sensitive by reason of his spectacular victories at Rocroy and Lens. In his conceit he wanted nothing less than control of the kingdom, an ambition rivalled only by that of Gaston of Orleans, the veteran of a score of intrigues against Richelieu and Louis XIII. The remainder took arms to avenge an insult, settle an old score, or because they had nothing better to do. The count of Alais marched against the *parlement* of Provence because it had denied his claim in a land suit, Gaston's daughter raised her own army to bargain for her cousin the king's hand in marriage, and Madame de Longueville, a restless beauty married to a dullard, relieved the tedium of her life by inciting lovers to deeds of martial valour. For the nobles and their ladies the Fronde became an exciting game in which foreigners of their own class were welcome to join, exiled cavaliers from England and princes of the Empire bored by the return of peace to their territories.

Anne of Austria rode out the storm with great courage and determination, enduring danger and indignity to protect her two sons while Mazarin bobbed and weaved his way through the tangle of intrigues. Twice he left France in order to deprive the *frondeurs* of a common enemy, twice he returned to negotiate private settlements when they fell out with each other. Condé was the first to be isolated, since no one could withstand his disdain, and he took his revenge by entering the service of Philip IV. At this, his rival Turenne returned to his allegiance, and there ensued a dramatic struggle between them for the mastery of Paris, in the course of which Gaston's daughter, forfeited her chance of marrying Louis XIV by training the Bastille's artillery on his army. Condé ruled for a while in Paris, the hero of the mob, but he was driven out by 1652 and the nobles began to tire of a conflict which had become so confused as to be unprofitable. When Louis XIV, still in his teens, proclaimed his majority, he provided the occasion for most to make their peace. The end of the regency signalised the end of the

Fronde, and, though Condé remained defiant at the head of a Spanish army, Mazarin was swiftly restored as director of the administration by the end of 1653.

Meanwhile the Fronde had given Spain an unlooked-for advantage in the years following the peace of Westphalia. By concentrating her sea-power, by bringing the Dunkirk squadron into the western Mediterranean, she established local maritime supremacy, recovered control of the Tuscan coast and forestalled a French attempt to intervene in Naples. The fleet was also of value in running a blockade of the Catalan coast while the army laid siege to Barcelona. After fifteen months, in 1652, the city capitulated, to be granted an amnesty by Philip IV, whose chief concern was no longer to enforce the policies of Olivares, but to secure recognition of his own authority. Once this was realised by the Catalans, the revolt began to crumble, although French troops remained in the kingdom until 1659.

So successful were the Spaniards that in 1656 the French proposed to end the war. Agreement was reached on most territorial issues but Mazarin could not bring himself to grant an amnesty to Condé, who wished to be restored to his lands and titles. The war continued, therefore, but with the French government determined to find an ally with sufficient naval power to tilt the balance against Spain. The Dutch were the obvious choice, but John de Witt welcomed the preservation of Spanish power in Flanders as a useful buffer between France and the United Provinces. It was to England, therefore, to the victor of the Anglo-Dutch war, that Mazarin applied for aid, despite the apparent difficulty of reconciling a Puritan regicide to alliance with a Catholic monarch.

The Spaniards in fact had already come near to succeeding. They had offered Cromwell the opportunity to win Calais and Bordeaux, but would not go so far as to allow freedom of worship to English traders in Spain, nor freedom of trade throughout the Spanish empire. Mazarin, however, had prepared the ground with due caution in 1655 by a commercial treaty. Thereafter it was an easy matter to encourage English ambitions in the West Indies, where Blake was despatched to take Jamaica, to remind Cromwell that many leading cavaliers were serving in the Spanish army under Condé and to offer the prize of Dunkirk if Spain were defeated. In 1657 Cromwell agreed to join France.

Finding an ally was one thing: it was equally important to deny assistance to the enemy, and to this end Mazarin hoped to derive advantage from the Imperial election which followed the death of Ferdinand III in 1657. 'The electors', he instructed his ambassadors, 'have a unique opportunity of showing all Europe that the Imperial dignity is not the patrimony of a single house and in the gift of the council of Spain, as it has been until now, but does in fact depend upon their votes.' Despite massive expenditure to purchase these votes, the French failed not only to secure the election of Louis XIV but also to prevent that of Leopold, Ferdinand's heir. Nonetheless, the election of 1658 was made on terms which guaranteed Austria's continued neutrality in matters relating to Spain.

In the same year, Mazarin took under his wing the League of the Rhine princes. Led by the three ecclesiastical electors of Mainz, Trier and Cologne, it also included the Protestant states of Brunswick-Lüneberg, Hesse-Cassel and the Swedish administrators of Bremen and Verden. Its aims were unexceptionable–unity and peace–and it proved useful to France in denying Spain assistance in the Rhineland.

Mazarin's careful diplomacy had achieved its ends: without allies, with straitened finances and with Portugal still actively in revolt (see below), Spain could not survive England's entry into the war. Turenne, his army reinforced by 6000 Ironsides, defeated Condé in the Battle of the Dunes in June 1658, and recovered possession of Dunkirk and Gravelines. Philip IV immediately sued for peace. Mazarin enjoyed a free hand in the negotiations, because of Cromwell's death, and, for the sake of securing additional benefits by the marriage of Louis XIV and the infanta, was persuaded to give way over Condé. The territorial clauses were straightforward, and the final terms of the Treaty of the Pyrenees were signed in 1659.

1. Roussillon and Perpignan in the Pyrenees were restored to France after a century and a half of Spanish rule.
2. To France were ceded Montmédy in Luxemburg and other fortresses controlling the routes between Metz, Toul and Verdun; Artois, with its capital of Arras; and the towns of Béthune, Gravelines and Thionville (see map 22).
3. England was given Dunkirk.
4. Spain recognised all French acquisitions in the Peace of Westphalia.
5. France agreed to pardon Condé for his treason, and to deny further aid to the Portuguese and Catalans.
6. Louis XIV was to marry the infanta Maria Theresa, Philip IV's sole heiress. She renounced her rights to the Spanish throne, but the

French insisted that the renunciation be dependent upon the payment of her dowry, which Philip IV was unlikely to be able to afford.

The Catalan revolt ended with the Peace of the Pyrenees, but the Portuguese were not to be disposed of so easily. Their own recovery of Brazil from the Dutch in 1654 was critical to their survival, since from the profits they derived from the trade in sugar and slaves they were able to finance their war of independence. In 1658 they won a major victory at Elvas in Alemtejo and launched an attack into Spain itself, to lay siege to Badajoz. In the following year they were deprived by the peace settlement of further help from France, but Charles II of England came to their rescue in 1661 when Catherine of Braganza brought him a dowry of £800,000, along with Bombay and Tangier. By dispensing with imperial outposts they could no longer defend, the Portuguese saved their homeland, for Charles sent them an experienced soldier, Schomberg, who led them to victory in 1663 at Ameixial. Philip IV, in a last desperate effort to restore unity to the peninsula before death claimed him, raised every available soldier to put 23,000 men in the field at Montesclaros in 1665. In the last and fiercest battle of the war of liberation, Schomberg triumphed and the news of defeat brought about Philip's death. Three years later Portuguese independence was officially recognised.

At the end of more than half a century of warfare, Spain could only add up the bankruptcies, the defeats and the humiliation. The United Provinces, to whose defeat all else had been subordinated since the death of Philip II, were independent and powerful, and the unity of the Iberian peninsula had been broken by the loss of Portugal. The Austrian Habsburgs, saved by Spain after the defenestration of Prague, abandoned her after 1640 to pursue their own destiny in the Danube valley, and the triumph of France in 1659 marked the end of a century or more of Spanish domination of European affairs. The Treaty of the Pyrenees was more than a fulfilment of the ambitions of Henry IV and Louis XIII. No longer content to think merely in terms of containing the action of what had once been the most powerful state in Europe, the French, by the marriage of Louis XIV to Maria Theresa, clearly planned to absorb what was left of it within a Bourbon empire which would dominate Europe in its turn.

Bibliography

A. ENGLISH PUBLICATIONS AND TRANSLATIONS OF FOREIGN
WORKS

(More detailed bibliographies are found in, for example, Kamen,
Pagès, Polišenský and Rabb (ed.))

ASTON, T., *Crisis in Europe 1560–1660* (London, 1965).

BENECKE, G., *Germany in the Thirty Years' War* (London, 1978).

BELLER, E. A., *Propaganda in Germany in the Thirty Years' War* (Princeton,
   NJ, 1940).

BURCKHARDT, C. J., *Richelieu*, (3 vols.) (New York, 1964–72).

CARLETON, SIR DUDLEY, *Letters &c.*, 2nd ed. (London, 1775).

CARTER, C. H., *The Secret Diplomacy of the Habsburgs 1598–1625* (New
   York, 1964).

CHUDOBA, B., *Spain and the Empire 1519–1643* (Chicago, 1952).

CHURCH, W. F., *Richelieu and Raison d'Etat* (Princeton, 1972).

COOPER, J. P., (Ed.), *New Cambridge Modern History*, vol. IV (Cambridge,
   1971).

COUPE, W. A., *The German Illustrated Broadsheet in the Seventeenth Century*
   (Baden-Baden, 1966–7).

DALTON, C., *Life and Times of Sir Edward Cecil in Dutch Service* (London,
   1885).

DANSTRUP, J., *History of Denmark* (Copenhagen, 1948).

EDMUNDSON, G., *Anglo-Dutch Rivalry* (Oxford, 1911).

——, *History of Holland* (Cambridge, 1922).

ELLIOTT, J. H., *Imperial Spain* (London, 1963).

——, *The Revolt of the Catalans* (Cambridge, 1963).

EVANS, R. J. W., *Rudolf II and His World* (Oxford, 1973).

FREYTAG, G., *Pictures of German Life* (London, 1862).

FRISCHAUER, P., *The Imperial Crown* (London, 1939).

GARDINER, S. R. (ed.) *Letters & c. England–Germany 1618–20*, 2 vols (The
   Camden Society: London, 1865 and 1868).

——,*History of England from the Accession of James I to the Outbreak of the Civil War*, 10 vols (London, 1883–84).

GEYL, P., *The Netherlands Divided 1609–48* (London, 1936).

GINDELY, A., *The Thirty Years' War* (New York, 1884).

GREEN, M. A. E., *Elizabeth, Electress Palatine and Queen of Bohemia* (London (Aberdeen), 1909).

HALEY, K. D., *The Dutch in the Seventeenth Century* (London, 1972).

HOLBORN, H., *History of Modern Germany*, vol. I (New York, 1959).

JONES, J. R., *Britain and Europe in the Seventeenth Century* (London, 1966).

KAMEN, H., *The Iron Century* (London, 1971).

KAMEN, H., and HUGHES, M., '*The Thirty Years' War*' *in European History* (1976).

LEONARD, E., *History of Protestantism* (London, 1965).

LYON, F. H., *El Conde de Gondomar* (Oxford, 1916).

LYNCH, J., *Spain under the Habsburgs*, vol. II (Oxford, 1969).

MANN, G., *Wallenstein* (London, 1976).

MACARTNEY, C. A. (ed.) *The Habsburg and Hohenzollern Dynasties*, (London, 1970).

PAGÈS, G., *The Thirty Years' War* (London, 1970).

PARKER, G., *The Army of Flanders and The Spanish Road 1567–1659* (Cambridge, 1972).

POLIŠENSKÝ, J. V., *The Thirty Years' War* (London, 1971).

——,*War and Society in Europe 1618 and 1648* (Cambridge, 1978).

RABB, T. K., *The Struggle for Stability in Early Modern Europe* (New York, 1975).

——(ed.), *The Thirty Years' War* (Boston, Mass., 1972).

REDLICH, F., *De Praeda Militari. Looting and Booty* (Wiesbaden, 1956).

——,*The German Military Enterpriser*, 2 vols (Wiesbaden, 1964–5).

ROBERTS, M., *Gustavus Adolphus II* (London, 1958).

——(ed.), *Sweden as a Great Power 1611–1697* (London, 1968).

SCHILLER, F., *The History of the Thirty Years' War* (London, 1901).

SCHWARZ, H. F., *The Imperial Privy Council in the Seventeenth Century* (Cambridge, Mass., 1943).

STEINBERG, S. H., *The 'Thirty Years War' and the Conflict for European Hegemony* (London, 1971).

TAPIÉ, V. L., *The Rise and Fall of the Habsburg Monarchy* (London, 197).

TREASURE, G., *Richelieu* (London, 1972).

WANDRUZSHKA, A., *The House of Habsburg* (New York, 1964).

WATSON, F., *Wallenstein. Soldier under Saturn* (London, 1938).

WEDGWOOD, C. V., *The Thirty Years' War* (London, 1938).

WILLIAMS, H. N., *A Gallant of Lorraine* (London, 1921).
WILSON, C., *The Dutch Republic* (London, 1968).
YATES, F., *The Rosicrucian Enlightenment* (London, 1972).

B. WORKS PUBLISHED IN FOREIGN LANGUAGES

(see in particular Dahlmann, F. C. *and* Waitz, G., Quellenkunde der Deutschen Geschichte, 9th edn (Leipzig 1931–32) ed. H. Haering and others)

ALBRECHT, D., *Richelieu, Gustav Adolf und das Reich* (Munich, 1959).
——, *Die Auswärtige Politik Maximilians von Bayern 1618–35* (Gottingen, 1962).
ALEKSEEV, V. M., *Tridsatiletnyaya Vojna* (Leningrad, 1961).
BASSOMPIERRE, F. DE, *Ambassade en Espagne 1621* (Cologne, 1668).
BLOK, P. J., *Frederik Hendrik Prins van Oranje* (Amsterdam, 1926).
BRANTS, V., *La Belgique au 17ème siècle, Albert et Isabelle* (Louvain, 1960).
BRAUBACH, M., *Der westfälische Friede* (Münster, 1948).
DENIS, E., *La Fin d'indépendence Bohème* (Paris, 1890).
——, *La Bohème depuis la Montague-Blanche*, i (Paris, 2nd edn, 1930).
DEVÈZE, M., *L'Espagne de Philippe IV* tome 1 (Paris, 1970); tome 2 (Paris, 1971).
——, *L'Espagne et le Portugal sous le règne de Philippe III* (Paris, 1965).
DICKMANN, F., *Der westfälische Friede* (Münster, 1965).
DIWALD, H., *Wallenstein* Ullstein paperback edn (Munich, 1969).
ESSEN, H. VAN DER, *Le Cardinal Enfant et la politique européenne de l'Espagne* (Louvain, 1944).
FRANZ, G., *Der Dreissigjährige Krieg und das deutsche Volk* (Jena, 1940).
GINDLEY, A., *Geschichte des Dreissigjährigen Krieges*, i–iv (Prague, 1869–1880).
HANOTAUX G., and DUC DE LA FORCE, *Histoire du Cardinal Richelieu*, 6 vols (Paris, 1893–1947).
HAUSER, H., *La Prépondérance espagnole 1559–1660* (Paris, rev edn., 1948).
HAYWOOD, F., *Histoire de la Maison de Savoie* (Paris, 1943).
HOUTTE, J. A., VAN, *Economische en sociale Geschledenis van de Lage Landen* (Zeist, 1964).
JOBART, J., *De Luther à Mohila, la Pologne dans la crise de la Chrétienté* (Paris, 1974).
LEFÊVRE, J., *Spinola et la Belgique* (Brussels, 1947).
LEMAN, A., *Richelieu et Olivares* (Lille, 1938).

——, *Urbain VIII et la rivalité de la France et de la Maison d'Autriche de 1631 à 1635* (Lille, 1920).

LONCHAY, H., and Cuvellier, J. (eds), *Correspondance de la cour d'Espagne sur les affaires des Pays-Bas XVIIe siècle*, ed. Cuvelier (Brussels, 1923).

LOOSE, H. D., *Hamburg und Christian IV von Dänemark* (Hamburg, 1963).

MARAÑON, G., *El Conde-duque de Olivarès*, 3rd ed. (Madrid, 1952).

MARAVALL, J. A., *La Philosophie politique espagnole au XVIIe siècle* (Paris, 1959).

MARTINELLI, V., *Le Guerre per la Valtellina* (Varèse, 1935).

MECENSEFFY, G., 'Die Beziehungen der Höfe von Wien und Madrid während des Dreissigjährigen Krieges', *Archiv für Geschichte*, CXXI (1953).

MOUSNIER, R., *Les Progrès de la civilisation européenne et le déclin de l'Orient* (Paris, 1951).

PAGÈS, G., *Naissance du Grand Siècle* (Paris, 1948).

PFISTER, A., *Georg Jenatsch, sein Leben und seine Zeit*, 2nd ed. (Basel, 1939).

PIRENNE, H., *Histoire de Belgique*, vol. III (Brussels, 1923).

POLIŠENSKÝ, J., *Angle a Bila Horn* (Prague, 1949).

PRINSTERER, G. G., VAN, *Archives et correspondance de la Maison d'Orange–Nassau*, 5 vols (Utrecht, 1841–61).

QUAZZA, R., *Politica europea nella questione Valtellina, la lega franca–veneta–savoiarda et la pace de Monçon* (Venice, 1921).

——, *La guerra per la successione di Mantova et del Montferrata 1628–1631*, 2 vols (Mantua, 1926).

——, *Storia politica d'Italia. Preponderanza spagnola 1559–1700* (Milan, 1950).

RITTER, M., *Deutsche Geschichte im Zeitalter des Gegenreformation und des Dreissigjährige Krieges* (Stuttgart, 1889 and 1908).

——, 'Das Kontributionssystem Wallensteins', *Historiche Zeitschrift*, 1903.

RODRIGUEZ VILLA, A., *Ambrosio Spinola* (Madrid, 1904).

——(ed.), *Correspondance de l'Infanta avec le Duc de Lerma* (Madrid, 1906).

RÖMEIN, J. M. (ed.), *Algemene Geschiedenis der Nederlanden*, vols IV and V (Utrecht, 1957).

ROTT, E., *Henri IV, les Suisses et la Haute Italie* (Paris, 1882).

RUDOLF, H. U., (ed.), *Der Dreissigjährige Krieg. Perspektiven und Strukturen* (Darmstadt, 1977).

SCHUBERT, F. H., *Ludwig Camerarius* (Kallmünz, 1955).

STURMBERGER, H., *G. E. Tschernembl* (Linz, 1953).

——, *Aufstand in Böhmen* (Munich, 1959).

206 EUROPE AT WAR 1600–1650

EUROPE AT WAR 1600–1650

206 EUROPE AT WAR 1600–1650

206 EUROPE AT WAR 1600–1650

206 EUROPE AT WAR 1600–1650

206 EUROPE AT WAR 1600–1650

206 EUROPE AT WAR 1600–1650

206 EUROPE AT WAR 1600–1650

TAPIÉ, V. L., *La Politique etrangère de la France et le début de la Guerre de Trente Ans, 1616–1621* (Paris, 1934).

VAINSHTEIN, O. L., *Rossiya: Tridsatyilyetnyaya Voyna* (Leningrad, 1947).

VILAR, V., 'Un gran proyecto anti-holandés', *Hispania*, LXXXVIII (1962).

VILLARI, R., *La Rivolta antispagnola a Napoli. Le Origini 1585–1647* (Bari, 1967).

ZELLER, G., *La Guerre de Trente Ans et les relations internationales* (Paris, 1947).

——, *De Christophe Colomb à Cromwell*, vol. II of *Histoire de relations internationales*, ed. P. RENOUVIN (Paris, 1953).

ZOLLNER, E., *Geschichte Österreichs* (Vienna, 1961).

Index

Entries analysing the relations between countries are made under the country rather than under the individual responsible for the conduct of these relations. Numbers in italics indicate the number of the map.

Bavaria *and* the treaty of Ulm
(1620)
Charles I, king of England 98, 101,
106, 108, 112, 113, 156, 157,
161, 176, 191
Charles, duke of Lorraine 133, 137,
146, 153
Charles Emmanuel, duke of
Savoy 13, 17, 24–5, 41, 42,
57, 58, 65, 66–7, 74, 95, 101,
105, 116, 118, 130
Charles Louis, elector Palatine 156,
179, 181, 185
Cherasco, treaty of (1631) 130, 185
Christian II, elector of Saxony 17
Christian IV, king of Denmark 53–
4, 78, 102–21 *passim*, 152, 157,
169–70, 172, 173, 176
Christian of Anhalt 16–17, 20, 36,
58, 61, 65, 66, 69, 76, 108
Christian of Brunswick 87, 93, 94,
96, 97, 98, 108, 109, 110
Christina, queen of Sweden 139,
153, 169, 172, 180, 189, 193,
194
Chur 5; 26, 60
Cleves 2, 6, 7, 13, 20, 21; 9, 14, 28, 33,
34, 40–4, 100, 166, 180, 185
Coblenz 10; 75
Coeuvres, marquis of 99, 101, 107
Cologne 2, 3, 7, 10, 15, 16, 20; 9, 13,
14, 15, 40, 43, 67, 96, 132, 151,
181, 200
Compiègne, treaty of (1624) 99;
(1635) 145–6, 152
Condé, prince of 161, 163, 172, 198,
199, 200
Constance, lake 9, 95, 140
Copenhagen 19, 23; 159, 195;
treaty of (1660) 196
Córdoba, Gonsalez de 86, 87, 92,
93, 96–7, 116, 118, 120
Cromwell, Oliver 192, 199, 200
Cueva, cardinal; *see* Bedmar

Dampierre, Henry Duval 59, 63, 67
Danube, R. 2, 3, 9, 11, 15, 18; 90,
132, 133, 135, 142, 166, 172

Danzig 4, 23; 21, 22, 46, 189, 195
Davos 5; 26, 60, 89
Denmark 4, 14, 23
Christian, king of 53;
campaigns in north Germany
107–8, 110–21 *passim*;
relations with
England 102, 107–8;
Spain 157;
Sweden 22–4, 54, 169–73, 176,
195–7;
United Provinces 45, 46, 54,
107–8, 114, 172, 173, 176, 195,
196;
see also Christian IV, Frederick II,
the Sound and the treaties of
Knäred (1613), The Hague
(1626), Lübeck (1629),
Brömsebro (1645), Roskilde
(1659) *and* Copenhagen
(1660)
Dévots 43, 95, 98, 106, 120, 124
Dessau 14; 104, 110
Deulino, treaty of (1618) 55
Diest, mutinies of 29, 30, 34
Donauwörth 3, 15; 15, 142, 172
Dortmund 122;
treaty of (1609) 41
Downs, the 157
Dresden 15; 139, 141
Dunes, the 200
Dunkirk 1, 6, 16, 20; 10, 29, 96, 155,
176, 181, 199, 200;
privateers of 29, 96, 109, 128,
138, 155, 157, 176, 199
East India Company (Dutch) 4, 37,
46–7, 82, 177, 178, 186, 191
Ebersdorf, compact of (1634) 143,
146
Ehrenbreitstein 10, 15; 75, 132
Elbe, R. 9, 11, 14, 18, 20, 21, 23; 54,
103, 104, 108, 110, 113, 123,
138, 153, 180, 185
Elbing 4; 102, 122
Elizabeth, daughter of James I 56,
76, 77, 78, 83, 87
Emmerich 7; 44, 85